Editor's Note

Jonathan Wilson, Editor

The original *Blizzard*, the weekly newspaper set up in Sunderland in 1893, ran to 12 issues. When we started *The Blizzard* two years ago, taking inspiration from "the organ of Mr Sidney Duncan" as it described itself, my initial target was just to get through the first year and then, beyond that, to make it to 12 issues so we could at least claim to be the longest-running *Blizzard*. We're not there yet, but as we celebrate our second birthday, there's no reason to think we won't be here next year with Issue Twelve and hopefully for a long time after that.

For that, there's a huge number of people I have to thank. To start with, everybody in the office in Sunderland for having faith in the project, for seeing so many ways to improve it and for working so hard to make it happen. Then the sub-editors, illustrators and designers for taking the raw words and turning them to the form you're reading now. Then the stockists (a full list is available on the website), particularly those who took a gamble on us before we were established. And then the writers, for continuing to produce the ideas and content. All of these people, at least initially, put in time and effort without any guarantee they would ever receive any financial reward. Let's not pretend they're making huge amounts now, but at least there's some recompense from the profit-share scheme.

And then there's the readers. I confess I was sceptical about the pay-what-you-like model but thanks to your sense of what is fair, it's been a great success. The plan was devised to try to make *The Blizzard* accessible to as many people as possible and that would only work if readers respected the model; by and large, I'd say you have. So huge thanks for that — especially to those who have helped spread the word. We have no advertising budget so please do keep telling people about us.

And it's that last point, I think, that is most important. With *The Blizzard*, more than with any other venture I've been involved with, there's a great sense of collaboration, among *Blizzard* staff, contributors and readers. That comes across most strongly at the Q&As we've done — in London, Sunderland, Leeds and, this month, Swansea. There's a great sense of community, of people who see the value in what we are doing and like to discuss football in a particular way. That's something we'd like to develop, partly through further Q&As across Britain and, perhaps, beyond, but also with some changes we'll be making to our website.

So look out for future events and for those new developments, but most of all accept my thanks. For *The Blizzard* is a collaborative process and it wouldn't have survived these two years without everybody's involvement.

March 2013

Contents

The Blizzard, Issue Eight

FSC
www.fsc.org
MIX
Paper from responsible sources
FSC® C008152

6

Cyprus

"...overlooking the stadium is a United Nations watchtower, while barbed wire surrounds the pitch..."

The Wrong Side of the Border

After decades of stalemate, Northern Cypriot football may be about to come in from the cold

By Jacob Steinberg

At the top of the one of the stands of the Taxim Stadium in North Nicosia, a young man sits on his own, an umbrella in one hand and a can of Coke by his side. It seems a lonely existence, a strange thing to be doing on a Thursday afternoon in October, especially given that the heavens look likely to open at any moment. He is not, after all, waiting for anything special, just for the players of Çetinkaya to come out to train. Nothing more than that. When they do emerge, no one else joins the fan. He is on his own but he does not care. He just wants to see his team put through their paces; his dedication reflects the love of football that exists in Northern Cyprus.

Yet there is a poignancy to this story, for this small, derelict stadium is a symbol of the problems that have blighted Turkish Cypriot football for longer than most people would care to remember. On the surface, it looks like a normal stadium, albeit one in desperate need of renovation — the rain in Nicosia that day had been so heavy that most of the pitch is covered in water, meaning the players can only train on one half of it. But that is not the real issue. The real issue is that overlooking the stadium is a United Nations watchtower, while barbed wire surrounds the pitch, almost giving the ground the look of a prison courtyard.

The reason for the UN presence is easily explained by Cyprus's troubled history. This is a tiny island divided, with Greek Cypriots residing in the South and Turkish Cypriots in the North. Tension has long reigned in Cyprus — independence from British rule was achieved in 1960 — and reached boiling point in 1974 as unrest grew, prompting an invasion by the Turkish army to protect territories in the North which ultimately led to Nicosia being split in two. The UN still monitors a border known as the Green Line.

Unfortunately the Taxim Stadium's proximity to the border, plus its crumbling façade, makes it impossible for Çetinkaya to play their matches there — instead they use the Atatürk Stadium elsewhere in Nicosia. Çetinkaya, who were formed in 1930 and who are the most successful side in the history of Turkish Cypriot football, find themselves banished from their own home because of politics. That the UN allows them to train there at all is itself a minor miracle.

There was a time when Çetinkaya and other Turkish Cypriot clubs were part of the Cyprus Football Association (CFA), playing alongside teams from the south, but in 1955 they decided to declare independence and set up their own league, forming the Cyprus Turkish Football Federation (KTFF). That followed a decision by the CFA, which was set up by six Greek clubs and two Turkish clubs in 1934, temporarily to suspend the Turkish clubs to prevent clashes between the two communities in stadiums because of growing unrest on the island. Çetinkaya were the last Turkish Cypriot club to win the Cypriot title, lifting the trophy in 1951. Now they are no longer a professional club, they cannot use their own ground for its primary purpose and their players all have other jobs. It does not take a genius to work out that the consequences of that decision in 1955 have been disastrous, although there is of course far more to it than that.

It was the declaration of independence made by the North in 1983 which was the root cause of football's appalling decline in Northern Cyprus. Not legally recognised as a country by the rest of the world, they are banned by Fifa from playing professional football. There are 48 teams divided into four divisions but they are not allowed to play anyone from outside the Turkish Republic of Northern Cyprus (TRNC), not even in friendly matches, as those still have to be sanctioned by Fifa. The lavish riches on offer in the Champions League, the billionaire owners and players on £200,000 a week that are so common elsewhere in Europe belong to a different world, one that is denied to Turkish Cypriots by a mixture of politics and red tape. Whereas the CFA became a member of Fifa in 1948 and Uefa in 1962, the KTFF has been left with its nose pressed to the window, looking in from the cold.

For years, they have been unloved and unnoticed, cast aside by the wider footballing world, and left to fend for themselves. After all, if you cannot hear the cries for help, then who cares?

However, the situation was brought into sharper focus in October, when the Cypriot side AEL hosted the Turkish side Fenerbahçe in a Europa League group match. AEL were beaten 1-0 by their more prestigious opponents thanks to a late header from Egemen Korkmaz in a match that was never likely to capture the imagination abroad but, in Cyprus, it was treated with the utmost importance. A Europa League group match was given the status of the Champions League final. You would expect nothing less for a match between the Cypriot champions and Turkish giants, which was reflected by the 900 police officers who lined the streets of Nicosia.

With AEL's stadium not up to Uefa standards, the game was moved from Limassol to the capital and played at the GSP Stadium, the home of Apoel, who made history last season by becoming the first Cypriot side to reach the quarter-finals of the Champions League, where they were well beaten by Real Madrid.

As one taxi driver put it, this was more than a game, which was hammered home by the presence of the guest of honour, Sevim Ebeoğlu, an 83-year-old Turkish Cypriot who played for AEL in the 50s. In 1955, he was AEL's top scorer as they became the last side to win the league title when it involved clubs from across the island. In that same season, Ebeoğlu also persuaded the club's president to change AEL's strip from white shirts and blue shorts to the yellow and black of Fenerbahçe. "Our shirts were white and were always getting dirty because there was no grass on the ground," Ebeoğlu said. "And I knew the president of our club was a Fenerbahçe supporter. We had the idea to change the colours and they have been the same ever since."

Ebeoğlu's enduring popularity at AEL proves that, when it comes to football, the split is essentially a waste of everyone's time. The widespread support for Fenerbahçe in the region is of particular concern. When the Turkish side came to Cyprus, 1,400 of the travelling fans were actually Turkish Cypriots who had crossed the border for the match. While there is nothing wrong with supporting a bigger, wealthier team from Turkey, that so many choose to do so indicates the abject state of football in the North. Fenerbahçe should not have a bigger presence in the north of Nicosia than Çetinkaya, the most decorated team, but that is the current reality.

Football is on life support in Northern Cyprus and for years those trying to revive it have been unable to find a solution. The frustration is palpable and is only matched by the desire for change.

Orçun Kamal, the director of international relations at the KTFF, is vociferous in his view that a solution must be reached, which happily does look more likely following recent positive talks with the CFA. Kamal, who played football in the Turkish Cypriot league for 16 years, moved into coaching after his playing career before joining the KTFF three years ago. He also coaches a wheelchair basketball team. The 44 year old, once a powerful midfielder — like Bryan Robson, he proudly claims

— has an MA in business management but bringing football to the North is his passion, although not one that can last indefinitely, not if politics keep getting in the way of sport.

"I played for 16 years," Kamal said. "I won trophies but I couldn't leave. There are no friendlies against international sides. How can you show what you can do?" Until 1983, foreign teams could play friendlies — Galatasaray, for instance, were regular visitors from Istanbul — but not now. Leyton Orient were once ready to play against Çetinkaya but permission was never granted.

"How do you tell the young that they cannot play football because of politics?" asked Kamal, who seems to know every one of the 260,000 citizens in North Nicosia. "How can you tell them to wait for the political situation to improve?" He was keen to stress that football and politics must not mix, that there is no desire for that. This is not about unifying Cyprus or even getting the Turkish side recognised by the international community, this is merely about being allowed to play football. "I am not a politician," Kamal said.

Mistakes have been made, however, and cries for help have fallen on deaf ears. Within the KTFF, which is finally on the rise, there is acceptance that they have had a PR problem, that they have expected others simply to solve their problems without really knowing where to begin or even what the issues are. In the end, as with anything in life, the way to stand up for yourself properly is to do it yourself. They are at last starting to realise that nothing worth having comes without a fight. "The mistake is to think everybody knows us," said Kamal. "We think people will give us everything. If the baby doesn't cry, it doesn't get food — but no one knows us in Europe. It's normal."

For a while, they were their own worst enemies. Hoping to join Fifa independently was never an option and money was frittered away on hosting tournaments such as the ELF Cup in 2006, a competition for sides unrecognised by Fifa that ended up including the futsal teams of Tajikistan and Kyrgyzstan. Then, when they went for meetings with the CFA and Fifa, there was too little discussion of football and too much discussion of politics. After several meetings, Fifa's proposal was that the KTFF should be subsumed into the CFA but the Turkish side were not ready for that and talks ended after the Northern Cyprus elections in 2009. Retaining their independence is of paramount importance to them, whatever the consequences, but they might eventually have to accept this proposal. As it is, they cannot play, the CFA has all the power and the KTFF has none. "We have to inform the people they need this agreement," says Kamal. "It would not affect the situation for the country. People are scared of losing their cultural identity but don't think of politics."

Think of the football is the message. It is difficult to argue with the insistence that the divide has to end. The dream for Turkish Cypriots is that they will be able to have their own league. Unfortunately without the power to change the rules, the reality is they need to compromise. They need to be canny and play the hand dealt to them intelligently. Not having the best cards does not mean they cannot get what they want. "We have no voice at Fifa and Uefa," said Kamal. "Someone has to give us an opportunity. There are no direct flights here and no trade but we wear Nike and Adidas to play so in our own way we are contributing to football, with nothing coming back to us. This is the people's game but there is no chance for youngsters. We need to find a compromise. We want to play football. Let's put the football over the politics." It is a message he drives across time and time again.

Kamal does not know how he can tell his daughter that she cannot play football. Once he wrote a letter to Fifa's president and signed it as his four-year-old son. "I am four years old," it read. "My family never got a chance to play football abroad. Give me a chance." There was no response. "They are killing the hopes and dreams of young people," says Kamal. "At least let under-18s play and be free. What's that Pink Floyd song? Leave our kids alone."

The damage caused is clear. In most countries, professional football offers a path to untold wealth but in Northern Cyprus it is nothing more than a dead end and the knock-on effect that has on the sport is depressing to see. The support for Fenerbahçe means that money is not poured into improving the local infrastructure but instead goes to Turkey. People are not stupid. They have eyes and ears. They can see the Champions League, the Premier League and La Liga on their televisions. They can see Lionel Messi and Cristiano Ronaldo on their televisions but never in front of them. What's worse, they can see Greek, Greek Cypriot and Turkish sides taking on these teams and players in European competitions. They have been denied that privilege and they know their football is not up to scratch.

There are 3000 active players in the league. Players do come from abroad after a formal invitation from the KTFF — there are lot of players from Africa — and everyone is paid, but not much. Despite it all, a mobile phone company, Telsim, sponsors the league and the satellite television channel, BRT, bought the rights to show matches, acquiring them for 50,000 Turkish lira (£17,000).

Most of the stadiums in Northern Cyprus are still tiny. After the war some teams left and moved to the South so they could still play — they are known as immigrant teams. Anorthorsis Famagusta are one of those sides and in the 2008-09 season they qualified for the group stage of the Champions League, twice taking on Internazionale. Yet they do not play their football in Famagusta, a commercial port in the North. Those days are long gone. It is not hard to see why. There the biggest local team is MTG Famagusta, who play at the Canbulat Stadium near Othello's castle. Indeed it looks like a fortress, with Famagusta Castle overlooking the ground. On one side of the pitch, there is a small stand; on the other there is a wall separating it from the local port. People stand on the wall watching the games but it can be a problem if the ball flies over. You might hear a splash.

MTG did not always play there. They moved from the nearby Dr Fazıl Küçük Stadium, which is now used by a second division side called Dumlupınar. The stadium is not far from the restricted area in Famagusta, which is closed to citizens. Houses and hotels have been emptied and the Turkish army are inside. On the coast, it feels like a holiday resort, until you turn around to see what looks like a ghost town. Reminders of conflict are never far away.

Even so, it is not as if the two sides cannot exist peacefully together. In 2003, the Green Line was opened, allowing the border to be crossed, while in the small town of Pile, Greeks and Turks live side by side. One day, it could yet be the same on the football pitch.

Lifting the ban on crossing the Green Line meant that some Turkish Cypriot players were able to try their luck in the South. However, these moves have often been controversial. Sabri Selden was the first to move and was helpfully called a traitor by the former TRNC president Rauf Denktaş. Coşkun Ulusoy tried his luck with Nea Salamis but lasted only two seasons and there was more anger last summer when Mustafa Yasinses joined Alki.

This is not viewed as the definitive answer, however, even though they know they need players to move abroad. It is easy to get a Greek Cypriot passport and a visa but there is unease over whether that would truly benefit Turkish citizens, even if it would allow Turkish Cypriots to develop their talent and play professionally. "It is not the solution," said Kamal. "Then you are not representing your people. Kids should play at home. How can you send your kids away? The sacrifices are too big. How can you go to the South every day? Don't use the young people in politics."

Perhaps it will take the emergence of another Ebeoğlu for people to alter their views. He played in the Cypriot league for AEL in the fifties, finishing as the top scorer twice and winning the title three times. He was the only Turkish Cypriot in the top division but he was not out of place. Far from it. Having started his career in football with Limassol Turkish Sports Club in 1946, he shows that Greek Cypriots and Turkish Cypriots can thrive together. "We are waiting to play," said Ebeoğlu, whose living room is packed with AEL regalia, his medals, trophies, awards and photographs of him with various dignitaries and politicians. "There are many football players in the North. Very good players." He was one of them. More can follow his example, if the politics allow it.

There was no problem for a Turkish Cypriot to play in the Cypriot league back then as the Turkish sides were part of the CFA. Ebeoğlu moved to AEL in 1951, spending seven years at the club at which he would make his name and become a legend. He even played for Cyprus twice, travelling to Jerusalem with the squad. They played the Israeli side Hapoel Tel Aviv. However his is still a tale of missed opportunities. In 1952 he was supposed to play in a World Cup qualifier for Cyprus against Egypt, but it was deemed unsafe to go there after the British invasion. Still, they would play against Olympiakos and other Greek teams.

Turkish Cypriots were able to play for the national side without any hassle and Ebeoğlu's brother-in-law also played for Cyprus. "There were five Turkish players, five Greek and one Armenian," says Ebeoğlu. "But there cannot be a combined Cyprus team now." He stopped playing in 1963 when the troubles worsened, becoming a coach and a referee for a while, and it is a

scandal that no one has been able to follow in his footsteps.

Despite the obstacles, the feeling for football in Northern Cyprus remains strong. That it does is testament to their love for the sport, because the challenges are fierce. In October, a game between Bagcil and Gençlik Güku had to be postponed after 37 minutes because of the weather and it was rearranged for a Wednesday afternoon. The score was 1-1 at the time.

Always conscious of following Fifa regulations, the match kicked off at the 37-minute mark on the rearranged date in front of a small but boisterous crowd. There could not have been more than 100 people inside the ramshackle stadium — there are English Sunday League sides with better facilities — but no one seemed to mind. This was grassroots football at its very core, even if there wasn't very much grass on a pitch that badly needed some attention.

There was only one stand and flies everywhere, while the football was technical but not up to much. That was hardly a surprise, though. The lack of a proper infrastructure ensures the quality is low. In the end, the match finished 3-1 to Bagcil after two well-taken goals in the second half, although the thunder in the distance as the final whistle approached was the signal for most people to leave. "Careful, they'll have to cancel the game again," someone remarked.

It is not an exaggeration to suggest, based on the evidence, that a non-league English side would have thrashed either Bagcil or Gençlik Güku. But the fact that so many people turned out to watch a keenly contested match and were so vocal in their support on a Wednesday afternoon shows why a compromise must be reached if football truly is the world sport we want it to be.

For Kamal, it was a friendly organised against Liverpool veterans two years ago that revealed the depth of feeling among Turkish Cypriots. Although Fifa does not allow professional sides to play friendly matches in Northern Cyprus, they do not need authorisation to invite former professionals so along came Robbie Fowler, Jamie Redknapp, Michael Thomas, Mark Wright, Jason McAteer, Don Hutchison, David Fairclough and Phil Babb and in a packed stadium, 2,500 fans watched Liverpool win 2-1. "This is when we understood," said Kamal. "This is when we understood we have to do something for the people."

However, there is light at the end of the tunnel. The appointment of Hasan Sertoğlu in 2010 has seen the KTFF's stock rise. Sertoğlu oversaw the league's sponsorship and television deals, while their new headquarters are based near the border. "We worked from the inside to start with," Sertoğlu has said. "Now we are working for change on the outside."

It seems that the increased media attention on football in Cyprus has accelerated the process. In October, Kamal seemed pessimistic, talking about how he could not work for the KTFF for ever, not if there was no prospect of change. However since then, both sides have appeared more ready for the issue to be resolved. It has been put to them by outside mediators brought in to speed up the talks and bring professional football to Northern Cyprus that if

Palestinians can play in the Israeli league, then there should be no problem in Cyprus. No one has been able to come up with much of a counter-argument.

So in November the CFA and the KTFF met for informal talks in Limassol, before an official meeting took place at the CFA headquarters in south Nicosia. In a historic twist, it was decided that second meeting would be held between Sertoğlu and the president of the CFA, Costakis Koutsokoumnis, at the KTFF headquarters in north Nicosia on 17 January. "The presence of the media shows that the footballing community of Cyprus wants a solution to the 'football' problem," Koutsokoumnis said. "We need to move quickly, we think the ground is right to find a solution for the unification of football on the island and I am certain that both sides are determined to solve this problem that has existed since 1955."

At last, the end is in sight. There is a way to go yet but Koutsokoumnis suggested that an initial plan would be in place within two months. "The island has suffered thanks to politicians and our focus is only on football, not on politics," Sertoğlu said. "I believe that with good will we can find a resolution to this problem. Everyone expects a solution from us. I have a strong belief that we will not disappoint anyone."

They have surely come too far for that now. At times the CFA and the KTFF have resembled two warring siblings who have needed to have their heads banged together but there is acknowledgement about the need to compromise and a meeting in January was reportedly extremely positive. As the success of Ebeoğlu all those years ago demonstrates, this would not only benefit the Turkish Cypriots but the Greek Cypriots too. It can improve their league, which has never been in better shape.

Some will doubt whether clubs from the North can compete with their more illustrious neighbours from the South. The gulf in wealth at the moment is eye-watering. Yet few people will care about that at the moment. This is not about money. It is simply a moral imperative that football is made available to everyone and also a reminder that sport and politics rarely, if ever, make good bedfellows. Football purports to be the world game. The people's game. It is hard to take that seriously while there are those who are not allowed to take part. Ⓑ

The Hangover of War

Almost four decades after the Turkish invasion, the shadow of conflict hangs over the Nicosia derby

By Cyrus Philbrick

Rivalries are formed most often out of geographical convenience. Teams fight for bragging rights to a neighbourhood, city or state. As geography also shapes race, religion, class and politics, such divides can cut deep. But some rivalries are so political that they defy geographical boundaries, born not from arbitrary locale, but from ethos. A few such conflicts exist in Cyprus. The largest, Apoel v Omonoia, nearly splits the republic's mind in half.

Those new to the politics of the island — a triangular battleground of influence between Greek nationalism, independent Cypriot identity and Turkish occupation — can struggle with what Cyprus even means. "Cyprus the island" has always referred to the geographical mass of land, which points, like a spade drill bit, between the coasts of Turkey and Syria. After 1974, "Cyprus the Republic", or just "Cyprus", has referred to the southern two-thirds of the island, divided from the north side by a Turkish invasion. Cyprus is currently a member of the EU, which doesn't recognise the occupied north or, by extension, its football league.

Over a drink at a football clubhouse, I asked an elderly man about the rift between Omonoia and Apoel. In Cypriot baritone, he reminded me to start at the beginning. "Look, everybody conquer Cyprus," he said. "But Greeks, they do it best." For thousands of years, Cyprus was passed from one empire to the next as an enticing, but not crucial, portage between Africa, Europe and the Middle East. Mycenaean Greeks began this chain of conquests some 3,500 years ago, first installing Greek roots. In the Archaic period, waves of Greek settlement 'Hellenised' the island with Greek language, art and religion. Fast forward a dozen or so regimes (Assyrian, Roman, Byzantine, Frankish and Venetian, among others) and Cypriots living under decaying colonial rules — first the Ottoman[1] and then the British — kept the strongest cultural connection to Greece. Under the British, Cypriots expressed a growing desire for re-unification with Greece. By 1950, over 95% of the country voted in favour of a referendum for union. But the British responded with harsher control measures.

Forming athletic clubs served as a way for Cypriots to identify with Greece under the noses of their British

---

[1] *During Ottoman rule, between 1571 and 1878, Turks settled on the island. Their descendants are referred to as Turkish Cypriots.*

occupiers, who brought club football to the island. Anorthosis Famagusta, the first Cypriot club, was formed as a literary society that aimed to educate children and promote the goal of 'rectification', a more loaded word for re-unification. The club added athletic pursuits like football, in 1913, to bolster its influence. Apoel, which stands for "Athletic Football Club of Greeks of Nicosia," was formed in 1926. These clubs played against a smattering of British and other Cypriot clubs in the Cyprus Football Association, which was officially formed in 1934. "First the best teams were all British," said the elderly man, whom I later discovered had played for 25 years for a first division club in Limassol. "But we learned."

After the Second World War, as Britain's colonial grip weakened, a war-torn Greece scrambled for its own identity in the vacuum left by the fascist exodus. Like much of eastern and southern Europe at the time, Greece teetered between Western and Communist control. The US and Britain tried to ensure a West-leaning government by supporting military strikes that squashed Communist organisation. The Greek Civil War, largely fought between these two political affiliations, lasted from 1946 to 1949. The tensions spilled over into Cyprus. As a sign of solidarity with the Hellenic Amateur Athletic Association (Segas), the Apoel board required its players to sign affiliation to the new right-wing Greek government. The requirement, however, violated a club statute that outlawed political affiliation.

"About seven or eight players refused to sign," said Konstantinos Scambilis, a writer for *Haravgi*, a leftist newspaper from Nicosia. "They disagreed with the idea and left to form their own club. The same thing happened at other clubs. Nea Salamina (Famagusta), Alki (Larnaca) and Orfeas (Nicosia) also formed leftist clubs. Together, they formed their own league. And today these are still regarded as the leftist clubs in the country."

Scambilis emphasized that the East-West tension in Cyprus wasn't as violent as in Greece. "Apoel let the players go," he said. "The players weren't persecuted or prosecuted. There was no Cypriot government at the time. It was British. So no one interfered ... You can imagine it wasn't too hard to form a new club in those days. You found other people close by who thought like you and who could play."

During the 1950s, Cypriots escalated their push for independence from Britain. Independence represented a long overdue goal in Cyprus favoured by both left- and right-wing supporters. Such common ground and a desire to bolster Cypriot football against British influence, pushed the two leagues to reunite in 1953 under the Cyprus Football Association (CFA), which was large enough to allow promotion and relegation. Based on merit, Omonoia was initially the only leftist team accepted into the Cypriot first division.

Although the struggle for independence united the nation against the British, it also revealed the different visions of the future of the country held by different factions. "What you have to realise," Scambilis said, "is that the war for independence wasn't really for independence. It was for union with Greece and freedom from British rule. So as a political tactic it is really different from fighting for independence or an independent nation. All political formations, like the communist party and the church, supported union. But the church, and the more right-wing part of society, used much more strongly the idea of union. 'Union and only union,' it was said. The left, though, accepted the idea that there could be some form of independence or self-government in union before the final goal of independence. Like Puerto Rico in the US, I think. They have some form of self-government and the idea was that you could have some form of government even though you were still a colony. Then eventually you would go for independence of the country."

Conflicting notions of independence again pitted Cypriots against Cypriots. Some insurgents pushing for Greek union pushed harder and more violently than anyone else. They lashed out against those standing in their way, which meant both leftists and Turkish Cypriots. "The struggle started with the idea of union as its target," Scambilis said. "The leftist Cypriots were not as much a part of the struggle, not as invested. In many villages in Cyprus there are actually records of killings of leftists by the insurgents. And also killings of Turkish Cypriots [who almost certainly didn't favour union with Greece]. The British would place Turkish Cypriots as police officers. And these positions were targets for insurgents. So killings started happening."

In 1955, Çetinkaya Türk SK, the lone Turkish Cypriot team in the First Division, withdrew from the CFA because of the escalating tensions between Greek and Turkish Cypriots. Even at this time, many Turkish Cypriots supported a divided island. Along with other Turkish Cypriot clubs, Çetinkaya Türk SK formed the Cyprus Turkish Football Federation (KTFF). This federation still exists in the occupied north of the island, although it isn't recognised by Fifa.

Britain finally relinquished independence to an increasingly stubborn but increasingly fractured Cyprus in 1960. The Zurich-London Agreements established an independent, and not Greek, republic. Throughout the sixties, a large portion of the population still pushed for union with Greece. The fervour peaked in 1974 when a right-wing coup, supported by the Greek government and Nato, tried to overthrow the Cypriot president, Archbishop Markarios III. Chaos ensued as the island ignited in conflicts between Greek Cypriots and Turkish Cypriots. The Turkish military invaded, it claimed, to protect both the constitutional rights of the country and the safety of the minority Turkish Cypriots. The coup and its aftermath crystallised both political and football loyalties.

"Apoel took a stand supporting the coup," Scambilis said, "and Omonoia took a stand against it. So you had a lot of tension at that time, riots at stadiums. Leading up to 1974 you had serious violence. You had guns and death. It's safer now obviously. But you can still see it today. When you go to games you see Apoel fans holding Greek flags. And you see fans of Omonoia holding Cyprus flags. And in the stands you hear songs about each side being traitors.

"Apoel fans still hold to those Greek-loving feelings and affiliations. They leap back to that era. They know that this was their main cause, even though they know it's not as realistic now." Apoel fans largely cling to Cyprus's past, while Omonoia holds hope for a new future. "I'm a fan because of our past," an Apoel fan told me. "Because it's important — where we come from as a people, as a country."

After 1974, tensions cooled between the two sides. But unlike in most other European countries, in Cyprus hooligan violence has increased in recent years. Brawls have bloodied both sides. "When you hear about football violence today, it's mostly not for political reasons," Scambilis said. "It's hooligans creating violence because they're hooligans. Unfortunately, some of the people that are members of Ultras groups are in it only for the hooliganism. So they go to the ground looking for a fight, not because they like or believe in their club." Conflict mostly plays out verbally, in supporter chat rooms and in warring chants that echo around the walls of the GSP stadium in Nicosia, the largest in the country with a capacity of around 25,000. During derbies, the stadium is perfectly divided, green and white shouting across at blue, yellow and orange — spring yelling at summer. Cypriots of all ages spew some of the dirtier chants in the business. "Mostly they call us Communists or Turks, and we call them Fascists," Panayiotis Kouis, an Omonoia supporter, said. Kouis puts it gently. One chant, screamed at AEL Limassol[2] fans, translates roughly as, "You are pussies, you are pussies / Turks fuck your mother / and AEL, and AEL / You are the bitch of Apoel." But Omonoia fans

are most comfortable with the classic anti-Apoel chant: "Sons of a whore, you fascist right-wingers!"

Blatantly political chants are banned by the CFA. Both Omonoia and Apoel played a match in April match inside an empty stadium. But the league misses, or ignores, a number of arguably political chants. According to Kouis, Apoel fans frequently get away with yelling, "Die Christofias!" in reference to the Communist president. As elections approach, Kouis says, the chants take on political edge: "If a match is near the presidential elections or the parliamentary elections, you will see flags of the parties on the stands, you can hear songs about parties, and feel more political aggression."

Beneath the league's official position against political ties, however, there lies powerful political support for both clubs. "Although nobody officially admits it, Omonoia and Apoel are run by the two political parties," Scambilis said. "Behind the two parties, if you see the people that are managing the teams, financially, administratively, these are people you see five or 10 years later becoming members of parliament."

High-reaching affiliation has caused suspicion on both sides of match-fixing. "If you ask any fan in Cyprus, they will say that there is political intervention in the championship," Scambilis said. "On numerous occasions there have been reports. You hear it through the years from both sides. But it is hard to prove.

[2] *AEL beat both Omonoia and Apoel in 2011-12 to win their sixth league championship, the fourth highest total behind Omonoia's 20 and Apoel's 21 since 1934.*

Twenty and more years ago, I think there were real problems with match-fixing based on the political background of the officials or politicians. But recently match-fixing has become financial, based on pay-offs. It doesn't happen as much. But I think it's still a problem."

Scambilis cites increasing media coverage and more foreign players as the main reasons why any political match-fixing doesn't happen in the modern game. "Most of the players at any club today are foreigners," he said, "so how can you ask them to fix a game for political reasons? Money maybe ..."

When Cyprus joined the EU in 2004, the league abandoned caps on foreign players. Now the league has over 70% foreigners, the highest percentage in Europe. Some teams start zero homegrown players and maintain what are viewed as "token Cypriots" on the bench. Omonoia and Apoel typically fielded one or two home-grown players this season. More foreigners and higher contract values even allowed a few player swaps between Omonoia and Apoel, which was previously unthinkable.

"Before it was impossible, physically impossible," Kouis said. "But in the nineties, players got paid enough not to care. Still though, only about three [players] in 15 years shifted teams, that I can remember. Two from Omonoia to Apoel. And one from Apoel to Omonoia. And it was a big deal."

Since the nineties, players have largely divorced themselves from club political affiliations. They lash out only when prodded. After a match in 2010, for example, a group of Apoel players lapped the pitch while draped in a Greek flag. They did so in response to witnessing an Omonoia ultra torch a Greek flag during the match. Omonoia banned the fan, who tried to plead insanity upon arrest, for life for desecrating a sacred emblem.

Kouis also remembers a rare statement by Omonoia players. After the first goal against Apoel, Omonoia players lifted their kit to reveal Che Guevara shirts. The stark Guevara icon is a common sight amid green and white Omonoia Ultras, or "Gate 9." Guevara is a natural emblem for them. Like other Che-clad hordes, Omonoia's Gate 9 has real, if idealistic, beliefs in the necessity of both social revolution and unity beyond national interests. For many fans, the club represents not only Communist beliefs, but hope for a unified island. The word Omonoia literally means "not fighting." Their green and white represent hope and joy, or peace and unity, depending who you ask.

Omonoia have never played a match against a Turkish Cypriot team, but veterans of leftist teams have played friendlies against veterans of Turkish Cypriot teams in events held to promote unification. Kouis admits the dangers of staging a friendly match. "It could turn out to be a boomerang for the country," he said. "It could turn other teams and other parts of society against Omonoia. There could be a lot of hatred. It would be something really challenging and maybe courageous. But it should be tried."

"There were a few attempts," Kouis noted, "from the leftist teams Salamina and Alki, to sign Turkish Cypriot players. But the players were prohibited from signing by the pseudo-government [on the occupied side]." The pseudo-government declared that playing for the CFA would imply recognition of the Cyprus government. Last season, a Turkish Cypriot team from Nicosia threatened to join the CFA after receiving a 13-match ban from the Turkish Cypriot Football Federation (KTFF) for a pitch invasion. The KTFF answered the threat, which may or may not have been intended seriously, with one of its own. It stated that any attempt to join the CFA, which the CFA would be unlikely to accept, would breach the KTFF constitution, and that the club would be exiled from the KTFF.

Omonoia's lobbying power, bolstered by thousands of optimistic youths, holds the potential to undercut the refusal of both sides of the island to recognise one another, or communicate. In the mould of other socially conscious Ultras groups, Gate 9 claims to be a mouthpiece of worldly values. Some of its effort goes towards supporting a re-thinking of Cyprus's relationship with Turkish Cypriots. Gate 9 once hosted a group of 500 Turkish-Cypriots in the stands at a match against Apoel. Together they unveiled banners, in both Greek and Turkish, on which were written a single word: PEACE.

The Gate 9 website includes a lengthy manifesto that, towards the end, says: "The Cypriot educational system teaches hatred towards the Turkish people from a very early age due to the political tensions among Cyprus, Greece, and Turkey. After the separation of the island in 1974 ... the hatred grew even further. We as anti-racists accept the Turkish people and the Turkish-Cypriots as fellow human beings, without promoting the hatred that others impose on us. We condemn the invasion of the Turkish army as we do all militaristic interventions. We condemn the nationalist upraising on the island which led to the invasion. Gate 9 condemns all nationalistic actions whether they are governmental or social."

Omonoia fans are particularly proud of stunts that combine their ethos with digs at their enemy. When the Iraq war started in 2003, Gate 9 unveiled a banner that read: "Do not throw bombs at Iraq, save them for the Apoel fans."

In one sense, the story of these two clubs is not unique. Other politicised rivalries pepper the rawer areas of Europe, Africa, and the Middle East. But it is rare that two fan-bases stand in such perfect deadlock, defined by the other while trying to devour them. The rivalry constantly re-polarises itself. And only Cyprus cares. For many Cypriots, these clubs stand as surrogates for the two major political parties, for lines in the sand that most Cypriots are unwilling to breach because of two different versions of national pride. In this way, the Apoel-Omonoia rivalry helps preserve the political stalemate within Cyprus, and between Cyprus and the occupied north. Maybe beyond the vitriolic chants, the "Fascist sons of a whore!" and the "Communist bastards!", lies a fragile space for meaningful dialogue, for country-swaying change. But compromise over national identity promises to be at least as difficult as any previous overthrow of empire.

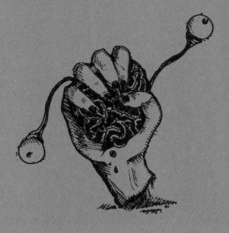

21
Interview

"It's not Uefa which has a different
view. It is Monsieur Platini."

Sepp Blatter

The president of Fifa admits he may stand for re-election in 2015 and reveals concerns over the Qatar World Cup

By Philippe Auclair

We're in the small hours of the morning in one of Moscow's better hotels, late in the autumn of 2010. A few journalists are sharing gossip around a bottle of Chablis, of which the bar's wine list offers a bewildering selection. All of us have been invited to see at first hand how Russia is coiling the spring in its bid to host the 2018 World Cup. Fifa's decision will be made public in a few weeks' time. 'Made public', not 'made', as it's quite clear to all those who follow these sorts of things closely that a significant majority of the 22 remaining ExCo members (Amos Adamu and Reynald Temarii, both of them suspected of corruption, had been suspended in November) are keen on the Russians. And the Qataris. Quite naturally the conversation drifts to the stories which shroud the process in a smog of allegations, about which most of the bidding nations seem quite happy to give 'private briefings'. No-one's found the smoking gun yet, but everybody's convinced it's been fired a few times. Quite naturally, the name of Sepp Blatter is mentioned time and again. The septuagenarian Blatter, the supreme football politician of our age, must be pulling the strings. But if there are strings to pull, they're of the kind that enabled Christopher Reeve to fly like Superman in those old pre-CGI movies. You just know

the special effects squad must have used something but the editor's done a brilliant job. Superman's revving the planet faster than Sputnik, with no strings attached.

"One thing people forget, or fail to get," one of our group says, "is that, at heart, Blatter is a romantic." The natural response might be to laugh. Isn't it agreed that Joseph S Blatter is a *bad thing*? But we're all listening, as the man who's speaking knows him better than most — certainly better than any of us. He's worked with Blatter for over a decade; he's been party to discussions that we'd all have loved to witness and write about; we also know him to be trustworthy and sincere; he didn't ask for water when the second bottle was brought to our table. Blatter-bashers would struggle to understand how he could have served such a master for so long without becoming tainted himself. But he did, within Fifa, and wasn't. So Sepp is "a romantic", really? Our friend wasn't referring to Blatter's tenure as the President of The World Sociey of the Friends of Suspenders, a position he was elected to in 1973. The story of how the amateur Swiss footballer from Visp and one-time general secretary of the Swiss Ice Hockey Federation placed himself in the wake of João Havelange, climbed up the Fifa ladder and became the ruler of that empire in June 1998, gazumping Lennart Johansson in the process, is well-known and, at first glance, anything but 'romantic'.

But let's take a step back. Joseph Blatter joined the Fifa 'family' in 1975, as the organisation's Technical Director, becoming its General Secretary six years later. Fifa was near-bankrupt in the 1970s. Attendances were falling in almost every single domestic and international competition. Is football a better game to watch now that it was then? The change to Law 12 — a change of which Blatter had been a vocal advocate — banning keepers from handling a back-pass, was met with scepticism when it was introduced in 1992 by the International Board. Few would now question that it had a hugely positive impact on the game, perhaps more than any other such change since the 1925 modification of the offside law. Dangerous tackles from behind were made red card offences in 1998. Again, Blatter had pleaded in favour of a measure that many believed unenforceable or even detrimental to the game. They were wrong. Africa has staged a World Cup. Women's football has developed to an extent that was unthinkable when its first World Cup was held in 1991 in China. Fifa's coffers are bursting with cash — over £740m — which, no matter how questionable the manner in which these millions have been harvested and might have been misused by certain individuals, help finance thousands of grass-root

schemes throughout the organisation's 209 associations. Football is objectively healthier now that it was when "the man who has fifty ideas a day, fifty-one of them bad", according to a German wit, decided to throw in his lot with the now-discredited Havelange.

So, yes, perhaps the arch-manoeuverer, the political virtuoso who is always one step ahead of his adversaries, is also a 'romantic', if only for his capacity to turn the conviction that he is acting for the good of the game into a formidable weapon in the fight to gain and hold onto power. Those who dismiss Blatter as an out-of-touch, quasi-senile buffoon because of his suggestions that women footballers should wear "tighter shorts" (January 2004) and gay fans "should refrain from sexual activity" when they attend the 2022 World Cup in Qatar (January 2010[1]) make a mistake that has proven fatal to many of his former rivals: they underestimate him. Meeting the Fifa president face-to-face for the first time, as I did for this interview, conducted on the occasion of the International Football Arena in Zurich[2], I was struck — as many others before me have been — by the agility of his mind, his personal charm and his ability to suggest one thing while saying quite another. As is the rule on such occasions, a list of topics (Brazil 2014, Qatar 2022, financial fair-play) had been agreed upon before I could be led into the inner sanctum of Fifa's headquarters, which can only be accessed once your

[1] *Homosexuality is illegal in Qatar and is punishable by up to five years' imprisonment.*

[2] *This interview was conducted in French, one of five languages that Blatter speaks fluently: German is his mother tongue; English, Spanish and Italian are the others.*

guide's fingerprints have been scanned by a laser beam. Joseph Blatter, the romantic schemer, the man who put chips into footballs, is clearly in favour of cutting-edge technology.

⚽ *Mr President, Brazil 2014 is now a year and a half away and there are still many doubts as to whether the country will be ready to welcome the World Cup...*

...and we'll have had the Confederations Cup by then.

⚽ *...Do you share any of these doubts?*

Listen, as in every process of organising a World Cup which I have lived through for a number of years, there are always delays in the building work. But, ultimately, all the games take place. So, in my case, it is not necessary to be pessimistic and say, "They won't be able to do it." If Brazil, the sixth largest economic power in the world, with its 200 million inhabitants, a footballing nation *par excellence*, were unable to deliver a World Cup... they'll do it. Yes, there are delays, there's a bit of this, a bit of that. But you've got to say that the political organisation of Brazil plays a role in this. You've got a central government, but this central government has delegated the mission to organise this World Cup to the governors of the various provinces, and within those provinces, you've got the cities, and, naturally, politically speaking, the system isn't the same everywhere, which creates interferences and delays from time to time. I assure you, in the end, everything will be fine even if, as I have seen it with my own eyes before — in Portugal, at the 2004 Euro — you've still

got to apply a lick of paint on the opening day of the competition.

⚽ *The difference, this time, is that there are a number of important, powerful people within Brazil who are openly critical of the whole process, especially as far as the financing is concerned, people who think this money would be better used in other fields. Can this not have an adverse effect on what is happening there?*

I am in regular touch with the Brazilian president Dilma Rousseff. She delegated all her powers [in this matter] to her sports minister, Mr Aldo Rebelo. We at Fifa have asked our general secretary Jérôme Valcke and his staff to take care of all the administrative details. Now, as you know, Brazil is going through a very dynamic phase of economic development... and social development too. When you've got a big event like [the World Cup], people say, "Yes, football's fantastic," but others add, "We've also got another big event to take care of!" The Olympic Games, of course. They take place in a single city, of course, but they affect the country as a whole. Brazil "saw big." And Brazil has to digest it.

⚽ *Didn't Brazil see too big?*

I don't think so. It's a great country. I'm certain Brazil will be able to deliver a great World Cup. You'll see. As soon as we play the Confederations Cup there [from 15 to 30 June 2013], things are going to move, things are going to get hot! Not like in other countries where football isn't anchored as deeply as it is there in the people. Everyone's a footballer in Brazil. We're going back to the essence of football. Of course, the

English will tell you (adopting a mock British accent), "We are the country of Association Football," but Brazil hasn't won five World Cups by chance. They last had a chance to organise it in 1950. Three generations ago. It is only fair that they get a chance to do it again. Brazil will deliver.

Going beyond 2014 and looking ahead to 2022, we've recently heard a number of officials — your Fifa vice-president Michel Platini among others — recommending that the Qatar World Cup should be held in winter, more precisely in November and December 2022, in order not to clash with the Winter Olympics. Are you open to this switch? Would you be in favour of it?

The World Cup is going round the world. We'll be in Russia in 2018, as no eastern European country has ever hosted a World Cup, and the last major global event to take place there was the 1980 Olympics. Then Qatar. Good. The basic conditions — not just for Qatar, but for all the candidates — were the same. It means that the Fifa World Cup is played in June and July. That's the basic condition. And it is on this basic condition that the Executive Committee took the decision to give the 2022 World Cup to Qatar. Now, naturally, a bit late perhaps, we realise... we already knew that it gets very hot in Qatar at this time of the year. The other candidates had battled for their bids on the basis of a World Cup that would be played in June and July. Now, who can change that? Firstly, it is not us, Fifa, who are going to take the initiative

to do so, even if eminent... or important members of our Executive Committee[1] have expressed themselves [in favour of a winter World Cup]. The basis remains the same: June, July. If someone wants to change that, the request must come from Qatar. Qatar should present a request to Fifa — which Qatar hasn't done yet. No discussion has been held. *Voilà*. And if you changed something, what would the reaction of the other candidates be? They'd say, "If the basic condition is changed, what's going on, what's happening now?" That's one thing. The other thing is the international schedule — even though, with all parties in agreement, an international schedule can be changed.

Some leagues are completely opposed to this, however. Wouldn't that create a political storm? Wouldn't that be detrimental to football?

I can tell you that Qatar hasn't finished being a subject of preoccupation in the football world.

Should Qatar 2022's Supreme Committee turn to you and say, "Mr Blatter, we've gone deeper into air-cooling technologies, and we really think it'd be better if the tournament was played in November and December," would these words find a sympathetic ear — or would you tell them, "Perhaps it'd be better to reconsider the bid from A to Z?" What would Australia say, or the USA?

Or Japan, or Korea! Listen. If I had to govern the football world with 'ifs'...

---

[3] *ie Michel Platini, the only ExCo member who had asked for a switch to winter at the time this interview was conducted.*

[laughs] In any case, I cannot give a personal answer. I have to abide by the decisions that have been made by Fifa. It is my duty, my responsibility and my right to defend Fifa's principles. And one of these principles was: June, July.

⊕ *In what respect would a summer World Cup in Qatar represent a step forward for football?*

The important thing for me was that the World Cup should travel round the world. I remember how, when South Africa was chosen to host the 2010 World Cup, I had told the crown prince of Saudi Arabia — who was a passionate supporter of Morocco — that, for me, Africa lies south, not north of the Sahara. He replied, "Mr President, I invite you to think, one day, about the Arab world, and give it the World Cup." That is the case with Qatar. It is the realisation of what I'd said in June 1998, when I was elected president of Fifa. I'd been asked, "What is your programme?" and I'd said, "To give the World Cup to Africa and to go round the world with the competition," so that it wouldn't remain the privilege of Europe and the Americas. We're now facing a problem. But perhaps it's a false problem and the technology [to cool stadiums] will be there in 2022. As Fifa president, I repeat: June, July.

⊕ *Wouldn't the Americans, the Australians, the Japanese and the Koreans turn against Fifa if it was decided to switch the tournament to winter? Wouldn't that be a plain breach of tender?*

In any case, it wouldn't improve Fifa's reputation, I can tell you that.

⊕ *...which Fifa could do without — which leads me to the question: now that a new Ethics Committee has been named, are you satisfied with the progress that's been made in terms of governance?*

We're in the last bend before the last straight. We initiated the reform in 2011 and we have a road map that leads to the 2013 congress [which will be held in Mauritius from 30 May]. The Ethics Committee now consists of two entities, each of which has a completely independent chairman. That's done. What's left to do is to elect the members of the tribunals, which we'll do at this Congress. We'll do the same thing for the Disciplinary and Appeals Committees, in order to have complete separation of powers within Fifa. Second, the Audit and Control Committee, which is an internal FIFA organisation — but with an independently-chosen president — has been set up. Third, there are the statutory changes, which we're now in the process of identifying in consultation with the national associations. We'll have their feedback in February, their answer to questions like: "Should the ExCo be chosen by the Fifa congress, or by the confederations? Should there be an age limit? Should there be a limit to the number of terms that can be served?" All of this is supervised by the Independent Governance Committee which is presided over by Dr Mark Pieth, whose work will be concluded in 2013. This means that we now have safeguards in place — off the pitch. But that's not enough. Fifa, that's 300 million people. You can't have a single tribunal for 300 million people. It only means something if it goes down to the 209 national associations and the six confederations.

The system can only work that way. At Fifa level, on 1 June, it'll be done. And then we'll get on with the electoral campaign for 2015 [laughs]. I'll be able to say, "My Fifa is now in calm waters, I can leave the boat in two years' time."

⊕ *Are you really counting yourself out for the 2015 election?*

[Pause]

⊕ *You're in very good health, you...*

...Listen...[laughs]

⊕ *Never say never?*

Never say never again? Well, there'll be candidates. I'm sure of that. I'll have been at Fifa for 38 years in February. We've created a Fifa that is about democracy — all the associations have one vote, the small ones like the big ones — and solidarity. The World Cup must remain the number one competition, because it is our only source of money and, with that money, we can develop football in the whole world. It's been accepted now. But there is now a trend, by which clubs think that they're more important than the rest of the world, than the national teams... but that's not true. Ask any citizen of any country how important he thinks his national team is. Solidarity between clubs and national teams is essential. Fifa stands for discipline, respect, fair-play, not just on the field of play, but in our society as well.

⊕ *As you mention fair-play, how do you view the 'Platini reform' and the introduction of FFP by Uefa? Could the regulations that are phased in in Europe serve as a model for other confederations, in Asia, for example, where the problem of 'financial doping' is just as acute as it is in Uefa countries?*

I must say that, within Fifa, financial fair-play is already safeguarded by our Audit and Control Committee. Each [national] association must exert that control. I'd say that the phrase "financial fair-play" has a pleasant ring to it... but I don't know if there's fair-play in financial matters. In financial matters, it's about the bottom line, profit and loss. Simply call it "audit and control", and you've got it. For the whole world. And it might be a bit simpler to say, audit and control, rather than [respect] fair-play. In "fair-play", there is the word "play". And you shouldn't play with finances. Those who do are gamblers.

⊕ *When you see what's happening at PSG, and sovereign funds — Qatar, in this case — which are willing to commit unbelievable amounts of money to football, how do you react as a football man and as president of Fifa? Can it work?*

As long as you've got serious investors who wish to put money into football, I applaud. It proves that football is attractive. What upsets me, what I find scandalous is when clubs accept fools. We've seen that in England with Portsmouth, we've also seen that in Switzerland. Three clubs have fallen into that trap and succumbed, Neuchâtel-Xamax among them[4], of which I am still the honorary president. But as long as

---

[4] *FC Lausanne-Sport and Servette FC are the other two.*

you've got investors who are paying the players...You also pay the great stars of cinema and theatre, the singers who give four or five concerts a year and are paid huge amounts of money. Why shouldn't footballers be paid, players who put on a show twice a week for thousands in the stands and millions on television? If it's done seriously, I find nothing shocking about that, either as a football man or as Fifa president. What happens is that you've got clubs which are more popular than others, because they've got the better players, and the others say, "Why not us?" But go back fifty years. Look at the great leagues. The Italian one, for example. Fifty years ago, who was playing for the title? Inter, Milan, Juve. In England, it was between the Liverpool, Manchester, Birmingham and London clubs. What's changed? Same in Spain and Germany. As the saying goes, "You only lend money to the rich." So, if [new] investors can pull a league up, it's a good thing, I think. What matters is financial equilibrium, audit and control.

But people in France will tell you that it is impossible for a PSG to balance its accounts in the short or medium term. They'll never recoup their investment.

This investment is never rewarded. You have investors, like the Americans in the Premier League, who provide bank guarantees. You have patrons like Abramovich, who give their money to their clubs. You've got Qatar, which is one family [the al-Thani dynasty]. If they put money into football... I haven't got anything against it. How long they'll put money into football is another matter. Will they carry on or not?

So this new money, going into new clubs, disturbing the established order, can be a good thing?

Yes, of course. As long as these investors are serious. Look at Switzerland again. Lausanne, Servette... what happened is that it was not properly controlled by the league or the association. As to PSG, if they've got the money, what's the problem?

One last question: we remember your reaction at the 2010 World Cup, when Frank Lampard scored a 'ghost goal' against Germany, and you said, "I never want to see that again." Fifa has now completed extensive tests of goal-line technology — but how do you reconcile Fifa's promotion of technology with Uefa's reluctance to embrace it?

It's not Uefa which has a different view. It is Monsieur Platini. It is not Uefa. If you go to the associations which compose Uefa, or ask the professional leagues, you'll see what they say. That — that is a Michel Platini idea, Platini who, for a reason... has put it in his head that he didn't want technology on the goal-line, because if you put it on the goal-line, tomorrow you'll use it for off-side decisions, and so on. That's him. When the majority of fans, leagues — and referees — thank Fifa for introducing goal-line technology, that's not very positive for the development of football.

30

Theory

"...at some clubs, you can fine players a fortnight's wages and it's a cup of tea to 'em."

Mourinho's Cult of Personality

How the Real Madrid manager's charismatic authority fosters loyalty

By Roy Henderson

José Mourinho still has a tendency to refer to Chelsea as "My Chelsea'. Isn't that odd?

I mean, the club's in rude health, isn't it? In the last five years alone, they've won six domestic trophies (including a domestic double) and reached two European Cup finals, winning one. OK, so the owner is a bit eccentric, but the mere fact he deems that kind of return unacceptable says something in itself. The club has cash and talent in abundance — but despite all that, there's still that lingering and distinct whiff of Post-Mourinho Syndrome about the place, isn't there? In the latter part of the Villas-Boas era in 2011, Stamford Bridge still chanted Mourinho's name. Can't they just move on and get over it?

It's easier said than done. You see, on moving to Chelsea in 2004, José Mourinho had just about mastered the darkest of managerial arts — the construction of a textbook personality cult. Whether wholly conscious or not, I firmly believe it's the central pillar of Mourinho's methodology.

Let me explain myself.

A long established and ubiquitous term (Karl Marx made casual reference to it in a letter of 1877), "personality cult" broadly fits the sociologist Max Weber's model of "charismatic authority" and describes the situation that develops when a compelling individual, in an auspicious context, establishes a public persona seductive enough that followers subjugate their individual reason and free will in favour of the will of their leader. A clear pattern emerges from there and the results aren't always too healthy.

Mourinho artfully established himself as just that kind of charismatic leader, and his players, his staff, the national media, and to a great extent football at large found themselves hanging on his every word — a situation that persists to this day. When he arrived at Chelsea, he was the shepherd and we were simply his latest dutiful flock. By that stage, he'd already been refining his methods for some time.

The Basic Prototype

In modern times, you'd think it would be difficult to establish yourself as some kind of messiah. Scientific reason, a free press, human rights... there are all kinds of obstacles in place for the aspiring modern day despot. But we're not nearly as collectively clever as we like to think.

Take Vernon Wayne Howell, for example. We know him better as David Koresh, the man who in 1993, along with 75 of his devoted followers (including 21 children), died in the fiery conclusion of an FBI siege in Waco, Texas. Illiterate and dyslexic, Koresh had suffered a lonely and directionless childhood. At the age of 11, however, the foundations were being laid for the man he would later become, developing an early taste for rumpy pumpy, and somehow memorising the entire New Testament. It seems from that point on he spent his time pestering Christian girls to 'mate'.

After several years of mixed success in that regard, Koresh eventually found his way to Waco, where he stumbled upon an interesting, hospitable group known as the "Branch Davidians". Led by a 76-year-old 'prophetess', the group happily accepted his claims that he was also a prophet and that God wanted him to father the 76 year old's child, with said child destined to be some kind of messiah. Conception being a little tricky at 76 years of age, the prophetess told Koresh he could 'teach his own message' while they kept working on it. Her son, meanwhile, was a little pissed off with these developments, and eventually ran Koresh off the property at gunpoint with 25 of his new-found devotees following in his glittering slipstream.

Koresh had stumbled into control of his very own personality cult. The group found new premises, and he set about recruiting new followers using the standard personality cult toolset:

1. Proclaim that you're 'special' and that you have a vision.

2. Define simple behavioural rules based on that vision.

3. Enforce the behavioural rules by ensuring your followers buy into them.

4. Make sure everything the group does relies on you.

Koresh's idea of glorious martyrdom wasn't the most sustainable of visions, of course, but his story, while tragic, illustrates the basic template for establishing a personality cult — a template similar to the one Mourinho had refined since first attempting its use during his brief stint with Benfica at the turn of the millennium.

Contextual Catalysis

Charisma and context are key to this process, of course. "Catalysis" is generally defined as the increased rate of chemical reaction after the introduction of some 'new' substance into the contextual mix — the 'catalyst'. Assemble a room full of journalists and cameramen and walk Bill Shankly in? Certain people, when introduced to a certain context, can leave the people in that context electrified.

Contextual catalysis is key to points 2 and 3 in the four-step template. Sometimes a group's rules are already largely defined and sometimes the group already buy into those rules to such an extent that they're just waiting for a leader with the right qualities to set the whole thing off. When a leader walks into a new leadership role, he's wise to sit and wait for the right opportunity — the right context — to present itself.

In that respect, Chelsea, like any ambitious club on the rise, was a context tailor-made for a man with Mourinho's skill set: a group of phenomenally talented footballers (assembled at almost unprecedented expense and levels of expectation) who desperately craved a working template for success, and a footballing 'establishment' (media, fans, competitors, and authorities) collectively waiting for (and largely dreading) the arrival of someone who could 'light the blue touch paper' and deliver that success — hungry young men who needed a guiding father figure and a football industry crying out for a little genuine drama.

Mourinho is careful in his selection of role, of course. Luís Lourenço, in his biography, betrays to some extent the early contextual lessons he learned on this front. Mourinho says, "I am the son of a coach, and I watched my father coach many different clubs all over Portugal. I can never forget the most painful days for a football coach. It isn't a new idea, and it's been used time and time again through the decades: the psychological whipping. I saw my father being sacked several times, too many times. I never knew of anyone who would first phone him to give him some sort of justification."

This youthful awareness of how precarious the managerial working context can be was compounded early in his career in his abortive stint at Benfica, where presidential elections and internal politics undermined his work with the squad. Looking back on the circumstances of his departure from the club, it's clear from Lourenço's biography that Mourinho at that stage was not sufficiently confident of his 'mythos', his reputation and marketability within the game, to do what his instincts told him he should do. "A touch of personal pride made me stay on at Benfica," he said. "I felt I couldn't leave without showing them I could do a good job. Today, I admit it was a mistake to stay. My insistence can be put down to age and inexperience. I was a 'kid' who needed to prove his worth to others, and that's why I stayed. I wouldn't do it again today."

That's not to say he didn't experiment politically, as the then-Benfica president would point out. The early signs were there of a clever man feeling his way into his role with an understanding of his circumstances that perhaps belied his level of experience and tender age. That sensitivity to the human forces at play (members, players, board), coupled with the self-awareness to recognise his own naivety, would inform his approach in later roles.

In contextual terms, as well as learning more carefully to manage his job selection and demands for his working environment, Mourinho learned the importance of selling his 'project' to the key stakeholders from that point on — a practice he uses to this day.

The Bible in PowerPoint

When Mourinho was approached by the owners of União de Leiria, he drafted a report which presented to the owners his plans for the club. Impressed, they immediately offered him the job. Jorge Nuno Pinto da Costa, the Porto President, had years before told Mourinho "your time at this club will come", and shortly thereafter Mourinho wheeled out the projector to deepen Pinto da Costa's commitment to his methodology. The Lourenço biography provided a glimpse of an approach he would later use with Abramovich. Mourinho said of the Porto presentation, "I think this document is extremely important, because it guides and directs an entire process. This document is a PowerPoint presentation that I gave to the president. The very first diagram sets out the idea that is the basis for the whole programme: 'The concept of club is more important than any player.' This concept is presented by itself on the first slide and is the basis for the entire structure of the document. It is a belief that must be taken on by everyone in the club, especially in the junior ranks."

Of course, while outlining basic suggestions on the structure of player contracts, on having no more than two senior players for each position, and so forth, what this document amounts to is a request for the project sponsor's buy-in. But the language and imagery used goes further than that. No 'player' is bigger than the club. But the manager? The document calls on the president to provide his tacit blessing to the establishment of the personality cult. There may in fact be some sleight of hand at play, where Mourinho allows the President to believe these are *his* ideas. Mourinho perhaps hints at this in saying, "respect for the club, for its norms, for its philosophy, etc, is much more important than any individual. The document I drew up, and which some now refer to as the 'Bible', is totally in line with this principle. Also, the stand taken by the president, Pinto da Costa, had been a great help in terms of having these ideas adhered to in the club."

In August 2004, Mark Honigsbaum reported in the *Observer* that Mourinho had "sent Abramovich a PowerPoint

presentation with a detailed breakdown of Chelsea's squad, his assessment of which players should stay and who should go and what he expected from the club in terms of training, scouting and medical facilities. The result was that, when Mourinho finally met Abramovich on his yacht in Monaco the day after the Champions League final, Chelsea's owner already had all the information he needed."

The article went further, hinting at Mourinho's having learned the need to be punctilious with 'difficult' owners, particularly when applying a methodology such as his, which would increasingly capture the hearts and minds of those involved under his management.

This pattern would be repeated following his departure from Chelsea with Marca Ingla and Txiki Beguiristain of Barcelona, and presumably with Moratti, Florentino Pérez and whichever other clubs approached him with offers of work. In Barça's case, however, this ritual proved an unlikely contextual filter for the club, convincing them that Mourinho was a bad fit for them, and that they should instead appoint the then Barcelona B manager, Pep Guardiola. Graham Hunter, in *Barça: the Making of the Greatest Team in the World* [an extract of which appeared in Blizzard Issue Four], revealed that, "Mourinho had prepared what Ingla and Beguiristain remember to be a brilliant PowerPoint demonstration. His self-belief was clearly intact; he had deduced from a distance what was going wrong and had clear views on the best way out of the mess they were in. In normal circumstances the material, and the man, on show would have been so dazzling, so convincing that the argument would have become whether to give him the job there and then."

Ingla would later conclude, "I just don't like him."

Some may feel that Barça's sidestep would later fuel Mourinho's ambition to supplant them at the pinnacle of the European game, but for better or worse, the presentation had done its job. If there's likely to be a cultural problem with the club acquiescing in the Personality Cult approach, as was the case with Barça, the opportunity is there for the hiring club to pass.

Charismatic Authority

Max Weber, in his theory of the tripartite classification of authority, theorised that there are three categories of authority:

- Traditional Authority — you have authority because it's habitual;

- Rational-Legal Authority — you're backed by a 'mandate' that everyone accepts;

- Charismatic Authority — you have authority because people want you to.

With Traditional Authority and Rational-Legal Authority, the context itself bestows the authority. However, with Charismatic Authority (akin to our 'personality cult'), you have some chance of managing and engineering your authoritarian context in ways that support your methodology.

Weber defined Charismatic Authority as: "The authority of the extraordinary and personal gift of grace (charisma)... Men do not obey him by virtue of tradition or statute, but because they believe in him."

Mourinho's messianic arrival at Chelsea in 2004 provides maybe the best example of him establishing just that brand of authority, indelibly stamping our minds with his vision in the process. "I intend to give my best, to improve things and to create the football team in relation to my image and my football philosophy..." he said. "We have top players and, sorry if I'm arrogant, we have a top manager... I'm not a defender of old or new football managers. I believe in good ones and bad ones, those that achieve success and those that don't. Please don't call me arrogant, but I'm European champion and I think I'm a special one."

Visionary, prophetic language you might say: creation in his own image... a special one. As he said himself: "God, and after God, me."

By that stage of course, just as he'd previously done with his squad on joining Porto, Mourinho had written to his players and reinforced points 2 and 3 in the standard issue personality cult template: establish behavioural rules in support of your vision and obtain the group's buy-in to such an extent that they themselves enforce those behavioural rules. "From here each practice, each game, each minute of your social life must centre on the aim of being champions," Mourinho wrote to his squad in early July 2004. "First-teamer will not be a correct word. I need all of you. You need each other. We are a TEAM." He concluded the letter with the equation, "Motivation + Ambition + Team + Spirit = SUCCESS."

Having achieved buy-in from his owner, the letter systematically moved the establishment of his vision on to his playing squad, a process that was, of course, on-going and which has betrayed repeating patterns — recipes — in his exhaustively reported career since. That he was constantly refining his own 'manual' was beyond doubt. Use what works, refine or jettison what doesn't. On the subject of the letter, Honigsbaum noted, "It was almost word for word the same letter that he had sent to Porto players when he was appointed manager in January 2002."

It's maybe in this that the 'My Chelsea' tag, a tag that the club's players and fans still seemed to enjoy, at least until the Champions League victory in Munich, is so enduring. The notion, in the context of securely established charismatic authority, is a powerful and emotionally evocative one. As a metaphor, its nature is essentially paternal and when combined with the obvious martial imagery, the bond it builds can be dangerously persistent, beyond notions of reason or what's best for the group itself in the longer term. It certainly appeals to football fans, who will often have undergone the rite of passage and transmission of 'lore' from their father or substitute parental figures related to playing or supporting the game.

Meanwhile, as a manager, Mourinho's portrayal as 'club as child' traces back to his time at Benfica. In Lourenço's biography, he explained that he started to identify the Benfica team as 'his' when players assumed his mentality: of irreverence, of ambition and of internal solidarity. Talking in typically dramatic terms after a draw with Braga in which his side had dominated his visitors, he said, "That day was also set to mark the reconciliation between the fans and the team, despite the final draw... At the end of the match, the team went onto the pitch to receive its members' ovation, as players and fans made up. All the factors involved in this game, and the way in which everything took place, resulted in a turning point in the mindset of the Benfica players. From then on, nothing was the same. 'My Benfica' began there and then."

'My Benfica'.
'My Leiria'.
'My Porto', 'My Chelsea', 'My Inter'...
'My Real Madrid'?

Reinforcing the House of Cards

When describing Charismatic Authority, Weber acknowledged that of the three categories, it's the least stable. If those who follow experience doubt as to the leader's 'powers', his authority loses its legitimacy. Ideally it's best to engineer the situation in such a way that your group does the reinforcement for you — and it's here that Mourinho really extends the basic four-step template and demonstrates his team-building prowess.

The dynamic at work is illustrated by a 1967 experiment by an American high school history teacher with his sophomore students, known as "The Third Wave". The idea was to illustrate that even the most enlightened and educated groups can find themselves swept up in the power of charismatic authority and, in the process subjugate the kind of reason they may have formerly taken for granted, given the right combination of context and catalyst.

The teacher began the experiment by encouraging his students to respond immediately to his questions without thought, ideally with yes or no answers. He insisted on discipline and obedience, introducing group symbols, slogans, and gestures that allowed the group to identify with each other, their 'movement' and their leader.

Ambiguity and disorder were kept to a minimum, with certainty and security their perceived replacement. The teacher introduced the idea that this movement was bigger than any of them realised — that it was sweeping the nation and would lead the nation to a simpler, better way of life. But to his horror, the movement spread beyond the class to the rest of the school, gaining momentum as more and more students became involved and eventually giving rise to bullying and ridicule for those who chose not to become involved (to the extent that the teacher brought the experiment to a sensibly premature close).

Such is the power of symbolism when a group craves a sense of oneness. The leader establishes a clear vision, and supports that vision by:

- Introducing a simple symbology and 'code' to communicate;

- Introducing vigorous discipline;

- Insisting on immediate obedience;

- Removing ambiguity and disorder;

- Promoting a sense of security and certainty;

- Associating the project with something greater than the group itself — the fans, God... whatever works.

Chelsea again provide the clearest illustration of Mourinho's approach in this regard. After telling the world's media at a press conference that he's special, Mourinho quickly went on to establish a comprehensive symbology for those involved at the club. For example:

- The Chelsea club badge changes, with his approval, featuring a lion that "looks arrogant";

- Using a subtle rebranding of established coaching practices, he introduces a 'colour box system' to instil coded tactical call-and-response in his players at all levels within the club (see "guided discovery", "resting with the ball" and so forth);

- Each member of staff receives two books, *Mourinho's Drills* and the *Chelsea Bible*;

- Members of the playing squad increasingly talk of "the Chelsea Family";

- A few games into their first season under his management, the squad receives crystal clear messages in terms of what's to be expected if behavioural rules are contravened (Joe Cole is dressed down, Hernán Crespo is unceremoniously dispatched to Milan, Adrian Mutu fails a drugs test and is cast out);

- After a particularly physical away encounter against Mark Hughes's Blackburn, the players defiantly throw their shirts into the away end at Ewood Park.

Alongside all of this, of course, Mourinho maintained a consistently convincing demeanour both with his staff and with the media (tone, posture, attitude, projection of invulnerability). It was difficult not to be seduced by it all.

Of course, buy-in to Mourinho's methodology is possibly harder for those on the footballing side than any of the other parties under his influence. In the coaches' and players' case, active work was required and not only on the physical and technical aspects of the game. Lourenço's book betrays the peculiar notion of 'fitness' used by Mourinho and his staff — relating a concept central to every athlete's sense of self-worth to the broader goals of the group and, in particular, the manager. The comments dated from his second season at Porto — a time when the players were being asked to depart from their standard 4-4-2 setup and accommodate greater squad rotation in pursuit of trophies on all fronts. "For us, to say that this or that player is in great physical shape is a mistake," Mourinho said. "The player is either fit or not. And what do we mean by being fit? It is to be physically well and to be part of a game plan which a player knows inside out. With regard to the psychological side, which is essential to play at the highest level, a fit player feels confident, cooperates with and believes in his teammates, and shows solidarity towards them. All of this put together means a player is fit and it is reflected in playing well."

That this all takes time is of course also central to Mourinho's 'message', despite later claims that 'long-term is a big excuse for coaches'. Shortly after

starting mid-season at an underachieving Porto, he said, "When a coach begins his work halfway through the season, he can always make one of two choices. He can opt for a psychological beating — which I don't believe in — or he can choose a methodological beating... the methodological beating... produces long-lasting effects because it brings about structural changes. In this case, changes in the work philosophy and the model of play can be seen."

That this methodological beating paid off in footballing terms at every club since Porto is beyond doubt, of course. But the language he uses is illustrative, some might think.

The Empathetic Father Figure

At the end of his short stint at Benfica, Mourinho said, "I felt incredibly angry that I was raising a child I would have to abandon." It's an interesting turn of phrase and a theme that again has followed him throughout his career. Mourinho, for all his peculiarities, is demonstrably warm — demonstrably 'human.' A family man whose friends appear to have remained close and loyal throughout his adult life, he has at certain times in his managerial career demonstrated his empathy to his players, and behaved in a manner befitting his charismatic 'father figure' aspirations.

When César Peixoto's anterior cruciate ligament ruptured in 2004, Mourinho attended the operation. When Petr Cech's head was controversially injured against Reading, his sense of concern was palpable (although his comments related to the medical professionals involved may have been ill-advised).

Didier Drogba was famously reported as being in tears upon hearing of Mourinho's dismissal from Chelsea. Wesley Sneijder, on winning the Ballon D'Or in 2010, dedicated his award to Mourinho, with Mourinho visibly moved by the gesture. Marco Materazzi's embrace outside the Bernabéu following that season's European Cup final victory encapsulated the bond that Mourinho is capable of forming with his players and staff. That he boasts pure uncut charisma is beyond any doubt, of course, but these are often intelligent, independently motivated men. Michael Essien, on joining Real Madrid on loan, repeatedly referred to Mourinho as "my Daddy". Wesley Sneijder said, "I am a bit like him. He could have been my father."

The broad emphasis in his coaching and man management style is inclusive. His explanation of the 'guided discovery' approach in tactical work betrays his sensitivity. "It is not easy to put this theory (guided discovery) into practice, especially with top players who are not prepared to accept everything they are told just because it comes from you, the authority..." he said. "I will arrange the training sessions to lead along a certain path, they will begin feeling it... all together, we reach a conclusion." So while he talks of "methodological beating", it's done in ways that allow the players to feel they 'own' the conclusions reached as a group — much like his PowerPoint-based approach with the men in suits.

This sensitivity is also illustrated in the way he picks his fights with certain players. Helder Postiga, Joe Cole, Mario Balotelli and Karim Benzema have all been singled out for criticism over the years, and in each case, clear messages were sent to his squads in terms of the behaviour and standards of 'fitness' expected of them. The cases of Sergio Ramos, Iker Casillas, and Cristiano Ronaldo, all of whose comments on Mourinho have caused controversy during his time with Real Madrid, provide an interesting counterpoint. Mourinho, like all the canniest man-managers before him, knows which fights to pick — a strength that's proven particularly crucial to him in his current role, not least in obtaining at least begrudging buy-in from his players to his methods.

Lourenço's biography tells the story of Mourinho's 2002 Porto training camp, which illustrates how central the buy-in of his group is to his approach. A few nights into their retreat, Mourinho gave the players the afternoon and evening off. He said, "The only thing I asked of them was to be back at the hotel by 11.00pm... It was around twenty to eleven when a taxi arrived with the first group of players. Immediately after this, all the other players began to arrive as well. I was completely taken aback, not only because they'd arrived before the stipulated time, but also because they all arrived at the same time. Jorge Costa walked past me, and I asked him, 'Jorge, what happened?' 'We all went out together. We have a great group here, Mister.'"

That unity of purpose has characterised his teams ever since. Arguably, that is, until now.

The Routinisation of Charisma

Given his recipe for team building, Mourinho's current tenure at Real Madrid provides an interesting contrast to his time with Chelsea. Charismatic authority is the least stable of Weber's three categories, since it wholly depends on the group's perception of the figurehead — their belief that he is 'special'. The model applies just as much at any football club and if you find yourself with a realistic chance of consolidating (let alone establishing) your authority, you've already done a sterling job.

Weber believed that instances of Charismatic Authority "cannot remain stable; they will become either traditionalised or rationalised, or a combination of both." He called this "the routinisation of charisma".

It's here that managers with genuine dynastic-level ambition set themselves aside — for case studies, see the careers of Stein, Busby, Shankly, Herrera, Michels, Clough, Ferguson... the peculiar combinations of charisma and context in each case dictated their fortunes to a great extent.

In some situations, routinisation is relatively easy. Managerial life would have been far easier for Bob Paisley at Liverpool, for example, than for Brian Clough or Jock Stein at Leeds United. As a rule, however, it's extremely difficult for a manager to control the conditions he needs to control if he's to stand a chance of routinising his authority. Even with the most accommodating owners, it helps to be a master of the dark arts to get your way. (Stein in particular proved himself supreme in handling his stakeholders, whether in the boardroom, referee's room, tunnel or press room. Alex Ferguson, of course, received a comprehensive education from the great man in the more Machiavellian nuances

of his craft while working as his assistant with Scotland.)

In Mourinho's case, the situation at Chelsea ultimately proved too difficult even for him to handle. Despite the appearance of an ideal 'catalytic context', the club at the time (and arguably to this day) featured a host of characters seemingly vying for influence over Roman Abramovich, from the level of Bruce Buck and Ron Gourlay/Paul Smith, through Frank Arnesen and Avram Grant, to several of his senior players. When Mourinho was ousted, the media reported it as a "shock"; however, in light of Weber's model, it was perhaps predictable. Having been unable to routinise his charismatic authority (something all but impossible with Abramovich at the helm, other than with his blessing), Mourinho found himself vulnerable to challenge throughout his time at the club, despite appearances to the contrary. The authority, though clearly established, was never routinised.

Mourinho would of course go on to quit his job with Internazionale, where his authority had clearly been as routinised as far as was possible with Moratti's consent. His time in Italy had been tough on a personal level, as he appeared to find it difficult to adjust to the peculiarities of its footballing life. Mourinho, on winning the European Cup, said, "There are many things [in Italy] that I haven't liked and for three to four months I've been thinking of going... I am not leaving Inter, I am leaving Italian football. This group of players have given me great satisfaction and I will always have Inter inside of me."

Mourinho had, of course, ruffled feathers among his managerial peers, while possibly betraying one of the central conditions of his employment. He famously said, "While I choose the team that goes out on the pitch, other coaches don't do that... If anyone told me what to do with my line-up, the next day my office would be empty and I would have my suitcases packed."

Mourinho had perhaps grown accustomed to the kind of reception he'd enjoyed in England. Ian Hawkey, writing in the *Sunday Times* in February 2010, neatly encapsulated the contrast, while underlining the persistence of (and Italian football's comparative disdain for) his self-appointed 'Our Father' persona: "The last time he sat in an executive box to watch Chelsea come back from a goal down to win against Fulham, he told reporters he recognised the gutsiness of the performance as that of 'my Chelsea'. Barely a month later, he beamed after Inter's win over Milan in the Serie A derby: 'Now I can say this is an Inter team built in my image.' There are folk in Italian football who wonder whether something built in Mourinho's image is a good thing... Much of this is the familiar knockabout that was part of his routine in the Premier League and in Portugal's Superliga. But Mourinho's eagerness to turn spats with rival coaches into something personal ... is viewed here as vulgar and vain."

The Real Madrid Routinisation

In terms of Weber's model, the cards seemed stacked against him from the off at Real Madrid. After all, at a club like Real Madrid your chance only ever exists within clearly defined limits — ultimately, Real Madrid are at the whim of their fickle socios. Whoever rides in on

the next presidential ticket will propose whatever they most care about. The trick is to get them to care about you — to believe that you're special.

That Mourinho was due to move to Real Madrid in the summer of 2010 was perhaps the worst kept secret in world football at the time. Mourinho commented early on the defining theme of his early tenure in Madrid — his working relationship with Director General, Jorge Valdano. Gabriele Marcotti, in the *Times*, quoted Mourinho as saying, "I have no doubt that the relationship will work because Valdano knows to respect the autonomy of his job and my job... We can talk to each other about transfers and the like, but his role is clearly delineated."

Mourinho, on formally assuming the role (the situation leading up to his appointment saw him somehow leading the club while still being at the helm of Inter), applied the standard template as usual, but taking on a squad of newly ordained World Cup winners, his miracle-working mythos perhaps impressed the senior players a little less than had been the case at his previous clubs. And not only that, this was Real Madrid — a place where no man is bigger than the club.

In spite of that, however, and despite Barcelona's ongoing and unprecedented success, Mourinho successfully set about establishing his vision, bedding in his methodology, and establishing the standard set of behavioural rules. Xabi Alonso, whose footballing role for the club remains pivotal, not least in tactical terms, gave the impression in the early stages that, as usual, Mourinho's approach had been consultative and inclusive — a sensible gambit with such an accomplished squad.

After a goalless draw in his opening game, his team steamed through domestic round after domestic round into the winter, and enjoyed early success in the group stages of the Champions League. Mourinho perhaps suffered from this early success upon their first encounter with Barcelona, however, setting his side out at the Nou Camp in open, offensive mode, only to run into an epoch-defining 5-0 defeat hailed by many as the greatest team performance of all time. This was a setback to establishing his authority at the club, since to bed himself in, and to keep those who had already 'bought in' on side, he would need to persuade them they'd achieved some degree of footballing success, while simultaneously attacking the forces with the potential to undermine his position.

A few months later, the football world was debating whether he'd achieved that to an acceptable extent. Vicente Del Bosque would no doubt confirm that a single Copa Del Rey does not generally equate 'success' at Real Madrid. So in a season that saw him push Barcelona in the league, but ultimately falter, coupled with their head-to-head humiliation and the ignominy of being knocked out by their great rivals in the semi-final of the Champions League on their own pitch... ordinarily you'd have expected the manager to lose his job.

However, in line with his comments before joining the club, Mourinho had dedicated attention to the other big obstacle to his assertion of authority — Jorge Valdano. A post-match press conference early in the season saw Mourinho in familiar combative mode, reciting a litany of errors made by the referee. However, it appeared to some that his target was not solely the Spanish refereeing establishment. In the April 2011 edition of *FourFourTwo*, Simon Talbot explained his insight into the event: "There was something familiar about Mourinho complaining about the referee: it forms part of his armoury, another tactic for a master tactician... And yet, as he waved the piece of paper in the air, revealing that he had been handed it by someone from the club on his way in, it became clear that this was different. It was not really the referee he was complaining about. It was Real Madrid. This was another us versus them; only 'us' was the team, 'them' was the club hierarchy. And one man in particular: director general Jorge Valdano... This was less press conference, more a declaration of war."

Mourinho proceeded to air all that was grimy in the Spanish media, stating, "I don't like hidden wars... If I have wars, I have them in the open." Mourinho's brinkmanship having accompanied him throughout his career (shortly after his departure from Benfica, he apologised to their president for his 'blackmail' of threatening to leave for another club) he would surely have fancied his chances, despite Valdano's status as consigliere to Florentino Pérez's Don. Valdano's role had of course been central to the club's footballing direction for several years and, as well as being a trusted colleague and confidante, he was also Pérez's personal friend.

As time passed, and with the Madrid ultras defiantly chanting Mourinho's name, Mourinho set about systematically undermining the foundations of Valdano's authority. This would occasionally surface in pointed comments, such as "If I can talk to the number one, why would I talk to anyone else?"

Suddenly people were asking the question — what value is the middle man adding. Pérez, of course, had made the ultimate statement of defiance in hiring Mourinho: that Barça's rise would not go unchecked and that he would bring in the very best world football had to offer in pursuit of Real Madrid's return to the top. Mourinho was aware of the key bargaining chip at his disposal — if political subterfuge was seen to have undermined Mourinho's work with the club and he was to depart as a result, it wouldn't reflect too well on Pérez (footballing consequences aside).

As such, it was maybe no surprise when Mourinho brought the matter to a head, insisting, "I want to leave." Peréz had no choice but to act, taking unprecedented steps in meeting Mourinho's structural demands while making the inevitable changes in personnel. Valdano protested, "I have always respected Real Madrid. I've never turned the club into a battlefield... I always put my position as director general before who I am, and I have always avoided fighting that battle... I believe José Mourinho staying on is good for a club that's been unstable in the past. It needs to settle for a reasonable period of time. He's done a good job, I believe he is a good coach and I find it normal that he stays on. Real Madrid is great, which doesn't mean this new structure belittles it. The president came up with this solution to resolve a difficult situation that wasn't easy to manage."

Meanwhile, Pérez, while denying Mourinho had made any demands, confirmed them. "The experience of the season just ended has shown the need for new organisation at the club, giving autonomy to our coach..." he said. "This is the first step in our reorganisation process which we will develop in the coming weeks... Mourinho did not make any demands. He asked for more autonomy in line with how English clubs are organised."

Oddly, Barça's month-long assertion of dominance over Real Madrid in the spring of 2011 played into Mourinho's hands. If people had started the year asking themselves what value the middle man brought to the party, surely they ended this period demanding an answer. If Madrid could spend hundreds of millions of Euros assembling the most expensive squad in football history, and if they boasted the most celebrated manager in the modern game, then why weren't they the ones dominating?

The charges had been laid over the months, and all that was missing was the detonator. "We lack a striker," Mourinho had complained, despite having a squad replete with striking talent. "I don't have full control," Mourinho had complained, in response to subtle challenges from the Valdano camp relating to Mourinho's (and several of his players') relationship with the Portuguese agent Jorge Mendes. Suddenly, despite having won the Copa del Rey, they were out of the league and the Champions League, with Barça being hailed as possibly the greatest team of all time.

Mourinho had got his excuses in early and results forced action from Pérez:

Valdano was removed from his post. Pérez had already gambled the fate of his presidency on hiring Mourinho and his expensive coaching entourage and, having given him hitherto unimagined control over the club's footballing operations, Pérez found himself with a dilemma. Do what the club had done throughout the last decade and get rid of the manager, with massive expense and loss of face, or do the unthinkable and consolidate his power base at the club, with all the personnel and structural consequences that this entailed. And while the broader reasons may be many and varied, Pérez by the end of last season was able to point at results and make the reasonable claim that his team were in the ascendancy, a dramatic loss in the Champions League semi-final notwithstanding. Their league victory was impressive and was achieved against a stronger Barça side than any Real Madrid manager had ever faced.

2012 would prove a rollercoaster ride in terms of Mourinho's hopes of routinising his authority. The new year brought reports of training ground hostilities between Mourinho and the two club captains, Sergio Ramos and Iker Casillas. Meanwhile, support from the crowd was divided, with fans chanting Mourinho's name as he was whistled by other sections. Right on cue, rumours began to emerge that Mourinho planned to leave in the summer.

One terse press conference stood out. When asked if there were issues with his man-management, and whether there were cliques in the group, Mourinho replied, "I don't provoke cliques," the inference being that others in the group did. He was then spotted in London,

supposedly house hunting. Since the team were on course to wrest the league back from Barça, his position was strong enough to fire shot after shot across the club's bows. March saw him flirting once more with Chelsea. But ahead of their Champions League semi-final, his stance noticeably softened — artfully so, you might argue. Seeing his chance to cement his authority as a successful season drew to a close, he systematically buttered up his stakeholders, while appealing once more to their common goal — the mission that was bigger than any one person.

Sid Lowe reported him as saying, "I have a contract and I do not have any reason not to be here, but before the last game there will be sufficient time to talk to the players and the directors and decide what is best for me and for the players." He then turned to the players and compared them with his illustrious group at Inter, saying, "I look at this group today and I see the same hope and hunger." Lastly he said that working at Madrid "is an enriching experience and that has made me a better coach... I hope I do not fail to live up to people's expectations... It is about the way we work together, the way we create empathy... It is better to be [in charge] for three, four or five years than one or two because you can do more things... it is the players who are out there and I have faith in them." Continuing in this conciliatory vein, he said, "My feeling is that we still have the ability to grow as a team and the club can grow too. Clubs have to adapt to the evolution of time and to changing mentalities. A fantastic car in the 1980s is not fantastic in the 1990s or the 2000s. If the club thinks that I can still give something — and I know that they do —

and if the players think so as well — and I think they do; I feel like the empathy is increasing — I will continue."

Meanwhile, Tito Vilanova took the helm at Barça, and as many of Mourinho's key players set off for Poland and Ukraine to secure their third successive trophy with the Spanish national team, he waved them goodbye as the ink dried on his contract extension, securing his and his staff's services until 2016. Plans were made to revise further the club's overall structure, following his assertion that, "Real Madrid do not have a structure in accordance with their size." By this stage, his authority seemed about as well founded as it's possible for a manager to enjoy at Real Madrid.

Fast forward to October, however, and tensions surfaced once more. Against Deportivo La Coruña, Mourinho replaced Mesut Özil at half-time, exchanging harsh words in the dressing-room. Sergio Ramos indulged in some mischief, donning Özil's shirt beneath his own for the second half. When an observant photographer caught him in the act, Ramos pleaded benign ignorance. Meanwhile, Christiano Ronaldo sulked at the progress of his contract negotiations. Mourinho's authority was once again the focus of debate, and he hit back, saying, "Right now I don't have a team." As Christmas drew closer, he ramped up hostilities, accusing the media of a campaign against him, and complaining about his lack of influence over coaching and scouting elsewhere in the club's hierarchy, and saying the B-team coach Alberto Toril "has to decide if it's more important to form players for the first team or finish fourth or fifth." Once

again, some fans chanted his name while others whistled, to the extent that on December 3, he took to the field before the home game against Atlético Madrid having invited fans to direct their ire at him personally. Meanwhile the press reported a breakdown in his relationship with Florentino Pérez.

In the last weeks of 2012, with Vilanova's Barça streaking ahead in the league, Mourinho effectively conceded the title, saying, "The league's practically impossible." Casillas perhaps hinted at the root of the problem in saying, "If you gave me the choice of being 25 points behind in the league and winning the 10th [European Cup], I'd take it." Meanwhile Mourinho had supposedly talked off record about there being "three black sheep in the squad".

Thus the new year echoed its predecessor, with Mourinho confronting a senior player and tension surfacing. Mourinho did the unthinkable — he dropped Casillas in favour of his deputy, Antonio Adán. The football world was shocked, with his erstwhile rival Jorge Valdano commenting that it was "an exhibition of power, imposing himself on a legend of the club".

Adán's second game descended into farce when, six minutes into the game, he conceded a penalty and was sent off, Casillas taking the field while quietly ignoring the verbal instructions of his manager. Cue more media derision. Mourinho must have been almost relieved when Casillas was then ruled out for two months with a fractured finger. He was beginning to look anything but special, and clearly a few smelled blood. Florentino Pérez was forced to dismiss allegations in *Marca* that Ramos and Casillas had issued him with an ultimatum: "It's him or us." Pérez said the paper had "crossed an ethical line". *Marca*'s front page responded the following day with the words *"Marca no miente"* — *"Marca* does not lie" emblazoned on its front page.

From a stage in the summer when it seemed he stood a chance of establishing — against all the odds — long-lasting routinised authority at Real Madrid, things looked far less promising.

Residual Issues

Sustained success at any football club requires the establishment and sustenance of clear authority at the head of the footballing operation, be it via a European or English model. But establishing it via charismatic authority can be fraught with difficulty.

Mourinho is a one-off. His presence is such that his recipe tends to work not only on his players, but also on a chunk of the worldwide media. He lives large enough that his words in a post-match press conference can cause ripples at Uefa and at Fifa — even at Unicef. That's quite something and it's all down to his hypnotic allure, allied to his trophy haul.

People are fascinated by him in the same way they're fascinated by Hannibal Lecter or Count Dracula. We are afraid, but secretly a little aroused — maybe even infused with abstracted primordial blood lust. This is the danger with a powerful case of charismatic authority. It intoxicates as powerfully as any narcotic but, when it's over, it leaves your football club with a hell of a hangover.

The fact is, it's impossible for Chelsea to move on and get over it. In a very real sense, Mourinho is still in charge there. The winning mentality he instilled at the club has arguably contributed to a great deal of their ongoing 'success' since his departure, but some will doubtless claim it feels hollow without him and the sense of 'oneness' he represented. As Andre Villas-Boas puts it, "His is a presence ever felt in the club."

Villas Boas had, of course, experienced this spectre before during his time with Porto, but luckily his President, Pinto da Costa, understood the need for an exorcism, saying, "[Andre] needs time to mould his team. He can't do that as long as there are players, as I've heard, who exchange text messages with Mourinho." The same can't be said for Roman Abramovich. Both he and many of Mourinho's former players at Chelsea still exchange playful texts and phone calls with him. Mourinho, it seems, likes to leave his territory marked. Last year, facing the possibility of drawing Chelsea in the Champions League knock-out stages, he said, "People can't understand how much I love Inter and Chelsea and how much I love the boys." This came shortly after the annual round of rumours linking him with a return to the soon-to-be-vacant Chelsea hot seat — a link he and his representatives never seem to discourage (since as well as keeping his territory marked, it tends to help bolster his authority in his current role).

More than five years on from his departure, Mourinho still talks about Chelsea and its players in a direct and personal way. Contrast that with Rafa Bénitez, Chelsea's current interim manager, who in talking about the club, seems once removed from it. No sign of "my Chelsea", but rather, "I want to be at a top side and Chelsea is a top side with great potential." Of course, Marco Materazzi sought to highlight this contrast in recent weeks. It's unlikely to have disappointed Mourinho.

The challenge for Real Madrid was to attempt a complete and responsible routinisation of the process that absorbed Mourinho's best practice, while removing as far as possible the traces of Mourinho's charismatic residue. But is that possible? Some clubs can lay claim to just that kind of dynastic succession but Liverpool still has an air of Shankly about it, Ajax an air of Michels, Barça the distinct feeling of Cruyff...

As long as it's wielded responsibly and seen through to its logical conclusion, a fully routinised cycle of enlightened charismatic authority can only be a good thing for an aspirant club in a state of transition. But if the club falls short in its routinisation, it may find its progress hindered in the medium term while the people involved either squabble for scraps at the authoritative table, or pine for their departed, yet still glorious, leader. Ⓑ

The Lawnmower and the Teapot

Barry Fry discusses how to motivate players and how the world of management has changed

By Iain Macintosh

Barry Fry is one of English football's most recognisable characters. He's excitable and effervescent, controversial, noisy and ever so slightly unhinged. He'd be keen to remind you that he's also a bloody good football manager, having transformed Dunstable and Barnet, rescued Southend United from the drop and enjoyed ups and endured downs with Birmingham City before going on to manage and then own Peterborough United. In 2006, he sold the Posh to the property developer Darragh MacAnthony and has been the club's Director of Football ever since. Under Darren Ferguson, Peterborough are ticking over in the second flight and Fry now concentrates on identifying transfer targets and negotiating deals for incoming and outgoing players.

But what does he think of modern football? How has the game changed and what would he do differently if he had his time again? What are his philosophies? How does he operate? And is there ever a time when kicking a tray of tea out of Jeff Astle's hands is appropriate?

⚽ *So...football management, Barry. You've been doing this since 1974, haven't you?*

Yeah, that's right. I first become a manager at Dunstable in 1974; I actually lasted 31 years after that which is a miracle really. When I began I didn't have an assistant manager, I didn't have a goalkeeper coach, I didn't have a fitness coach or dieticians, you done it all yourself. You done training yourself, you put the nets up yourself, you cut the grass with a pair of scissors by yourself.

⚽ *Yes... weren't you done by the police for riding your lawnmower across the Barnet pitch in the middle of the night?*

Yeah, that was me! We had a game on Boxing Day and it was freezing cold on Christmas night. We had to get that game on because we were playing our local rivals and we always got the best gate of the season, so I was rolling the pitch and singing and then the police turned up and arrested me for being drunk and disorderly. When the ref come the next morning, he said, "Half the pitch is flat and playable and half the pitch is rutted and unplayable." I said, "I know mate, that's when the coppers fucking stopped me!"

⚽ *Do you think it's easier to be a manager now? With Darren [Ferguson], for example, he's got you dealing with long-term transfer policy, he's got an owner who's engaged with the wider plan for the future. Is it easier just to deal with the coaching?*

To be honest, yeah. The chairman, when he come in and bought the club off me, he obviously done due diligence and saw all the deals I'd done on the transfers and saw all the money we're still getting in two or three years on. So the one stipulation was that if he bought the club off me, I stayed as director of football and dealt with all the contracts regarding the players. And obviously every manager who's come in, he's said, not that Barry Fry picks the players, but if I've been to a game and I can recommend a player... I mean our best scout is our chairman, he's absolutely brilliant, he comes up with names that I haven't even heard of. I go watch them, I tell Darren, he sends scouts and we get 'em in like that. We don't fetch anyone into the club that the manager doesn't want to be fetched in. Really, I do what I'm told. The manager identifies the player who he wants and it's down to me and the chairman to get them, whether it's a million pound or a hundred grand. Likewise, when he doesn't want a player, it's my job to get rid of them.

That policy means that Darren meets the players and talks about football and I meet the agents and talk about finances. I used to deal with it all myself, I used to put in the bids, meet the agent, meet the player, and players want this, that and all the other and if I'm the one saying, nah you're not getting that, they can think it's a bit personal. It's not, it's all the budget allows you to do. This way, Darren can just concentrate on getting the team right on the Saturday and he hasn't got to have rows with the players and the agents.

🜂 *Is he happy with that?*

I'm not sure he's happy. I think Darren's the type of guy, he's like his dad, he

wants to run the whole caboodle, from the youth all the way up. But it's so difficult just running the first team that the chairman wanted him to concentrate on that.

🜂 *How much control does a manager have over the team and the players these days? In your era, you'd have almost absolute power, but is it harder to get through to them now?*

If I used to threaten to fine a player a couple of weeks' wages, it would hurt him. It was a big deterrent and he'd toe the line. But at some clubs, you can fine players a fortnight's wages and it's a cup of tea to 'em. It's got out of hand that way. In my time, you had a bit of power, they was all on less money and they needed that money for their families, for the HP on their cars, for their rent. Now they're millionaires in their own right. I don't think I'd last five minutes in management now. They'd just tell me to fuck off.

🜂 *So the mentality has changed that dramatically?*

It has, it really has. We, the clubs, have got ourselves to blame. Everyone blames agents, but they want the best for their clients and if you've got two or three clubs in, you can play them off against each other. I do that when I'm selling and you can get more than the player's worth. Clubs have tried to compete against each other and the game itself has got into serious financial problems. I'm really very fearful that several clubs will go bust and it'll be like a house of cards and it'll be fucking 20 or 25 going under. We've been spending too much. Players' wages have been escalating to ridiculous proportions. Sometimes the wages are 120% of the club turnover, so you're relying on individuals to prop the finances up. While they might have done that in the past, now their businesses have taken a hit in the recession and they haven't got the spare cash to do that. That's why the Football League have brought in guidelines now, protecting League One and Two. I go to all the meetings of the chairmen and all the clubs want the league to make the rule so they can say to players, "I'd love to give you extra money, but the league won't let me." But in previous years, we should have had the bollocks to say, "No, no, no. You can't fucking have it, 'cos you'll bankrupt the club."

Is that the root of the change in player's mentality? They know their own value now?

I get players leaving me, we're in the Championship, we're not big players, but they're leaving us for League Two. I get the chairman of a League Two club saying, "How much are they on?" I tell him and he says, "Well, he's asked for twice that amount." I just can't see where the agents and players are coming from, particularly in this day and age. More and more players are out of work, not getting fixed up.

When you took over at a football club, what was the first thing you did?

Normally when you get a job, it's because the club is struggling. They could be at the bottom of the league, with no money, the players' confidence has gone and you have to deal with that. When I took over at Dunstable, they'd finished bottom of the league eight years

on the trot. You have to get some belief around the place. My first gate was 34 people. I got George Best to play for us. I got some attractive pre-season friendlies. With a few months, I'd changed the mentality and people were coming to watch us. That year, we got a good side together, we scored 105 goals and we won the league.

Is that a priority at that level then, more so than, say, tactics? Getting a buzz around the club?

Yeah, buzz, team spirit, togetherness, a will to win together. We're all in the trenches, we're all helping each other. In them days, at Dunstable and then at Barnet, you trained Tuesday and Thursday, the lads come in straight from work, train and then we'd go in the clubhouse and have a beer together. We was a team on and off the field and the unbelievable success we had at Barnet, getting up, getting to the play-offs in our first year up, promotion the next season, it came from that. Nowadays, it's a bit more difficult to do that because you buy someone from Wales or Scotland or from a foreign country and they're all different. It's hard to get them all together. It was a lot easier in my day, you didn't have anything, you just did your best and hopefully if you picked the right players and got the best out of 'em, you'd win. It was wonderful.

But it must have been quite lonely? You walk into a dressing-room, you've got a room full of hairy bastards whom you don't know and you have to impose your will on them.

Yeah, it was frightening in a way, but I'm that sort of guy who's outgoing and loves football. I feel very lucky to be a part of football. I just think I took my enthusiasm into the dressing-room with me, with my players, and if you was good I'd praise you to heaven. I'd say you were amazing and you'd be playing for Man United and Real Madrid. If you was bad, I'd let you know you was bad. The thing was, I never fell out with anyone. I could have a right row with a player in the dressing-room and when he come in the bar afterwards, I was the first one to buy him a drink. I didn't bear grudges. Of all the players I've gone through over the years, I meet 'em now at functions, and I've sold some, I've upset some, but they all say they admired me because I was honest.

There must have been some scary moments though? When you're tearing strips off a six foot four centre-back, didn't you get worried?

Well, there was. I remember at Birmingham, bloody hell, I lost my rag a bit and had a go at Liam Daish. I bought him for fifty grand and sold him for £1.8m to Coventry, Daishy. He was my Captain Marvel. He'd head a Boeing 747 away, he was so strong. At half-time, I was laying into everyone, we weren't playing well, and I called Daishy a coward. Well, he got up and come over to me and I shit myself. He said, "What did you say?" Ha ha! So I ignored him and went on to someone else!

I remember big George Reilly at Barnet, he must have been six foot five and I come in and we had a big table in the middle of the dressing-room with all the tea on. I was so angry, I tipped up the table and this massive pot of hot tea went all over fucking George's foot and he screamed. He's took one stride from one side of the dressing-room to the other and looked at me from a great height and all I could squeak was, "Sorry, George!"

There was another time, again at Barnet, we was 3-0 down at half-time. I gave them a right bollocking and they went out second half and won 4-3. Magnificent performance. I was on the pitch at the end saying, "Well done, Ian, well done, Tom, well done, Dick, fucking marvellous. You, Codner, fucking empty shirt." And this is Robert Codner. He come up to me, face to face, he said, "What did you say?" I said, "You fucking empty shirt." And he went to headbutt me. But you know when someone draws their head back? I sort of jerked back myself and of course I fucking fell arse over tit in the mud. I got up, continued to say well done to the lads and then I went back in the dressing-room. I saw Robert, I said, "Robert?" He said, "What?" And I fucking give him a right-hander.

But we sat in the bath after and we had a right laugh about it. And then Stan come in, big Stan Flashman [Barnet's then-owner], and he said, "Barry, I want to see you." So I jumped out of the bath. "The FA are here, they was going to pick Robert for the England non-league squad, but I've seen what he done to you and I want him kicked out of the club." I said, "Fuck off, Stan. He didn't do nothing. I was abusing him, it was slippery and I fell over." He said, "It looked like he headbutted you." I said, "Look at my face! You'd know if he'd headbutted me."

I went to the FA afterward, I set them straight and they picked him. About six months later, we sold him to Brighton for £115,000. It just shows you how you can deal with things. If I'd made a fuss about that, we wouldn't have got that money, and that was a fucking lot of money in those days.

⚙ *Do you still get that sort of thing now?*

I never go in the dressing-room now, not since I was made director of football. I don't think Darren wants me hanging around, looking at his tactics.

⚙ *Did you know instinctively when to shout at people and when to praise them?*

Sometimes, you'd give people a bollocking and they'd vanish, they'd hide. You'd know for next time, that kind of player needs praise. Others you give a bollocking to, like Jeff Astle, and it works. Fuck me, I give Jeff Astle a bollocking once, he come in at half-time with the tea and we were 3-0 down. I kicked it out of his hands, told him to fuck off back out there. I told him he didn't deserve a fucking cup of tea. And we won that game 5-3, he scored a hat-trick. When he scored that third goal, he come running over to me, and gives me the v-sign and all that. He said afterwards, "Sorry, gaffer." I said, "No problem, I just wanted a reaction! But before we start next week's game, I'm going to kick you in the fucking bollocks!"

⚙ *In your experience, was that kind of man-management more important than tactical dossiers and drilling the players?*

I used to think so, yeah. We couldn't be that professional at the level I was at. When I started off, I was by myself, I only had the players to deal with. Although I had to be a bit aloof with them as I was

the manager, I was their mate as well. But management is entirely different now.

⚙ *What's changed?*

Well, press-wise, in my later years I was dealing with three TV stations, four or five radio stations, the whole written press, the weekly papers, the nationals and it was every day you were having interviews. The press become a big, big thing. It took half your day, every day.

⚙ *Did the mentality of journalists change?*

When I first started, journalists used to come on the team coach with us. If anything happened, it was kept quiet. You treated 'em like one of yours, you give 'em all the facilities, all the interviews and they respected that if there was a fight on the bus, they didn't report it. Now, you've only got to spit, fart or fucking giggle and it's on the front pages. Times have changed. But I've loved my time in football, I've spent my life in there. I'm 68 this year, I'm fat and happy and I'm still here. There ain't many of us left!

⚙ *Are you... erm... quite surprised that you are still here? I mean, you've had two heart attacks.*

I've had two heart attacks, two hip replacements, two knee replacements and my dick's fell off, but apart from that I'm happy as Larry. I must admit, my heart attacks were when I was still young, so I didn't expect to still be here at this age. People told me, people who weren't involved in football, that I had to be careful of the stress, but you keep going. They told me I should get out of it. But I decided early on that it was something I enjoyed and that I loved and if they carried me out in a box, well, that's the way I'd want to go anyway.

Did you have to manage your stress levels differently?

Nah, I was told to, but I've been on four tablets a day for 20-odd years now. I take them, I have check-ups regularly and I'm fine.

You sound like you're more machine than man.

Yeah! But I feel so lucky that I'm still in a job that I love. Football's been good to me. I almost lost everything trying to keep Peterborough afloat. That was a mistake. Well, it wasn't a mistake. I got out of jail in the end. But I jeopardised my family's future. I've got a lovely wife, how the hell she's put up with me for 35 years, I don't know. To put them in jeopardy for football was a bit wrong.

Would you do it all again?

Without a doubt. I might do it a bit differently. I used to have a go at all my chairmen when they wouldn't back me, when I needed extra players. Since I become an owner, I've phoned up all of my old owners and apologised for my behaviour. I, like them, have asked my managers, "Where do you think the fucking money comes from?" There's only so many second mortgages I can take out. But no, I wouldn't change a thing. **B**

The Bicycle Thief

Zlatan Ibrahimović has always been an individual — it's how he fits in

By Lars Sivertsen

Sometimes a single passage of play can demonstrate the essence of a player. When Maradona, in the immortal words of Bryon Butler, turned "like a little eel" and dodged a string of challenges to put Argentina 2-0 up against England in the quarter-final of the 1986 World Cup, everything that made him perhaps the greatest ever was put on display for a few, devastating seconds. When Johan Cruyff in the 1974 World Cup produced the Cruyff turn, his unique blend of balance, skill, creativity and spatial awareness combined in a single movement that was irrevocably etched into the sport's collective memory.

Zlatan Ibrahimović's moment came one late August afternoon in 2004 at the Amsterdam Arena. About 30 yards out, with his back to goal, he received a pass from an advancing full-back. After recovering from a poor first touch by muscling an opponent off the ball, he turned. A feigned shot with his right foot gave him some space on the edge of the box, but defenders kept coming in. Another feigned shot was followed by a series of dribbles which saw Zlatan move into space where there didn't appear to be any. Yet another turn took out both the goalkeeper and a defender, before the ball was calmly slotted home. As Zlatan himself would put it, many years later, it was an instant classic. The

physical strength to see off the first challenge, the balance and technique to slalom through a packed defence with no space to work with, not to mention the sheer audacity — if not stupidity — even to try it: it was a goal that could not have been scored by any other player. But that's not why Ajax's fifth goal in their 5-1 win over NAC Breda was so quintessentially Zlatan — the situation had a significant, now often forgotten subtext. But to understand that subtext it is necessary to go back a further decade, to a particularly rough part of an otherwise harmonious city in Sweden. You have to know the past to understand the present, and any attempt to decipher this most enigmatic of footballers must start in the troubled Malmö district of Rosengård.

Cultural and material exports have led the world to believe that all Swedish people are blonde, middle-class, live in IKEA-furnished houses, can produce catchy pop-songs given half a keyboard and are mostly named Ulf. This is largely the case, but that isn't the Sweden Zlatan Ibrahimović grew up in. Rosengård was built between 1967 and 1972 as part of a massive government housing program and it quickly attracted immigrant residents. Over the years that number increased. In 1972, 20% of the residents in Rosengård were immigrants; in 1998 it was 80%. By 2007, official statistics say "at least" 86% of Rosengård-residents are "of foreign origin", defined as "having two parents born outside of Sweden". The three most heavily represented countries were Iraq, Lebanon and the former Yugoslavia.

To put those figures into context, around 85% of the total Swedish population are ethnic Swedes — and 5% are Finns. The reported unemployment rate in Sweden as of August 2012 was 7.2%; in Rosengård it is thought to be around 60%. Recent figures from Statistics Sweden revealed that 71% of children in Rosengård live in relative poverty, school results are among the worst in the country and crime stats are high. Following a particularly troubling period in 2008, the Malmö fire department for a brief time demanded a police escort when responding to calls from Rosengård. It is, simply put, the closest thing to a fully fledged ghetto you'll ever find in Scandinavia. This is where Zlatan Ibrahimović grew up.

Ibrahimović's frank and wonderfully titled autobiography — I am Zlatan — was always going to make headlines. Tales of Zlatan screaming, "You have no balls!" to Pep Guardiola in the Barcelona dressing-room rightly got the international sporting press very excited indeed but the altogether more intriguing part of Zlatan's life story is his childhood and adolescence. Born to a Bosnian father and a Croatian mother, Zlatan's childhood had as much in common with the usual Swedish middle-class upbringing as Zlatan the footballer has with Erik Edman. "One day I fell off the roof at the kindergarten," he wrote. "I got a black eye and ran home crying, expecting a pat

on the head or at least some kind words. I got a slap in the face. 'What were you doing on the roof?' It wasn't like, 'Poor Zlatan.' It was, 'You fucking idiot, climbing up a roof. Here's a slap for you,' and I was shocked and ran away."

He insists that he loves his mother and that life was hard on her but also explains that, "She'd hit us with wooden spoons and sometimes they broke, so I had to go buy a new one like it was my fault she'd hit me that hard." "Us" being Zlatan, his sister Sanela and his brother Aleksandar. Once they all bought their mother a batch of wooden spoons for Christmas but apparently the irony was lost on her. When social services decided that this wasn't a healthy environment for little Zlatan, he was sent to live with his father, a caretaker named Šefik, instead. According to Zlatan, his father "had a big heart", but "the war really affected him a lot." Because this was the early 90s and for a Bosnian living in Sweden there was a lot of bad news from home to digest. Šefik Ibrahimović was a Bosniak born in Bijeljina. On 1 April 1992, Arkan's Tigers invaded his hometown. The death toll from the ensuing massacres is thought to exceed 1000. "The war ate at him and he became obsessed with following the news," Zlatan recalls. "He sat alone, drinking and mourning, listening to his Yugo-music." There wasn't always food in Šefik Ibrahimović's refrigerator in Rosengård but there was usually a healthy supply of beer. Although he may not have been the ideal provider, Šefik could be a fiercely loving father when he needed to. One night Zlatan fell badly ill and his father immediately called a cab, carried his son into the street, and screamed at the cab driver that she was to break all conceivable traffic rules to get to the hospital as soon as possible. It turned out Zlatan had meningitis. "His fridge was empty and he drank too much," Zlatan said. "But when the shit hits the fan, there's no one like him." When roused Šefik was driven, had a fierce temperament and a macho swagger. He taught his son to stand up for himself, that life is tough and that the only way to get ahead is to be even tougher.

When Zlatan was a boy, he had a bike that meant the world to him. The bike got stolen, so Zlatan started stealing bikes himself. He enjoyed the rush and after mastering the dark arts of bicycle-theft he graduated to other pilfering. A few years later, when his peers began to dabble in more serious crime, Zlatan had to opt out. By that point he had a burgeoning football career to safeguard. It's tempting to see Zlatan as yet another rebellious youngster from a bad neighbourhood who was saved by his ability to play football. But the idea of him as a loutish hoodie in want of an ASBO is only one side of the story. Zlatan was also an awkward, spindly kid with a big nose and a lisp. For a period, a speech coach would come to his school and teach him how to say the letter S. He thought it was degrading. Zlatan wasn't a terrible student but he wasn't overly keen on sitting still and paying attention in class. Because his parents moved he had to change schools a lot and at one of them an extra teacher was brought in and put on Zlatan-watch. The young boy was infuriated. Like most outsiders, the thing he wanted most of all was to not be an outsider. "There was talk of putting me in a special school," he said. "They wanted to brand me and I felt like a UFO. It started ticking like a bomb in my body."

One day, in gym class, the presence of the extra teacher enraged him to the point where he hit her in the head with a ball. The teachers were aghast. They called Zlatan's father and asked him to come to the school and discuss the possibility of getting psychiatric help for his son. Šefik Ibrahimović turned up in a rage, shouting at the teachers. "Who the fuck are you? To come here talking about psychiatric help? You should be sectioned, all of you. There is nothing wrong with my son; he's a good kid. You can all go fuck yourselves."

When he wasn't stealing bikes or causing trouble in school, Zlatan played football. On a small gravel pitch outside the apartment block where his mother lived, little Zlatan played incessantly. Still a thin and weak kid, he had to move his feet quickly and develop tricks to avoid getting clattered by the older boys. Gaining recognition for pulling off tricks became more important than winning. As he got older he grew, both in ability and stature, and he would challenge flocks of 10 to 15 younger kids to get the ball off him. If someone managed it, he'd buy them candy. Zlatan's temperament and love of tricks was fine for kickabouts on the gravel pitch, but more of an issue when he played organised football. He joined his first club, Malmö Boll och Idrottsförening, at the age of six. MBI had a mix of immigrants and ethnic Swedes playing for them, and "a lot of the parents whined about my tricks from the block. I told them to go to hell and changed club several times." He ended up at FBK Balkan, a club made up of players from the former Yugoslavia, where he had an altogether better time of it — apart from the time Zlatan tried his hand at goalkeeping and failed miserably: "One game I let in a lot of goals and I became furious. I screamed that everyone was shit, that football was shit, that the whole world was shit and that I would start playing ice-hockey instead. 'Hockey is a lot better, you fucking idiots! I will become a hockey pro! Go drown yourselves!'"

As it turned out, in order to play ice hockey you have to buy a lot of expensive equipment, so Zlatan stuck with football. His talent soon saw him move from FBK Balkan to the youth ranks of Malmö FF — Malmö's representatives in the Swedish top division. But Zlatan now vehemently denies the notion that he was seen as a big prospect: "It wasn't like, 'Oh, we have to be nice to that little talent.' It was more like, 'Who let the immigrant in?'"

Aside from a few other foreigners Malmö FF's youth side were mostly made up of middle- and upper-class Swedish kids — though of course for a kid from Rosengård the difference between the two was negligible: "I felt like I was from Mars." Where his teammates lived in villas and were driven to training in Volvos, Zlatan lived in a block in Rosengård and cycled in on stolen bikes. They passed, he dribbled. They played, he fought. Once, in a match, Zlatan was booked for arguing with one of his teammates. He told the referee that, "You can go fuck yourself as well," and was sent off. On another occasion, in training, one of his teammates put in a number of rough challenges, so Zlatan headbutted him. The player's father started a petition to get Zlatan removed from the team. "They talked about it all the time: Zlatan doesn't belong here. We have to throw him out." When presented with the petition,

the team's coach, Åke Kallenberg, tore it up. But Zlatan didn't necessarily have a friend in Åke. Later, when Zlatan was moved to Malmö's Under 18-squad a year ahead of schedule, Kallenberg benched him for almost a year. "I could feel the vibrations," Zlatan wrote. "'That Zlatan, isn't he too unbalanced?' It wasn't petitions anymore, but not far off it. And yes, I yelled at my teammates, I screamed and talked too much on the pitch. I could get into arguments with spectators. But it wasn't a big deal, I had my temperament and my style of playing. I was a different kind of player, I got angry. I didn't really belong in Malmö FF."

He still didn't really belong in school either. By that point Zlatan had started upper secondary school on a sports program, at the prestigious Malmö Borgarskola. There were posh kids everywhere, posh kids and a bicycle-thief from Rosengård. "At Borgarskolan they had Ralph Lauren shirts, Timberland shoes and shirts! I had barely seen a guy in a shirt before and I realised that I had to do something about the situation." Zlatan tried buying shirts and jeans but to no avail. "Nothing worked. I still had Rosengård branded on my forehead. I didn't fit in." In addition to the class divide Zlatan was physically awkward, having grown a full 13 cm over the summer (according to himself). He had been a small, skinny kid with a big nose, now he was a lanky, awkward kid with an even bigger nose and shirts that didn't look right. But in spite of being stranded on the bench with the Under-18's and struggling to fit in at school, Zlatan's cocky demeanour never left him. At one point he was thrown out of class and shouted back at his Italian teacher that, "I don't give a fuck about you. I'll learn the language when I become a football pro in Italy." He was still stealing bicycles. One time after training his stolen bicycle had been stolen, so he picked up a particularly nice-looking bike he found outside the dressing-room. He liked it and he made sure to park it far away when he took it to training so its owner wouldn't recognise it. Three days later the players were called in for a meeting, and there was considerable commotion among the staff. Apparently the assistant manager's bicycle had been stolen.

As Mike Campbell dryly notes in Ernest Hemingway's *The Sun Also Rises*, bankruptcy sets in "gradually, then suddenly". The same tends to be true with fame. One day Zlatan Ibrahimović was told that Roland Andersson, the head coach of Malmö FF, wanted to see him. For Zlatan, being called in for a meeting meant bad news. Meetings with teachers, headmasters and coaches had all inevitably led to him being told off for some reason or other. In his autobiography he remembers expecting more of the same. "I panicked, and honestly I started thinking: Have I stolen a bike? Have I headbutted someone?" He hadn't. Or, he probably had, but that wasn't what the meeting was about. Roland Andersson had decided to promote Zlatan to the senior side. He made six substitute appearances and scored his first senior goal as Malmö FF were relegated for the first time in 64 years. Those six appearances were enough. As Malmö prepared for life in the Swedish second flight, Superettan, the hype around Zlatan grew and early stages of Zlatanmania started to sweep the nation. The following season, Malmö's journey back to the top tier was to be chronicled by a film crew and turned into a documentary. Like all things involving Zlatan, it ended up being mostly about Zlatan. In the finished film there is a particularly fascinating interview with Zlatan on a train either to or from an away fixture. All of 19 years old, he is wearing a light blue shirt and a dark leather jacket and he's reading an article about himself in a newspaper. The headline is "*Superettans superdiva*". He seems perfectly content with the tag. When speaking to the camera, the young Zlatan displays an unlikely mixture of big-headedness and self-reflection. "I feel some times that I can be a bit too cocky," he concedes. "Everyone has their cockiness but everyone also has their limits. Maybe I sometimes take it too far. But it's not like people think, that I'm just a cocky idiot who doesn't understand anything. I have my limits, I can be humble sometimes. But I often choose to be cocky because otherwise people can get at me."

It's not entirely certain which people he believes will get at him and how, but considering his parents, his upbringing, his time as the outsider in school, as the unwanted foreigner in football teams, it isn't very hard to see why Zlatan instinctively feels the need to hide behind an impenetrable wall of bravado. He also addresses this attitude in his book. "My thing was that I would both talk and deliver," he wrote. "Not just talk, like 'I'm the best, who are you?' — of course not, nothing's worse than that. But neither would I just perform and say weak things like the Swedish stars. I wanted both to be the best and to be cocky about it." Cristiano Ronaldo recently said that "Too much humility isn't good. Back home in Portugal we say too much modesty equals vanity."

Zlatan no doubt approves. It almost seems as if to his mind humility is a form of cowardice, that by downplaying your abilities you also absolve yourself of responsibility and blame. When Zlatan enters a football pitch he believes, with a fair bit of justification, that he is more likely to make something happen than most of his teammates are. That being the case, why shouldn't he dribble? And in talking the talk Zlatan also put pressure on himself to walk the walk.

Sweden may be a social democracy where modesty and humility are important values, but Rosengård isn't really Sweden as such. Zlatan didn't grow up idolising mild-mannered blond men on skis, he grew up dreaming of Muhammad Ali. But of course, at this point Zlatan wasn't quite Ali, he was a 19-year-old striker playing in the Swedish second division. His teammates tell the film crew following Malmö FF that "he's not the star yet, even if he thinks he is" and that "he's fucking selfish." The young Zlatan is typically bullish in the face of such charges. "I like to dribble, all of Sweden knows that. So sometimes, instead of passing, I dribble. Of course my teammates can get angry but that's just how it goes. If you can't dribble then it's no fun, and football is supposed to be fun. If you're not enjoying yourself, then what's the point?" Relegation served Zlatan well, as it gave him playing time and more freedom to develop. With Malmö FF heading towards promotion there was leeway for Zlatan to do the tricks he'd practised and perfected on the gravel pitch in Rosengård, and the recognition he used to get from the other kids he now got from the stands. He may not have been the most popular player in the dressing-room but he did

finish the season as top scorer as Malmö FF were promoted.

Having delivered, Zlatan did as he had set out to: he talked, telling journalists things like, "There is only one Zlatan" and "Zlatan is Zlatan." Statements like these would become a regular feature of Zlatan's career and led many to believe that the man is a raging egomaniac. This may be the case but there is a significant element of premeditated, knowing bravado involved. In the early years of his career, Zlatan the footballer would do things on the pitch that were fun rather than effective. He would dribble when he should have passed, he would flick the ball first time when he should have controlled it. Similarly, Zlatan the media celebrity would say things that sounded cool, rather than the things it would make sense for a footballer to say. One glaring example of this came in the spring of 2001 when he was briefly engaged to a girl called Mia Olhage. When asked by a journalist what he had given her as an engagement present, Zlatan famously quipped "Present? She got Zlatan." "It was one of those comments that just came, a quote bouncing out of me, and it sounded cocky, right in line with my media image," he now explains. Like José Mourinho, a man with whom he would later form a powerful bond, Zlatan was by and large speaking for effect. But as opposed to Mourinho's more Machiavellian brand of media mischief, Zlatan's statements are spontaneous and instinctive.

Those two adjectives can also be applied to his style of play. Ajax had kept a close eye on Zlatan for a while, but the moment the Dutch giants decided to sign him came in March

1999, in La Manga. Malmö were playing the Norwegian side Moss in a typically uninspiring pre-season friendly, with Ajax's head coach Co Adriaanse and their sporting director Leo Beenhakker[1] in attendance. Fifteen minutes in, Zlatan lobbed the ball over two defenders, raced past them to run onto the ball, backheeled it over the last retreating defender and volleyed it in. Beenhakker was no longer wondering whether or not to sign the kid, he was worried about a possible bidding war. Looking back at the goal, Zlatan explains that, "It was one of those pictures that just appear in my head, a flash of lightning in my thoughts that I can never really explain. Football isn't something you plan. Football just happens." It's an explanation that could be applied to many of his most memorable goals. It often seems that Zlatan more than anything delights in doing the improbable, as if the instinct to impress the other boys on the gravel pitch in Rosengård has never really left him. On the other side of that coin, Zlatan seemed for a long time to be more adept at doing the outrageous than he was at doing the basics that are expected from a top-class striker.

After signing him for Juventus in 2004, Fabio Capello despaired at Zlatan's inefficiency in front of goal. Every day after training, Capello's assistant Italo Galbiati would take Zlatan aside and practise finishing with him. Balls were fired at him in the box from every angle, without pause and Zlatan was to blast all of them past a goalkeeper from the youth team. "I'm going to beat the Ajax out of your body," Capello told him. "I don't need that Dutch style. Play one-twos, play nice and technical, dibble through the whole team. I can do without all that; I need goals. You understand? I need to get the Italian mindset into you. You need to get the killer instinct." Capello may or may not have been aware that Zlatan's love of tricks and flicks had little to do with his time at Ajax, that when he had started out playing the game he valued tricks higher than goals. In a further effort to turn Zlatan into a striker who actually scored goals, Capello once sat him down in an empty room in front of a television and showed him a VHS-compilation of Marco van Basten's goals. "Study his movements, suck them in, learn from them," Capello's ordered. After watching the tape for 30 minutes Zlatan got bored and left: "Honestly, I have no idea if I learnt anything or not, but I got the message." Zlatan's goal return for Juventus was a passable 23 goals in 70 appearances. "I changed under Capello," Zlatan says in his book. "The toughness in him was infectious and I became less of an artist and more of a slugger who wanted to win at any cost. It's not that I didn't want to win before, I was born with a winning mentality. But don't forget that football had been my way of making myself visible. The tricks had made me more than just another kid from Rosengård. It was all the "Oh!" and "Wow, look at that!" which had inspired me in the first place. For a long time I would have thought you were a moron if you told me that an ugly goal was worth as much as a beautiful one. But now I was starting to understand — no one will thank you for your tricks and backheels if your team loses."

[1]*Beenhakker spoke of his pursuit of Zlatan and his time working with him in* The Blizzard *Issue Seven.*

In his last season with Inter before departing for Barcelona, Zlatan was top scorer in Serie A with 25 goals in 35 appearances. It would be a mistake, though, to say the Italian killer instinct had entirely replaced his flair for the improbable: the goal which saw him crowned *capocannoniere* was an instinctive backheel to clinch a 4-3 win over Atalanta.

When Leo Beenhakker flew to Malmö many years earlier to wrap up the Ibrahimović deal, he sat down in a hotel room with the lanky 19 year old. Looking him in the eye, Beenhakker leant forwards over the table. "If you fuck with me I'll fuck you two times back," he said. Zlatan was impressed; it was his kind of talk. He liked Beenhakker because he "radiated power and coldness" and "looked like a mafioso". Zlatan responds to strength. While many agents pamper and sweet-talk their clients, the following is a sample conversation between Zlatan and his faithful representative Mino Raiola:

— You like when people tell you that you're the best, right?
— Yeah, maybe.
— But it's not true. You're not the best. You're shit. You're nothing. You have to work harder.
— You're the shit. You just moan. You should work out yourself.
— Go fuck yourself.
— Fuck you.

Zlatan likes Fabio Capello, because, "You don't mess around with Capello, that guy could floor any star with just a stare." And naturally, for a man who believes in both walking the walk and talking the talk, Zlatan likes José Mourinho. However, Zlatan does not like Pep Guardiola.

A few years on, the thing that's truly inexplicable is that Barcelona thought signing Zlatan Ibrahimović was a good idea in the first place. Zlatan is the anti-Barça, both as a person and as a player. At Barcelona, Zlatan might as well have been back at Borgarskolan, with an invisible but impenetrable barrier between himself and the posh kids. Xavi, Iniesta, Messi *et al* were all polite, obedient students in Mr Guardiola's classroom and Zlatan was again the unruly yob from the wrong neighbourhood. In his book he maintains that he tried to fit in but that it came at a price. He left his Ferrari in the garage and drove the club's sponsored Audi to training, he behaved politely towards his teammates, he didn't shout at anyone. "I became boring," he said. "Zlatan wasn't Zlatan and that hadn't happen since back in school when I saw girls in Ralph Lauren shirts for the first time and almost shit my pants when I was asking them out." On the pitch things went reasonably well until Lionel Messi — according to Zlatan — went to Guardiola and said he wanted to play in the middle. To accommodate the request, Guardiola switched from Barcelona's usual 4-3-3-formation to something more resembling a 4-4-1-1, with Messi playing off the front man. It meant a more limited role for Zlatan, who was now supposed to act mostly as a foil for Messi. Zlatan decided to follow Messi's lead and have a chat with the boss: "You are not using my capacity. If it was a goalscorer you wanted, you should have bought Inzaghi or someone. I need space and to be free. I can't run up and down constantly. I weigh 98 kilos. I don't have the physique for it." Guardiola replied that he thought Zlatan could play like that but Zlatan insisted that they might as well put him on the bench. Guardiola took him at his word and gradually stopped playing him, then stopped talking to him altogether. Zlatan's account of his falling out with Guardiola is naturally one-sided and there are probably those who would question its veracity. What is beyond question, however, is that Zlatan Ibrahimović was always going to be a spectacularly poor fit for the Barcelona-model, both tactically and personally: "I play better when I'm angry. If you see me furious, don't worry. OK, I might do something stupid and get sent off. But mostly it's a good sign. All my career has been built on my desire for revenge." At what point did it seem like a good idea to try to integrate this man into Pep Guardiola's team of well-behaved boys?

Another point his relative failure in Spain brings up is that Barcelona adhere to a strict tactical system, but Zlatan has never shown any willingness to subject himself to a system of any kind. Why should he limit himself to being a target man when he also has the skill and vision to drop deep and create? Why should he limit himself to playing between the lines when he also has the pace and power to spearhead an attack? Most players have their roles defined by their limitations. Zlatan is a striker who is quick, strong, skilful, good in the air, can hold up the ball, can finish with both feet, demonstrably has an eye for a pass (if not always the inclination to play it), has the intelligence to drop deep and the explosiveness to threaten the space behind the back four. Ability-wise he has few, if any, limitations. Because of this versatility and his imposing personality, Zlatan has made himself the main attacking outlet of every team he's ever

played for — with the notable exception of Barcelona. The tendency inevitably becomes "pass it to Zlatan, and see what happens," both because he wants it that way and because more often than not the strategy will yield results: his run of eight consecutive league titles for five different clubs in three different countries is remarkable, and a feat not likely to be bettered any time soon.

His lack of success in the Champions League however remains a blot in an otherwise majestic copybook. It's a blot that's given rise to accusations that Zlatan lacks the mentality for big games. In his desire to do everything all at the same time, he has occasionally been prone to doing nothing much at all. Damningly in some people's eyes, the times he's gone missing have often been pivotal games in the Champions League. But the accusations of Zlatan lacking big game-temperament are deeply flawed. On the last day of the 2007-08 Serie A season Inter were on the verge of disaster. After being 11 points clear at the top of the table, Inter collapsed in the final weeks, allowing Roma to move within a point of them before the final game of the season. Inter were facing a Parma side desperately scrapping to avoid relegation and they were facing them away on a rain-soaked pitch at the Stadio Ennio Tardini. For many years Inter had an almost institutionalised propensity for self-destruction. A hugely embarrassing title concession looked a very real possibility. Zlatan, having been injured for months, was just about passed fit to play — but he was badly lacking match fitness. At half-time it was 0-0. The pitch was soggy, Parma were battling, nothing much was happening for Inter and Mirko Vučinić had given Roma a 1-0 lead over

Catania. The title was on its way to the South. But cometh the hour, cometh the Zlatan. Battling the elements, rising panic and the weight of history and blunders past, a half-fit Zlatan scored twice and won Inter the *scudetto*. This simply isn't something you do if you're a man devoid of big game mentality.

A more plausible explantion for Zlatan's failure in the Champions League, the very highest level of club football, is his tactical indiscipline. Football's gradual shift in emphasis from the individual to the collective has been well documented. The last decade the sport's biggest trophies have almost invariably been won by teams who are exceptionally strong collective units rather than a collection of individuals. "Unleash the Zlatan" way well be a fruitful tactic over the course of a full league season as lesser teams find him impossible to deal with, but the very best sides are more capable of marginalising him, and Zlatan's teams have tended to lack a plan B. These high profile failures in the Champions League have led many to believe that Zlatan is overrated, that his talent doesn't match his reputation and ego. In fact there is a case to be made that his raw talent is underappreciated: in terms of physique, technique and natural talent there has hardly been a more complete striker in the modern game. But his refusal to reduce himself to being just one cog in a well-oiled machine has made him ineffective at the very highest level, and is arguably the biggest reason why he will never be considered one of the all-time greats of the game. The contrast between Zlatan the individualist and the modern game's emphasis on the collective could scarcely be more

clearly illustrated than by his unhappy time at Barcelona.

A few months after his falling out with Guardiola, Zlatan was back in Italy with AC Milan, where the management accepted that the only thing you can really do with him is let Zlatan be Zlatan. Over the next two seasons he rewarded them with 42 Serie A goals in 61 matches, playing some of the best football of his career and merrily kicking teammates in the head at regular intervals. The subsequent move to PSG seems a logical next step, with him joining a club where he will likely get the freedom he needs and the iconic status he craves.

All of which brings us back to Amsterdam Arena, 22 August 2004. Zlatan had already scored once that afternoon as a corner from Wesley Sneijder landed at his feet and he duly thumped the ball in from close range. But celebrations were muted, with teammates offering only half-hearted cheers. A few days earlier Sweden had played a friendly against Holland, and Zlatan had visited his studs upon Rafael van der Vaart's ankle while forcing his way through the Dutch defence. Accidentally, deliberately or maliciously? TV replays were inconclusive. Van der Vaart, who at the age of 21 was already captain of Ajax, was carried off with minor ligament damage. He told the press afterwards that Zlatan, his teammate, had injured him deliberately. Zlatan called to apologise, "but Van der Vaart continued talking to the press and I just couldn't understand it. Why the fuck would he talk shit about his own teammate?"

Van der Vaart was young, handsome and Dutch; the press loved him. Zlatan was Zlatan, and the Ajax camp was split between the Dutch players and the foreigners. The head coach Ronald Koeman called a team meeting to clear the air, at which point Van der Vaart repeated his accusations. Zlatan, ever the diplomat, replied that, "I didn't hurt you on purpose, and you know that, and if you accuse me of that one more time I will break both your legs. And this time it will be on purpose." Somehow this did not calm things down. Team Van der Vaart said the outburst was final proof that Zlatan was aggressive and crazy, and the situation went from bad to unfixable. Zlatan told the sporting director Louis van Gaal that he refused to play with Van der Vaart again. The argument neatly encapsulates the central paradox of Zlatan: he claims that he has to be cocky so people can't "get" him, yet his cockiness is overwhelmingly the thing people attack him for. His abrasiveness is an obvious defence mechanism, yet it is also exactly the thing that keeps getting him into trouble. With Van der Vaart, Zlatan believed that everyone was against him and so he went on the offensive — and in so doing turned everyone against him.

While all of this was going on, Mino Raiola was attempting to engineer a move to Juventus before the transfer window shut. The match against NAC Breda took on unexpected significance. In the stands were people from Juventus whom Zlatan badly needed to impress. Also in the stands was an injured Rafael van der Vaart, as well as thousands of Dutch people who were deeply unimpressed with this lanky Swede from the ghetto who had mauled their media-darling. "It was insane. It felt like the Dutch were spitting on me. They were whistling and screaming, and high up in the stands sat Rafael van der Vaart and he was applauded. It was ridiculous. I was seen as crap, while he was the innocent victim." So when Zlatan scored a tap-in from a corner after 13 minutes, nobody got too excited. After 76 minutes it was a different story.

Zlatan claims that during his entire career he has been motivated by his desire for revenge and to prove people wrong. It also seems at times like he is battling his own sense of otherness. Either way, here he was fuelled by anger at having been cast as the bad guy yet again. The dismayed Dutch in the stands were like the parents petitioning for his expulsion, like all Swedes who sneer at the foreigners from Rosengård. As a footballer, Zlatan was formed by formless games against other kids from the block, and here the NAC defenders became the herd of children trying to take the ball off him for candy. Throughout his career he had been told he needed to pass the ball more often, but Zlatan insisted on following his flashes of inspiration instead. Here he moved with agility and balance no 6′ 5″ man should be capable of, turning players at will, and in the end scored a goal that was uniquely Zlatan. A player should know better than attempting that run, but Zlatan didn't and he scored. Nothing could more accurately sum up Zlatan the footballer. And having done the brilliantly unexpected, everything turned on its head. Teammates who seconds before had been against him cheered wildly and buried him under a massive pile-on. Fans who had been booing erupted in unhinged jubilation. In Zlatan's own words, "it was like all the hatred against me turned around, into love and triumph."

For an outsider constantly seeking acceptance through his particular way of playing football, the triumph and vindication could hardly have been more comprehensive. Zlatan Ibrahimović will continue to divide opinion but that goal deserves to be remembered. Either as a showcase of skill and lunacy or as a microcosm of a fascinating career. **B**

66

"The battery of devotion is dying
and you are unprepared for the
identity of the recharger."

But You Can't Change...

How a Watford supporter ended up being converted into a Millwall fan

By Mike Calvin

This is a letter that must be written, but cannot be received, because I've not overcome the space-time continuum. It is addressed to myself, as a boy on the edge of adolescence. It covers love and loss, passion and betrayal. It features two football clubs, and a cardinal sin, the transfer of allegiance from one club to another. It sees a boy's world, through a man's eyes. It seeks to share the lessons of a lifetime. It craves forgiveness, because I will shatter the illusion of innocence, but there is nothing to worry about. I've been blessed.

Dear Mike,

Happy twelfth birthday. It's Sunday, 3 August 1969. The first face you see, as you wake in the top bunk of the bedroom you share with your brothers, is that of Colin Bell. It's a full page portrait, torn from *Goal* magazine and sellotaped to the wall, alongside images of Tony Book, Glyn Pardoe and a mythical creature named Mike Doyle. They won the Football League for Manchester City in 1968 but you follow them by default. Mum bought you a City shirt, round necked and a size too big, last Christmas, because she liked its shade of light blue. It also had growing room.

Mums are practical like that. She has only the vaguest notion you support Watford, your home-town club, who are beginning their first season in the Second Division. Their players do not get many photo-spreads in *Goal* magazine, or in *Charles Buchan's Football Monthly*, the other drain on your paper-round money. Only one, Keith Eddy, gets the full-colour treatment. His picture is posted above the bed. He's straight-backed, steely-eyed, a prince in the guise of a lower League journeyman. Watford's captain wears the number four and seems impossibly glamorous.

You've got Gola boots, because Adidas World Cups are too expensive, and you're not good enough to wear George Best's side-laced Stylo Matchmakers. Mum and Dad have three jobs between them, trying to make ends meet, but they buy your first sports book for your birthday. It's *The Football Man*, by Arthur Hopcraft. Neither they, nor you, realise this will shape your life. You will cherish it, memorise it, refer to it as the years roll away. You will never forget the last lines of the introduction: "This is not a gallery of heroes. I am a reporter trying to reach to the heart of what football is."

Dad is a Rugby League man. You watch his home town team, Whitehaven, on family holidays but much prefer to play endless games of football with your cousins, on a pitch at the end of your grandparents' garden. It is, quite literally, in the shadow of the pithead. Haig Colliery is Cumbria's last deep-coal mine, and will not close until 1986. It leads down to a beach, where you pick black diamonds, washed-up deposits for the fire. Grandad, an imposing figure in belted trousers which extend to his armpits, sits in a high-backed chair, and tells of being out of work from the 1929 Stock Market crash to the Second World War. He fought, bare-knuckled, in pubs for pennies, and trapped rabbits for the stew-pot. As you grow older, you will discover the relevance of his reflections on the importance of honesty, humility and hard work.

The other important document, your Magna Carta, is at home, beneath your pillow. It is a letter, on headed notepaper, signed "R.E.Rollitt, General Secretary, Watford Association Football Club Ltd". It confirms the success of your application to be a Watford ball-boy for the 1969-70 season and requests that you report for duty, a minimum 50 minutes before home games. Your green rectangular pass, enclosed in a plastic wallet, is your boarding card for a journey which will take you to more than 80 countries.

You will watch football in Africa, in places like Bamako, the capital of Mali, where polio victims shuffle on all fours, chasing a ball made of rags. You will travel to the slums of Naples, to World Cups in Mexico, the United States and South Africa, to see its beauty, depravity and eccentricity encapsulated in one man, Diego Armando Maradona. You might not be fit to lace George Best's boots, but to cannibalise a line from an infinitely better writer than you, you will be in a succession of pubs to ensure no-one laces his drinks.

But, forgive me, we get ahead of ourselves. Let's dwell on what it means to wear those ancient, faded bottle green tracksuits, which chafe like Sir Thomas More's hair shirt. You luxuriate in the knowledge you are in The Show, on the inside. You change next to the home dressing-room and the smell of liniment is as evocative as the incense, released by your alter egos, the altar boys at High Mass. You check on the crowd through a frosted fanlight and carry out boxes of metal numbers, to place on half-time scoreboards which extend from A to Z down the side of the pitch. Vicarage Road is pretty scruffy, to be honest. You've previously bunked in, via the allotments, to stand on the shale of the bend beside the Rookery End. Now you are within touching distance of heroes who still get the bus to work. You will never lose the thrill of the setting, the intimacy of the insight football provides into the best, and worst, of human nature.

You will make your first away trip, in a neighbour's motorcycle sidecar, to see Watford lose 2-1 at Oxford on 6 September 1969. You will pay a shilling for the programme and throw up on the way home, because you eat a cheese sandwich. They didn't recognise food allergies in those days, did they? You stick to Bovril on match days after that. You listen to *Sports Report* on the kitchen radio when Watford embark on your first FA Cup run, winning 2-1 at Bolton Wanderers in the third round. First Division Stoke are beaten by a 30-yard drive by Colin Franks, who lives just down the road. The game is on TV, the equivalent of a state visit. When Gillingham lose 2-1, to two goals by new £7,000 signing Ray Lugg, a local photographer captures you hugging another ballboy, Keith Furphy, the manager's son. He is small, flaxen-haired and will go on to play professionally in the

United States. He will get the plum job, operating behind the goal at the Rookery End, when Liverpool arrive at Vicarage Road on 21 February 1970, for the quarter final.

In the next century, when matches are beamed into satellite dishes erected on the sides of houses, and are regarded as minor wars, you'll wonder why you were so excited by the build-up to the game. The *Watford Observer* — of which more later — publishes a 16-page supplement, previewing the game. Watford are duly patronised as plucky outsiders, or blithely dismissed as relegation fodder by national newspaper men who can barely conceal their distaste at the ambitions of a team of such low breeding. Funny, that. You will love covering such ties, when it is your turn to make the long journey from Fleet Street to the real world.

On this day, you'll be stationed on the Shrodells' side, in front of a low-roofed eyesore which shields the hospital in which Gareth Southgate will be born, later that year. You'll see a grown man cry, for the first time. He's a Scouser, a crumpled figure in a donkey jacket who weeps as he sags into a wire mesh fence beside the wooden hut that houses the Supporters Club. Bill Shankly's team lose 1-0 on a pitch that consists of rolled mud and you are centrally involved in the goal.

You collect the ball, in front of a sign advertising Double Diamond ("Works Wonders") and quickly toss it to Lugg, who takes a short throw to winger Stewart Scullion and moves into space to receive the return pass. He nutmegs Peter Wall, the covering full-back, and delivers an outswinging cross, directly in your eyeline. It is met by a diving header from Barry Endean, who runs behind

the goal to celebrate and is ambushed by, you've guessed it, Keith Furphy. God, how you envy him, caught up in a scrum of men whose gold shirts, with a hornet on the left breast, are caked with dirt and suffused with sweat.

Life seems suddenly simple. You want a piece of this. You look into the crowd and see men, lost in the moment. A football club, small and apparently insignificant, is woven into the tapestry of people's lives. You find it easy to express the emotions of the occasion, through the written word. You imagine the unity of strangers and sense the spirit of that broken man, on the wire. You will meet Shankly, just before his death in 1981 and ask him about the defeat which prompted him to break up his first great Liverpool team. He will tell you, in that Ayrshire rasp, that it was "a bitter day, son. Bitter."

So, too, is Saturday, 14 March 1970. For some reason, lost in the mists of time, the semi-final against Chelsea, at White Hart Lane, kicks off at 2.45pm. A fleet of coaches, carrying fans living in a twilight world of hope and disbelief, begins to leave Watford at breakfast time. Yours, caught in the inevitable jam, is eased to the side of the road, to let the team bus past, somewhere near Enfield. More than 40 years later, you will still be able to summon the freeze frame image of Eddy, sitting by the window and smiling at the forest of scarves being waved at him. He had suffered a cartilage injury and will miss the biggest game of his life. Some of your friends have stolen bedsheets, daubed them with gloss paint from the garden shed, and transformed them into banners. You wear a rosette, with a small silver-papered Cup at its heart. Your rattle, wooden, but with black metal gears, is so heavy it could stun a rhinoceros. Take a deep breath and recite after me the team which played that day in full schoolboy shorthand: Walker, Welbourne, Williams, Lugg, Lees, Walley, Scullion, Garbett, Endean, Packer, Owen. Sub: Garvey.

Names, faces, memories. Mickey Walker, who will go on to manage Colchester, Everton and Norwich (twice), has the piercing eyes and thin moustache of a spaghetti Western villain. Duncan Welbourne, who will play 280 games on the spin, is a full-back who looks like a Teddy Boy. He should, by rights, play in brothel creepers. Tom Walley, who will develop into a brilliant youth coach and produce such England internationals as David James and Ashley Cole, will also become a family friend. Many years later you will discover Endean, the hero signed for £50, working as a builder in his native North East.

You are a water molecule in the sea of humanity which ebbs and flows around the lower tier of the main stand at White Hart Lane. It will, in time, become one of your favourite grounds, intimate and atmospheric. You have been to Rugby League and Amateur Cup finals at Wembley, but this is something more elemental. The stands seem higher, the noise louder. The pitch is fringed with dull, under-nourished, grass, but is mainly mud, mixed with sand. Your silent prayer, that this will help Watford bridge the chasm in class, remains unanswered. Watford lose 5-1, but you are comforted by the fleeting euphoria of Terry Garbett's first-half equaliser, struck from just outside the box. It will be 14 years, two months, and five days before Watford finally reach their first FA Cup final.

You will be there, in a different guise. That's because of another two-line letter, which you will also secrete beneath your pillow. This, too, is on headed notepaper. It is signed, "ER Foster, Editor". He offers you a junior reporter's job on the *Watford Observer*. Mum cries. When you tell Keith "Trog" Turner, your headmaster at the local Grammar School, of your intention to abandon your A-levels, he responds as if you have urinated through his letterbox. "Calvin," he intones, "this will lead to nothing." He's right, in a way. When, many years later, you are invited back, to contribute to his valediction, you find your diary is full.

Your great good fortune is to have, as your first sports editor, Oli Phillips. He introduces you to Bob Dylan and fried tomatoes on toast. The latter is infinitely preferable to the former, who gives you aural indigestion. Oli is a talented writer, a warm and wise teacher. He gives you your first byline — Mick Calvin — for a report on the West Herts Bowls Club Dinner & Dance. You have your own page, to cover the Watford Sunday League, and are eased into the Vicarage Road rotation. Football is suddenly seen through a different prism.

Watford hit their lowest ebb almost as soon as you arrive. A 1-0 loss at Darlington, on 30 August 1975, leaves them 92nd in the Football League. You spend most of the season with the Under-18s, developing a working relationship with a quietly spoken lad of your age. His name is Luther Blissett. You will see him score a hat trick on his England debut, a 9-0 win against Luxembourg on the evening of 15 December 1982. AC Milan will sign him for £1m, and sell him back, for £550,000, within a year. He will end up as Watford's record goal-scorer, 186 in 503 appearances. His is the first of many lives you chart.

You are sent to play darts against Watford's new owner, in the Supporters' Club bar. His name is, or was, Reginald Dwight. He dresses as Elton Hercules John and arrives at the oche in platform boots, a pink satin suit and scarf fashioned from peacock feathers. His glasses resemble diamante-studded dustbin lids. You can't hit the board, let alone find the treble 20, but something weird happens. You converse as fellow fans, share memories and emotions. Elton knows what he has to do at the end of the season. He sacks Mike Keen, rejects the chance to employ Bobby Moore and recognises the potential of a young manager named Graham Taylor.

Your football education accelerates. Taylor is a force of nature. He transforms your club, sweeps away generations of grime. He's empathetic, inclusive, sensitive, and utterly ruthless. He's a dream-seller, a scene-stealer. He insists his players live in the town and replies personally to all signed letters from fans. The season develops into a crusade. It is no surprise that Watford win the Fourth Division by eleven points, having clinched the title with six games to spare. Elton had given Taylor five years to get into the Second Division. He needs two. You hitch a ride on a football special train to see Blissett score with two headers in a 2-1 win at Manchester United. This is getting silly. Watford are promoted for the second successive season, and reach the League Cup semi-finals, where they are beaten by Brian Clough's Nottingham Forest. The following season is transitional, but highlighted by an

extraordinary comeback. Trailing 4-0 from the first leg of a League Cup tie against Southampton, the First Division's form team, Watford win 7-1.

Your career matches the upward trajectory of your club. You cover your first Olympic Games, as chief sports writer for a chain of regional newspapers, in Brezhnev's Moscow in 1980 and begin to follow England around the world. Business can be matched with pleasure, because Watford remain a breaking story. Taylor builds a vibrant team around Tom Walley's products, like Blissett, John Barnes, Nigel Callaghan and Kenny Jackett, a kid from your council estate. As a fan, you bridle at Terry Venables's lazy description of Watford as long-ball Neanderthals. They reach the First Division in 1982, and win the FA Youth Cup for good measure. The mood of Venables, and his media acolytes, is not improved when Taylor is asked to oversee the England youth team, on a part-time basis.

Taylor has the common touch. When he criticises fans for lack of vocal support, they argue that it would help if the main terrace had a roof. He promptly walks out on to the pitch with a placard which reads, "I'm sorry." There's not a lot to apologise for. Watford's initial season in the top flight is incredible. Blissett scores four in an 8-0 thrashing of Sunderland. Watford do the double over Arsenal, win at Spurs, and have home wins over Everton and Liverpool. They finish as runners-up, and qualify for the Uefa Cup. Not for the first time, or the last, Elton is in floods of tears.

Your year as a TV reporter allows you to follow your club into Europe.

Kaiserslauten succumb at Vicarage Road. Watford win, in extra time, against Levski Spartak, a team run by Bulgaria's Interior Ministry. On a freezing evening 60,000 fans light bonfires to keep warm and stage proletarian protests. The sleigh ride ends in the snow in Prague, where Sparta win 4-0, but the spiritual journey has yet to be completed. That happens in 1984, when Watford reach the FA Cup final.

You are working in Fleet Street and permit yourself one last indulgence. You return home, drink in the estate pub before the game with your childhood friends. You envy your brothers, their face paint and replica shirts, because you have to be suited and booted. You take your Mum to her first football match, on a Metropolitan line train which glows gold and reverberates to Elton's greatest hits. Mum sits next to Freddie Starr at Wembley, near the royal box, and barely registers the result. You envy her sense of detachment.

You will neither forgive, nor forget, a posturing ninny of a referee named Roger Milford. This bubble-permed publicity junkie unjustly sends off Wilf Rostron in the build-up to the final and costs a great pro the chance to captain Watford at Wembley. Andy Gray joins Milford on the hit list, although you will work with him, and like him, in later years. He knocks the ball out of goalkeeper Steve Sherwood's hands to score the decisive second goal in Everton's 2-0 win. Like Graham Taylor, you will never be able to watch a recording of the final. It is too painful.

Looking back, it is the end of innocence. Taylor's attempt to redress the balance ends at the semi-final stage in 1987,

when he is forced to select a wine waiter, Gary Plumley, in goal. The son of chief executive Eddie, Plumley is recruited because of injuries to Tony Coton and Steve Sherwood and is predictably powerless to prevent Spurs winning 4-1. Watford couldn't even sell their full allocation of tickets. Taylor leaves at the end of the season, to be replaced, with disastrous consequences, by Dave Bassett.

We have entered the age of Heysel and Hillsborough. You are among the football hacks summoned to Downing Street by Margaret Thatcher. She has the eyes of a tawny owl and clearly terrifies her ministers, who dance attendance. She goes around the table, asking each visitor what they would do to solve football hooliganism. You might as well quote Afghani poetry, because her mind is made up before anyone opens their mouth. In her world, football fans are second-class citizens who have forfeited the right to trust and respect. They deserve to be caged, treated with contempt. You descend the staircase, framed by portraits of past prime ministers, with a sense of dread.

The more you understand the principles of power, and the closer you get to the sort of people who administer it, the more depressed you become. You are no longer prepared to take things at face value. Football is re-shaped by Super Sundays and institutionalised greed. The Premier League is marketed brilliantly and spawns a culture of grasping agents, preening players and celebrity nonentities. By 1996 Watford are back in the old Third Division. They have reverted to irrelevance and you have turned on Taylor.

His failure as England manager is a self-fulfilling prophesy, even though he loses only one of his first 23 matches. He is too below-stairs for his most vindictive critics, and never recovers from his visit to the tabloid vegetable rack. Being lampooned as a turnip, following a European Championship defeat by Sweden, sets the tone. He cracks in Rotterdam, before the game which costs England a place in the 1994 World Cup. He loses his temper in the pre-match press conference, becomes embroiled in a row with a reporter and comes across as paranoid, out of his depth. The Channel 4 TV crew, developing a fateful fly on the wall documentary, are doing handstands. You write a scathing piece, knowing the impact it will have on Taylor, his wife Rita and his two daughters. You feel a little ashamed.

There are brief moments of rapture, which never quite rebuild bridges, but rekindle an old flame. Watford win successive promotions during Taylor's second spell as manager. You are in bed in Brisbane, howling at the moon and following the game on a ruinously expensive phone line, when they make the Premier League for the first time, on 31 May 1999. It is 3.36am, the following day, in Queensland when Nick Wright's overhead kick sets up a 2-0 win over Bolton in the Championship play-off final at Wembley. The *Sun* hails Taylor as a national treasure. Go figure.

You still feel for the club and ignore professional protocol that September by standing in the old wooden press box at Watford and punching the air to celebrate Allan Smart's winning goal against Chelsea. It is a rare highlight in a season which ends in relegation. Gianluca Vialli,

Chelsea's manager that day, succeeds Taylor at Vicarage Road at the end of the 2000-01 season and is useful as an elephant on an ice floe. He lasts a year and Watford flirt with administration.

You are able take your sons to watch another Championship play-off victory, 3-0 over Leeds United at the Millennium Stadium in 2006, but something still does not feel right. Aidy Boothroyd, in his first season as manager, is a media myth, quickly exposed in the Premier League. Watford finish bottom, winning only five matches. The cycle of recrimination and boardroom intrigue intensifies. The battery of devotion is dying and you are unprepared for the identity of the recharger. He's Kenny Jackett, the kid with whom you played pick-up games on the estate.

He's Millwall manager, a Lion tamer. You contact him, in the summer of 2009, with an outrageous request. Give me complete access to your club, so I can search for football's soul. He agrees and you report for the first day of pre-season training. You are on the substitutes' bench at Wembley, 333 days later, when Millwall are promoted through the League One play off final. You are unprepared for the intensity of the experience. It prompts you to question basic beliefs, realign your principles and allegiances.

Players reveal the reality of their trade, the insecurity which cannot be diluted by surges of adrenaline, or testosterone. They allow you to become part of the dressing-room's fixtures and fittings. You get a sense of their professionalism, and the bitter cruelties of their trade. They are mostly family men, whose life is influenced by the vagaries of form and fate. Cut them and their nearest and dearest bleed. Jackett and his coaches give you the privilege of their trust, take you into their confidence. There are moments of tension and tenderness, anger and amusement.

Millwall remains a byword for strife and a lack of social cohesion, but you look beyond the stereotypes. The club plays an integral role in a multi-cultural, multi-faith community. There are no fairytales out there, but you unearth reasons to believe in football's restorative powers. Good people are doing a good job, without fuss or fanfare. You begin to understand the precious nature of the link between players and their fans. These are not the corporate grazers of the Premier League or the ogres of tabloid myth. They are true believers, your type of people. They agree with Grandad about the value of humility, honesty and hard work.

The deeper you delve, the more committed you become. You love the tall tales from the Old Den, where men were men and opposing teams wished they were anywhere else. You meet club legend Barry Kitchener, the embodiment of a working class hero. Like most hard men, he has an affecting gentility, and dignity. By the time he succumbs to cancer, with tragic speed, in the spring of 2012, you have admitted to living a lie. Millwall is the football club best suited to your nature and experience.

Honesty is a double edged sword, which wounds when you return to Vicarage Road on the night of 27 September 2010. Your host, in the chairman's suite, is Graham Taylor. He is polite, attentive, but seems ill at ease with his duties. You guess why when Watford's new

owner makes a late entrance. He is an interesting character, who changed his name from Laurence Bazini to Bassini when he was made bankrupt in 2007. Your antennae twitch. He's a little too glib and doesn't endear himself to his guests with a guileless quip about Millwall fans ripping out the seats in the event of defeat. To be honest, you loathe him.

Watford come from behind to beat Millwall 2-1, without a hint of trouble. It is an abject game between ponderous, fretful teams. You are desolate, and realise that the club that enticed you into falling in love with the game's infinite possibilities no longer exists. It has betrayed the love of that boy with half-formed dreams, in the bunk bed. Taylor will eventually leave the club, on May 30 2012. Two months later Baz/ss/ini will sell Watford to the Pozzo family, who transform it into a feeder club for Udinese in Serie A. Your instincts have been proved correct.

You wanted "your" team to lose when Millwall came calling. That's heresy and you know it. Dare you share it? There's no option really, because it is what is expected of you. Be true to yourself. You know it makes sense. Repeat after me:

"Mmmmmmiiiiiilllllll..."

Best wishes,

Mike

This is an extract from Life's A Pitch: Passions of the Press Box, *published by Integr8 Books and available for order through www.lifesapitch.co.uk.'*

Ⓑ

CLASSIC FOOTBALL SHIRTS.CO.UK

THE MOST EXTENSIVE RANGE OF ORIGINAL SHIRTS ONLINE
HUGE CLEARANCE SECTION FULL OF 1000's OF BARGAIN ITEMS

GETAFE	FC YOUNG BOYS	LYON TECHFIT	MARSEILLE TECHFIT	VALENCIA
£11.99	£19.99	£34.99	£22.99	£19.99

OKE CROUCH £29.99 **NAPOLI CAVANI** £49.99 **NAPOLI HAMSIK** £44.99 **SHORTS, SOCKS, BAGS, JACKETS ETC.**

In the Shadow of the Goldfish

Having lived the dream, Leeds have slowly drifted into a protracted doze

By Gary Hartley

To suggest that Leeds United have kept their descent into torpor rather quiet would most likely be met with cries of derision.

Of course all the key features of a very public fall are there. For an abridged version of the last decade, try: goldfish, admin, El-Hadji Diouf. The rest of the seemingly limitless archive of public domain material for the casual haters to quote doesn't seem worth mentioning anymore.

While our dirty washing has been hanging out, the strangest thing is that the mass of fun-pokers you encounter don't see a terminal decline at Leeds and are in fact often inclined to reel out the consolations of "big fan base" and "too big to stay down" when you start complaining. It's too late: the platitudes of outsiders aren't enough to keep us convinced.

There are some glaringly mistaken but extremely common beliefs: the main two being the inevitability of a return to the top flight for Dirty Leeds and the formidable nature of a trip to Elland Road. It's time we talked.

Leeds's old ground loomed over a record eleven defeats last term. There was a 5-0, a 4-1 (all four for Nikola Zigić)

and a 7-3. The season before there was a 6-4 from 4-1 up. Elland Road is quiet. Elland Road is mainly unpleasant for the home fans.

Mid-table obscurity is one of the best ways to keep mainstream interest from your door — a wall of silence masking the fact that these are dark, dark days. Remaining high up the Championship average attendance table — fourth — also proves a neat distraction for the unobservant. In the average attendance table for the Championship last season, all of the top 10 bar Birmingham and Leeds were filling 70% of their seats or more. St Andrews was respectably creeping towards two-thirds full. The South Leeds monolith was echoing to a nervous 57.9%. We got fewer than 20,000 for Everton in the Cup. More worrying still, at last count, an average of over 3,500 more fans were staying away per game than in 2010-11 — by far the biggest exodus in the league. Those doing other things with their Saturdays are probably not regretting the decision.

Most of the non-capitulation defeats last year weren't particularly hard-fought either, just grudging expectation of the worst devoid of any semblance of either creativity or fight. Oh sure, there were nine reds and 75 yellows picked up overall, putting us a lofty second in the disciplinary charts, but the majority of the faithful do see 'fight' as being a subtler thing. No, really.

Anyone we could get vaguely excited about in recent times has gone: Gradel, Howson, Delph, Beckford, and add to that last summer, Snodgrass and Clayton. The psychological knock-on effect of repeated exits is evident as each contract renewal for the diluted 'stars' still knocking around comes up. We have learnt to expect the running order of no agreement reached, player/agent officially derided as greedy, offer accepted from nowhere spectacular; often Norwich.

Players' undoubted affection for the club overshadows careerist pragmatism no more. There's just not much been going on around here to maintain interest. Of course there's suffering and selling all round outside the elites, worsened by relentless recession, but some say you have to spend your way out of one of those. It's safe to say that is not an approach Ken Bates signed up to.

Financial Fair Play offers owners like Bates a chance to preach false morality via their (loss-making) in-house media, but the club are taking fiscal responsibility into the absurd, with by a massive distance the lowest wages/turnover spend percentage in the Championship — 51% to be precise — just scraping into Uefa's suggested range of 50-70 per for the healthy club, and actually below the 60% maximum adopted by Leagues One and Two. Mid-table investment with top of the league income and expectation is a poisonous concoction.

To clarify, this is fiscal responsibility where playing staff are concerned. Elland Road, the property portfolio we don't even own, has been making progress all the time. Plans for a 350-room hotel — which spawned the ultra-sardonic 'Visit Beeston' motif from sceptical fan media — have gone somewhat quiet, but not to worry: we've got over twenty new and under-utilised executive boxes, a massive concourse to emphasise further the reduction in non-executive attendees and we'll probably have opened a museum by the time this goes to press. They were still making desperate pleas for stuff to fill it in late 2011.

And that's without mentioning the proposed casino. Considering the journey from destructive high stakes to today's absolute lack of even a tame gambler's vision when it comes to assembling a competitive playing staff, the irony is not lost here.

The truth is that a famously one-club city with a potentially massive support base is having to rely on its away following — in many cases older 'out of towners' living on reheated memories of the Revie years — to maintain the myth that Leeds can incite fear and respect when in full voice.

All this may well be seen as a treacherous breaking of a semi-official code of silence. We've kept it a secret well, but it's time to confess, to those that are still vaguely interested in what goes on at the side of the M621: the fortress is in ruins. Ironically right at the point the Chelsea Village of the North™ is taking fine shape.

If you're building facilities, you tend to need some folk to use them. That might be tricky here. The fanbase is mirroring the flab of the ageing nation and any discernible marketing strategy to attract new blood to keep the elders' dander up under the Bates regime seems to involve making the club nigh-on invisible: personal court appearances overshadowing club business, scant ticket offers and up until recently not even allowing high street sports stores to stock the shirt.

It comes as no surprise then that the colours of the Premier League hegemony float about Leeds these days as if the city has no team representing it. In essence, Bates has exploited the 'Leeds mentality' on this one — the idea that we don't need to reach out for fans, we are Leeds, no explanation needed for those who haven't heard the legend.

In a sense, the appointment of Neil Warnock can be seen as the last throw of a dying big beast. The gnarled antihero has been hand-picking cheap potential from even more desperate and budgetary-restricted outfits this summer, as the fans cling to the hope that he maintains his reputation of making warriors from cast-offs. The fear is, after having Tony Fernandes's wallet to play with of late, he may have forgotten how.

It's lucky then, that our Arab white knights have ridden in. Or have they? The idea that GFH Capital could be merely a cipher, with Bates still pulling the strings may sound like garbled conspiracy, but this sort of thinking has become the norm in the last eight years, and this writer is as sure as everyone else: not at all.

This piece was supposed to be entirely about the dark clouds hanging over Elland Road these days. But Leeds United, as contrary as ever, have gone and led us to believe again in possibilities of silver linings, albeit the shine increasingly scuffed by conjecture and social media. Message-board rumours in the early weeks of summer that Bates was on his way out slowly and painfully became real people talking to the BBC about a 'bright future' and suchlike, in the depths of December. The suggestion that the parent company, Gulf Finance House is considered at risk of insolvency by KPMG was initially considered nothing to worry about, so sure was everyone that our new-found public faces were just that — smiling brokers for serious investment geared toward enabling the fêted return to the glory, glory that timeworn song talks about.

Under long-term mists of despair lie fertile breeding grounds for delusion. And these latest assumptions, apparently, are false. GFH are going it alone, and right now we're struggling to see change: channelling the cup specialisms of 2003 Sheffield United (by assembling a good number of their personnel) hasn't masked continued intrigues, vague communications, a transfer request from our top scorer, and most pertinent of all, fairly dire league form.

So as we did all summer, we wait once more for something more tangible than occasional raised-games in knock-out competitions. Time will be offered to those in charge, but not much. The Bates Out banners are still hanging, quietly. The self-declared internet experts and insiders look less 'in the know' than ever. This famously forthright set of fans reduced to desperate, passive sitting around, idly speculating as if we really have a stake in things. We should have learnt better.

Paying the Price

Rangers' administration and relegation were about far more than a club that couldn't pay its debts

By Craig Anderson

In March 2012, not long after Rangers had gone into administration, the Kilmarnock chairman Michael Johnston was interviewed on BBC Radio Scotland and predicted that Scottish football would undergo an "Arab Spring". It was a crass and hyperbolic statement, but his prediction of a revolution in Scottish football proved accurate, the change coming from supporters rather than from the boardrooms.

The target of Johnston's comment was the voting system which allowed Rangers and Celtic to dominate the Scottish Premier League. Under this system, a 'Special Qualified Resolution' is needed to change a number of articles within the SPL rules, most notably those on commercial matters. A Special Qualified Resolution requires 11 votes out of 12[1] for a motion to be passed. In practice, that meant that the two Old Firm clubs could vote as a bloc to prevent any changes to the league's financial distribution model. And they both had good reason to — the current system sees 32% of the league's commercial revenue split between the clubs finishing in the top two positions, while the other 10 have to make do with 68%. The gap in prize money between 2nd and 3rd is larger than that between 3rd and 12th[2].

The other 10 SPL clubs had publicly expressed their unhappiness at this model on numerous occasions, but remained powerless to do anything about it. Rangers entering administration on Valentine's Day changed that, and the other clubs seized the opportunity to put the issue back on the agenda. The 10 chairmen held a meeting at which they discussed ways of using the situation to their advantage. The prospect of Rangers being liquidated and forming a 'newco' was already being discussed and there was a clear implication that some clubs were hoping to incentivise the Rangers administrators to vote in their favour by offering concessions to the newco should they apply to enter the league.

This was the first tacit admission by the chairmen that they might bend the

[1] More specifically, a Special Qualified Resolution requires at least 90% of clubs to vote in favour. 90% of 12 is 10.8.

[2] The 1st placed side gets 17%, 2nd gets 15%, 3rd gets 9.5%, then places 4-12 decrease from 8.5% to 4.5% in 0.5% increments

rules and procedures of the league for financial reasons. As Johnston put it, "The clubs are mindful of a sporting integrity aspect but the commercial benefits may outweigh that." The commercial aspect he touched on was the potential loss of revenue if Rangers were not in the SPL, particularly given the league's £13m per year TV deal with Sky and ESPN was rumoured to be based on a guarantee of four Old Firm matches every season, as were a number of key sponsorship deals. Without Rangers in the league, clubs would be relying on the goodwill of those TV companies and sponsors and, with a number of sides already in precarious financial positions, the desire to avoid a hefty shortfall in their income was understandable.

The financial arguments didn't wash with supporters though. Fans see football as a sport, not a business, and it's difficult to reconcile that viewpoint with the idea that special rules could be applied for certain teams. Fans of every other club in the country, apart from Celtic, knew that their club would not have been afforded the luxury of direct re-entry into the SPL if they went bust. Historical precedent dictated that when a club went out of business, a vacancy was created in the

bottom tier of the Scottish Football League (SFL)[3], and clubs would apply to fill that gap. That was exactly what had happened when Airdrieonians went bust in 2002[4] and again when the same fate befell Gretna in 2008[5].

In the pre-internet days, these fans would have been restricted to venting their frustrations with friends at the pub or via radio phone-ins and letters to newspapers. It would certainly have been unlikely that supporters of clubs at the opposite ends of the country would have been able to debate the issue with each other at length, so any resistance would have come from isolated pockets of supporters from each individual club. Any form of organised multi-club protest would have been unlikely. But now, fans across Scotland could instantly share their reactions with other like-minded supporters via Twitter and on messageboards as the story developed.

It has become clichéd to say that online social networking has left traditional media trailing in its wake, but never was that more true than in the Rangers saga. The Scottish football press has many fine journalists, but very few of them seemed interested in the story of Rangers' tax problems. It was left to an anonymous

[3] There are four national divisions in Scotland — the top tier broke away in 1998 to form the Scottish Premier League while the three lower divisions are administered by the SFL.

[4] Following the demise of Airdrieonians, a successor club, Airdrie United, applied for the vacancy created in the SFL, but they lost out to Gretna in the election. Undeterred, Airdrie United bought over Clydebank FC and took their place in the league.

[5] Gretna supporters also founded a successor club, Gretna 2008, but decided not to apply for a vacancy in the SFL and instead joined the East of Scotland League. The vacancy in the SFL went to Annan Athletic.

blogger to lay bare the extent of Rangers' problems. "Rangers Tax Case" started in March 2011, and over the next 18 months broke a number of stories well ahead of the mainstream media. For his efforts, the blogger won the Orwell Prize, the UK's most prestigious award for political writing[6].

In the past, it was difficult to take the media to task over sensationalised or factually inaccurate articles, but now supporters could disseminate and debunk those stories within minutes and post their rebuttals online. The same applied to statements from footballing administrators — when the SPL chief executive Neil Doncaster claimed that newcos were commonplace in UK football, citing Plymouth Argyle and Crystal Palace, fans took to Google and within minutes they had found clear distinctions between the scenarios faced by those clubs and that faced by Rangers. No longer could authority figures go unchallenged — the supporters were finding their voice and it would prove to be very difficult to shut them up.

On June 12, Her Majesty's Revenue and Customs announced that they would be rejecting the Company Voluntary Arrangement (CVA) proposed by prospective new Rangers owner Charles Green, thus making it inevitable that Rangers FC would be liquidated. The saga was more or less over for the old company, but it was only just starting for the Scottish football authorities. Green had already announced his contingency plan in the event that his CVA was rejected — he was going to buy the assets of the old club, including Ibrox Stadium, the Murray Park training complex and the registrations of the players[7] at a cut price and transfer them to his new company, the catchily named Sevco 5088[8]. He would then apply to transfer the old Rangers FC's share in the SPL and their membership of the SFA across to his new company, allowing them to carry on as though nothing had happened.

Unsurprisingly, this plan did not go down well with supporters of other clubs, who were angered by the possibility that Rangers could dodge a £50m+ debt to

---

[6] It did not, however, end particularly well for the Rangers Tax Case blogger, who had been predicting that Rangers would be unsuccessful in their appeal against their large tax bill. Following the announcement of the result of the tax appeal tribunal in November 2012, the blogger appeared to misinterpret the result as a "defeat" for the oldco Rangers, and then later that same day deleted almost all of the content from his blog.

[7] Legally, under the Transfer of Undertakings (Protection of Employment) regulations, any employee could reject the move to a new company, but Green attempted to circumvent this by retaining their footballing registrations. Nonetheless, a host of players rejected the move to the newco, most notably the Scotland internationals Allan McGregor, Steven Naismith and Steven Whittaker, and Uefa gave them temporary registrations to continue their careers elsewhere while the dispute is resolved.

[8] Rather confusingly, these assets were then sold on again to Sevco Scotland Limited, which was the company Green used to apply for a transfer of Rangers' SPL share and SFA membership.

the taxman[9] and yet retain their lofty position within the top tier of Scottish football. Their response was to instigate a "No to Newco" campaign, spreading the message via Twitter and messageboards. Lists of email addresses for Fifa, Uefa, the chief executives of the SFA and SPL and the chairmen of every SPL club were put together, and people were encouraged to email their thoughts to the relevant parties. Standard emails were written for those who didn't have the time or capacity to compose their own, but most produced individual and often passionate correspondence. The Dundee United chairman Stephen Thompson received "emails and letters in the hundreds" from his supporters and it was a similar story across the country as fans bombarded their clubs' inboxes.

On June 18, the SPL announced that a vote on whether to admit the Rangers newco to the league would be held on July 4. The choice of date was purely coincidental but the significance of the vote being held on US Independence Day wasn't lost on supporters. While their primary reason for opposing the newco entry was the integrity of the sport, a secondary aspect was the hope of a new era in Scottish football. A whole generation of Scottish football fans have never seen a club outside of the Old Firm winning the league and they saw this as an opportunity to break that cycle. The last non-Old Firm side to win the league was Alex Ferguson's Aberdeen way back in 1984-85, a success which marked the end of Scottish football's most competitive and prosperous era. By the end of that decade, Rangers had won the first of nine consecutive titles, resuming the Glasgow stranglehold over the trophy.

The fate of the newco Rangers lay in the hands of the SPL chairmen, with eight votes out of twelve needed to see them admitted to the league[10]. Supporters took the opportunity to crank up the pressure on their clubs to vote against their entry. Realising that they didn't want to be paying to watch a fixed league, they threatened to walk away from their clubs if the newco were parachuted into the SPL. Fans who had been buying season tickets for years, even decades, told their clubs they would not be renewing if they voted "Yes". Unlike their counterparts in England, SPL clubs still rely on gate revenue for a large proportion of their income, given the relatively modest nature of the TV deal, so these threats made the chairmen sit up and listen. They were now in a lose-lose situation and had to weigh up the potential loss of commercial revenue with no Rangers

[9] *At the time, it was not known whether Rangers would win their tax tribunal in what was known as the "Big Tax Case" — the result (which went in Rangers' favour) was only announced in November 2012, by which point the old company had begun liquidation proceedings. Even with that case removed from the equation, the club still owed £21.3m to HMRC.*

[10] *Initially, the decision was going to be made by the SPL Board, which has six members — four elected representatives from the clubs plus the chief-executive Neil Doncaster and non-executive director Sir Ralph Topping, with a simple majority needed, and Doncaster having the casting vote. The clubs unanimously voted to change the rule to allow them all to vote.*

against the potential loss of gate revenue. While it was far from guaranteed that every supporter would follow up on their threat, it would be a brave chairman who would bank on them returning.

On June 21, the voting intentions of a number of clubs became clearer. Motherwell announced that they would ballot the members of the "Well Society", the programme set up to help the club's transition into fan ownership. Given the overwhelming opinion of their support, this was almost certain to be a "No" vote. Later that day, Heart of Midlothian became the first club to confirm a "No" vote, with their outspoken chairman Vladimir Romanov — nicknamed "Mad Vlad" because of his idiosyncratic behaviour — releasing a typically ebullient statement on the club's website. They were soon joined in the "No" camp by Dundee United, who cited poor season ticket sales as one of the main factors. Within days, more SPL clubs jumped onto the bandwagon and it became clear that the Rangers newco would not be playing in the SPL in 2012-13.

This appeared to be a success for fan-power, but many remained suspicious about the timings of the "No" declarations, which almost appeared to be synchronised. As it turned out, they had every right to be suspicious. The SPL, SFA and SFL chief-executives had been busy drawing up a contingency plan to place the Rangers newco in the Scottish Football League's 1st Division, two tiers above where a new club would usually enter, in the hope that this would appease the supporters while minimising the potential financial impact on the top flight. The fact that this was even considered suggests that the authorities misjudged the strength of feeling among supporters, who were against any sort of special treatment being afforded to Rangers. This even applied to the Rangers support, the majority of whom preferred the idea of a fresh start at the bottom of Scottish football[11]. For many, this was born out of a desire actually to earn their place back at the top of the game, but it certainly would appear to be the case that the motivation for some was a thirst for 'revenge' against the SPL clubs who voted against them, with the hope that the potential loss of revenue might put these clubs in severe trouble.

Whatever their motivations, all supporters in Scotland now more or less agreed about the just fate for the Rangers newco. Nonetheless, the authorities continued to push the second-tier fudge, attempting to blackmail and bribe the SFL clubs in equal measure. Clubs were promised league reconstruction, extra promotion places to the top flight and a better spread of financial revenue if they voted in favour of this plan. An invitational breakaway SPL2 was mooted as a possible consequence of the plan being rejected and SFL clubs were threatened with the loss of the £2m a year settlement which they currently receive from the SPL as compensation for the original breakaway. The threats didn't go down well with some SFL clubs — the Raith Rovers chairman Turnbull Hutton gained notoriety for his blunt honesty, claiming "We are being bullied,

---

[11] *In a poll of Rangers season ticket holders, almost 80% wanted the newco to enter the bottom tier.*

railroaded and lied to... What kind of game are we running here? It is corrupt".

The SPL newco vote, which was by now a formality, was held as planned and 10 clubs voted against their application to the league. The Rangers oldco were the only club to vote in favour[12], while Kilmarnock inexplicably abstained[13]. The SFL announced that they would hold a vote on the plans to admit the newco on Friday July 13. The SFL would vote on two proposals — the first would be to admit the newco directly into the First Division with 22 of the 30 clubs needing to vote in favour of the plan, while the second would be to admit the newco into the Third Division, which needed a simple majority. Now it was the turn of the SFL fans to wield their power. The SFL clubs earned very little in the way of commercial revenue — just a low-profile TV deal with BBC Alba, which broadcasts in Gaelic, and a sponsorship deal with Irn Bru. As a result, they rely on gate income even more than the SPL clubs and would be foolish to alienate their loyal supporters.

Many newspapers appeared out of touch with the average Scottish supporter and were still pushing the SFL1 compromise. A nadir was reached with an article in the *Daily Record* by Craig Burley, who declared that the "future of Scottish

football (was) placed in the hands of a few nonentities from the lower divisions." The message was clear — only the big teams matter, and the other diddy clubs should do what they're told. The worrying thing was that these views seemed to be shared by some in positions of authority within the Scottish game. The SFA chief executive Stewart Regan was becoming increasingly desperate and was quoted as saying that there could be "social unrest" if Rangers weren't parachuted into the second tier, predicting "financial Armageddon" for Scottish football. His comments were no doubt intended to scare supporters and clubs into backing his plans, but instead they resulted in him being lampooned relentlessly by fans. Regan lost all credibility among supporters, culminating in him having to close his Twitter account after receiving abuse.

Come July 13, all eyes were on the SFL vote at Hampden. Supporters were glued to Twitter, news websites and forums as they awaited an announcement of the vote. The outcome seemed inevitable, with the number of clubs claiming they would reject the SFL1 move reaching double figures but until it was official nobody was getting too carried away. Around 2pm, it was confirmed that the SFL1 vote had been rejected, with 25 of the 30 clubs voting against it. The good

---

[12] *Bizarrely, the old Rangers FC still had a vote, because the liquidation process had not yet started and they remained members of the SPL. Part of Charles Green's agreement with the administrators of the oldco was that they would vote "Yes" to the share transfer*

[13] *The Kilmarnock chairman consulted supporters prior to the vote, and justified his abstention by claiming that only 36% of supporters had voted "No". It was widely suspected that this was a manipulation of the figures — it's alleged that the figure quoted was a percentage of the 2500 surveys sent out rather than a percentage of the responses he actually received.*

news for Charles Green and his newco was that 29 of the 30 clubs had voted to place them in SFL3, allowing them to take part in league football in the 2012-13 season. The spectre of SPL2 briefly reared its head but before long it was announced that the newco would indeed begin the season in the fourth tier. The supporters of all clubs, including Rangers, had prevailed and the integrity of Scottish football was preserved.

On 11 August 2012, Charles Green's Rangers kicked off their SFL3 campaign with an away fixture in Peterhead. Despite starting the game with eight international players, they needed a last minute equaliser from Andrew Little to draw 2-2. Their supporters were simply happy to have a team to follow, though the debate continues, among fans at least, about whether it is the same club. The SPL retained most of the value of their TV deal — the £13m a year from Sky and ESPN remained in place, but they now have to give £1m of it to the SFL for the rights to show Rangers games. The predictions of financial Armageddon seem unfounded at the moment — the only noticeable impact has been that most SPL clubs are working with slightly smaller squads than the previous season.

The dust hasn't quite settled yet though. The SPL's voting system has not yet been changed, Neil Doncaster and Stewart Regan remain in their jobs at the SPL and SFA, and at the time of writing the talk of league reconstruction still lingers with the '12-12-18' plan preferred by SPL clubs. Most supporters welcome the idea of a change to the league system but the timing evokes suspicions that it is for the benefit of one team rather than forty-two. Rangers still face possible sanctions, including the possibility of titles being stripped, over claims that their players were improperly registered. The saga led to a breakdown in trust between supporters and authorities, and those wounds may take a long time to heal.

It is no exaggeration to say that the events of last summer were among the most important in the history of Scottish football. Had the authorities allowed a club to walk away from its debts and carry on where they had left off, they may have irreparably damaged the image of the game in Scotland. Instead the supporters wielded their power and perhaps restored some integrity to a sport which has often lacked it. In the words of the former SFA president John McBeth, "if you look after the game money will follow, if you look after money, you will kill the game." **B**

87

"He had a kind of inspired, defiant
infantilism about him. Much better
than the other"

Franco Baresi

How the great libero staged a remarkable recovery from a knee injury to play in the 1994 World Cup final

By Sheridan Bird

The mood was funereal. Italy had beaten Norway 1-0 to kick-start their 1994 World Cup campaign but they weren't celebrating: their captain, Franco Baresi, had wrecked the meniscus in his right knee. Normal recovery time from such an injury: three to six months.

The three-time world champions braced themselves for a tournament without the peerless Milan defender but the gloom underestimated the resources of the hardy 34-year-old skipper. If there were only 24 days until the World Cup final, that's all the talisman with the lived-in face would need... should his team get there.

Italy had lost their first Group E match 1-0 to Ireland. An essential win from their second group match in New York with Norway on June 23 arrived at great cost. The erratic goalkeeper Gianluca Pagliuca was sent off after 21 minutes. Arrigo Sacchi, so fidgety that he occasionally resembled Basil Fawlty's shorter, Latin cousin, sacrificed the half-fit *fantasista* Roberto Baggio to bring on the reserve keeper Luca Marchegiani. The Divine Ponytail and Italian fans at Giants Stadium and around the globe were livid but hindsight shows it was a prudent switch.

It got worse. Early in the second half, the Norway midfielder Øyvind Leonhardsen

darted towards a clever through-ball. Sensing danger, Baresi sprinted across and jabbed out a leg to clear the ball, as he'd done a thousand times before for his country. On this occasion he landed awkwardly and hobbled off the field. As physios assessed Baresi, his team were down to nine men. The verdict came soon enough and he was substituted. Thankfully for Italy, the 'other' Baggio, the hard-working, lean and deceptively skilful midfielder Dino, outmuscled Henning Berg to head the only goal with 21 minutes left.

The Parma centre-back Luigi Apolloni replaced his captain against Norway, winning his second cap. Excellent in the air, Apolloni didn't have a tenth of Baresi's ability to anticipate and was not particularly mobile. Sacchi had the option of moving the attacking left-back Paolo Maldini into the centre with the inexhaustible and versatile reserve full-back Antonio Benarrivo, a Sacchi-favourite, slotting in on the left. But no re-jig could compensate for the loss of the stricken skipper.

But after the exacting victory grave news arrived from the medical department. Baresi, the best *libero* of his generation, had suffered a longitudinal fracture to his medial meniscus, the crescent-shaped strip of cartilage spanning the joint.

Some feared his career was over. But Italian World Cup campaigns are often fuelled by adversity. At a future World Cup Francesco Totti would declare, "We only perform when the water is up to our necks." In the USA, the tide was touching their noses.

It had taken great effort even to get Baresi to the US. Citing stress, he had quit international football in June 1992 to preserve his body for Milan. Failure to qualify for Euro 92 felt like the end of a cycle so the Italian federation (FIGC) had accepted their captain's decision and begun to prepare for the future, which they saw as Marco Lanna, a 24-year-old Sampdoria centre-back. He had made a catastrophic debut against Switzerland in a World Cup qualifier in Cagliari in October 1992. The 1990 World Cup semi-finalists only salvaged a 2-2 draw with two goals in the final seven minutes and a Lanna error almost let Stéphane Chapuisat in to score a third.

The new *libero* concerned everyone and convinced no one. *La Repubblica*'s headline read "Time to Start Again from Scratch at the Back". The piece beneath went on, "A defence this disastrous doesn't seem real. It laughed in the face of Italian traditions." It wasn't all Lanna's fault. The other centre-back, Alessandro Costacurta, despite his achievements in the European Cup, was less than confident at international level. Making only his eighth international appearance, the blue-eyed pin-up was comically unrecognisable from the totem of Sacchi and Fabio Capello's all-conquering Milan sides. The goalkeeper Luca Marchegiani, winning his third cap,

was calamitous. But the newest new boy was made scapegoat.

Less than a year into the job as national manager, Sacchi tried to coax his trusted lieutenant Baresi out of retirement. No chance. Teammates joined the appeal. No joy. Eventually head of the FIGC, Antonio Matarrese, got involved. Details are guarded but Italian state radio and the television station RAI claimed the rumpled leader was lured back by a very generous financial package. On 18 November 1992 Capitano Baresi was back with the boys in blue (albeit in the white away shirt) against Scotland at Ibrox. The 0-0 draw from their second qualifier for the 1994 World Cup 1994 was an instant improvement on Cagliari.

Perhaps the only Italian wary of the comeback was Gianluca Vialli, whose tenure as post-Baresi national captain lasted just two matches. The relationship between Sacchi and the forward, who wielded considerable dressing-room power, was rapidly deteriorating. The coach no longer wanted Vialli and within a month the *Juventino*, hitherto undroppable as skipper, played his last Italy game, aged only 28.

Baresi, with his permanent weary, narrow-eyed expression was a tough man. And not just on a football pitch. In 1977, when Franchino was 17, he and his two brothers and two sisters became orphans. Their father died in a car accident, just four years after they'd lost their mother. Franco's big sister Lucia became the family's surrogate mother at only 23. The strain created strong, resourceful people.

Franco had started his football journey in 1974. Failing to impress Inter at a trial, the 14 year old needed three attempts to convince Milan to sign him. The *Nerazzurri* felt he was too slight for the rigours of regular football. The *Rossoneri*, in one of their greatest victories over their rivals, welcomed the elegant prospect and gave him a league debut in April 1978. The quiet, slim boy gained a second family at the club. "I remember leaving my friends and village," he said. "The first few years living at Milanello was tough. I was training and studying at the same time. I lived in the Milanello college until I was 18. But I felt fortunate because my dreams were coming true."

His tender age and slender frame earned him the nickname '*Piscinin*', Milanese slang meaning something close to 'Little'un' or 'Young'un'. There were further setbacks. Baresi missed four months of the 1981-82 season with a blood disease. Milan were relegated that year, their second trip to Serie B in three seasons, finishing third from bottom. Baresi turned down big money offers to join other clubs and was made captain aged 22.

Piscinin's first international steps were no less problematic. The impeccable Juventus *libero* Gaetano Scirea blocked initial progress. Baresi was in the 1982 World Cup squad but didn't play. When Enzo Bearzot, Italy's genial, stubborn coach known for his pipe and his boxer's nose, did field the young Milan skipper it was reluctantly. Baresi was forced to play as *mediano* on his fourth Azzurri appearance, against Cyprus three days before Christmas 1983. He didn't even make Bearzot's 1986 World Cup squad. His big brother Giuseppe, a steady but never world-class defensive midfielder, did.

But the determined young man from Travagliato in the province of Brescia wouldn't be discouraged. The wiry, technical sweeper, considered by many at a shade over 5'9" to be too small for central defence, became the kingpin of Arrigo Sacchi's 1988 *Scudetto* winners and European champions of 1989 and 1990. By Euro 88 he was at the heart of Italy's famous defence. In November 1990, aged 30, he was made captain. Of all the player's qualities, his patience and mental strength are often overlooked.

Back at Italy's plush World Cup HQ in Somerset Hills, Martinsville, New Jersey, Baresi couldn't sleep the night after the Norway match. In the morning he told medics he couldn't straighten his leg. "The pain is absurd," he said. Baresi was rushed from New Jersey to New York, where he was examined at Lennox Hill. At the famous Manhattan hospital (where Ed Sullivan died in 1974 and Lady Gaga was born in 1986) scans revealed no ligament damage. That meant the injury could be rectified with a straightforward arthroscopic intervention. But this wasn't a pet dog or a 'normal' person with a gammy leg. It was the captain of the Champions League holders. Permission was required.

FIGC officials called the Milan director Adriano Galliani in Italy and received the all-clear. Next they tracked down the club doctor Rodolfo 'Rudy' Tavana in St Moritz, Switzerland. Tavana gave his blessing and broke off his holiday to join Baresi. Reports of the exact time conflict, but the operation took place between five and seven pm on Friday, June 24. Baresi went under full anaesthetic and the procedure, carried out by Dr Elliott B Hersham, knee specialist and team doctor of the New York Jets, assisted by the Italian team medic Andrea Ferretti, lasted approximately 20 minutes.

"We acted quickly because the player couldn't even bend the joint," Ferretti said. "It was a partial arthroscopic meniscectomy. It was simple because we didn't need to concern ourselves with the ligaments." The next day Baresi returned to Somerset Hills. His wife Maura, young son Edoardo and father-in-law Valerio flew in to keep his spirits up. Rossoneri doctor Tavana was on the same flight. "I want to stay with the squad, even injured. I want to contribute," Baresi told the press.

The patient was walking freely two days after his operation. The same couldn't be said of his teammates. All four teams in their group finished level on points, the only time that has happened in World Cup history: Sacchi's men progressed in third place, ahead of Norway on goals scored.

In the second round, against Nigeria, Gianfranco Zola was sent off with 15 minutes remaining and only a laser accurate 88th-minute equaliser and extra-time penalty from Roberto Baggio saw Italy through. As Baresi began jogging, his companions found their feet in the last eight against Spain, Dino and Roberto Baggio scoring memorable goals. A few days later Roberto eliminated Bulgaria with two moments of genius in the semi-final before acute hamstring pain forced him off.

Italy had lost their first game, they'd suffered two red cards and had the defender Mauro Tassotti retroactively banned for eight games after an elbow on Spain's Luis Enrique. Baggio was fragile. And yet Italy were in the final. Would Baresi captain Europe's representatives at the Pasadena Rose Bowl? He'd already had the same operation on his left knee in 1985 after injuring himself in the Coppa Italia final. That time he made a full recovery within two and a half months. But then he was a much younger man.

"I'll do anything to play. I can't miss a chance like this," Baresi told the journalist Gianni Visnadi. The unflappable *libero* made himself available to Sacchi, just three weeks after the operation. To put that into context, the 27-year-old English gymnast Beth Tweddle took 12 weeks to recover from the same injury and win a bronze medal at the 2012 London Olympics. In April 1989 Baresi's Milan teammate Ruud Gullit, 26, tore his meniscus in the second half of their European Cup semi-final second leg against Real Madrid. One month and three days after surgery the explosive Dutchman returned to score two in the final versus Steaua Bucharest. While understandable, his swift reappearance was foolhardy. Gullit's right knee hadn't healed. The Black Tulip managed only three games the next season. Only the Swiss skier Pirmin Zubriggen, who resumed competition without complications 19 days after a meniscectomy, recovered faster than Baresi. Zubriggen was 21.

Sacchi had much to ponder. Benarrivo's dynamic left-back performances convinced the former Milan boss he could shift Maldini to the middle. Costacurta's caution for an injudicious foul from behind on Hristo Stoichkov in the semi-final was his second yellow card of the tournament, ruling him out of the final. The dependable Apolloni was the 'fit' option alongside Maldini. But the prospect of Apolloni against Romário and Bebeto stirred memories of Lanna's Swiss calamity — and Sacchi knew Baresi and Maldini had played together in many high-profile matches.

The healed hero led his men out on July 17 against Brazil with the white captain's armband hugging his left bicep. Italy played a 4-4-1-1 with Roberto Baggio behind the bulky striker Daniele Massaro. Baresi and Maldini were the central pair at the back, with Benarrivo and the tireless, conservative Roberto Mussi, another Sacchi foot soldier from Parma and Milan, patrolling the flanks. The writer Fiorenzo Baini dismissed their opponents as "the most horrid Brazil ever. A truly Sacchi-esque, compact team in which everybody maintained the correct distances at all costs, to allow Romário and Bebeto to run at opponents."

Baresi's task was thwarting the slippery, stubby streetcat Romário under California's fierce midday sun. There were no signs of rustiness. The skipper had one of his best matches. He intercepted, tackled, blocked and neutralised threats. A defensive reshuffle when the flame-haired right-back Mussi went off injured after 35 minutes didn't disturb Baresi. He was equal to anything Brazil offered.

The South Americans poured forward and the *Milanista* kept them at bay with his anticipation and incredible short-sprint athleticism. Baini noted, "Baresi seemed the only one not frozen by fear. He even tried a few of his trademark breaks into their half, driving into the Brazilian defence, to shake things up."

After a positive start, the *Azzurri* dangermen tired rapidly. Nicola Berti, galloping *mezz'ala* and one of Italian football's greatest lotharios, fizzled out despite a spritely opening on the left. Roberto Baggio was compromised by his damaged right hamstring, wrapped in an ugly black compression bandage below his white shorts. Massaro was starved of service after latching onto a magnificent Baresi long ball and prodding an 18th minute chance straight at Claudio Taffarel. Roberto Donadoni, the ultimate all-terrain, no-frills yet indispensable winger, was the solitary cogent attacker. Italy were pinned back but Baresi's heroics continued.

Sacchi replaced the dashing Dino Baggio, 22, with the square-jawed, rugged 31 year-old Alberigo Evani on 95 minutes. The Sampdoria man had evolved from the *tornante* of his prime with Milan into a reliable defensive *mediano*. The substitution indicated Sacchi was playing for penalties. The Brazil coach Carlos Alberto Parreira threw on the broad-shouldered, bustling striker Viola to torment the shattered Italians in the second period of extra-time. The Corinthians fireball couldn't score but his direct running and zip bamboozled everyone — except Baresi.

Franchino's wispy, mousy hair looked more bedraggled than ever, his royal blue socks slumped around his calves. But Baresi was the ageing king among upstart princes. Los Angeles was witnessing a masterclass as the wizened legend organised his defence and prompted attacks as *regista*. Cramp briefly forced the No 6 off at the death. It reminded spectators that the titan with the familiar untucked shirt was flesh and blood.

After a goalless 120 minutes, the 1994 World Cup final was settled on penalties. The record books show Baresi missed his side's first penalty. They also note Baggio's failure. Both men sent their kicks high over the bar. Brazil won the shootout 3-2 and lifted their fourth world title. There are photos of the weeping comeback captain and drained Divine Ponytail consoling each other while Brazilian players dance in the background. No one did more on the pitch to drag Italy to the final than Baggio. No one did more off the pitch to be there than Baresi.

Brian Glanville

The doyen of English football writing discusses the forefathers of modern sports journalism

By Philippe Auclair

Writing what is supposed to be an introduction to a conversation with Brian Glanville about past masters of football writing, the temptation was to write a piece about Brian Glanville himself, who deserves that epithet more than most; indeed, perhaps more than anyone else. 'He invented the World Cup,' the *Guardian*'s Kevin McCarra once said, not without reason, as any reader of *The Story of the World Cup* would agree. No writer did more than the fearless, talon-sharp and unfailingly fair reporter of *The Sunday Times*, *The Observer* and countless publications besides to open the eyes and minds of the British public to international football at a time when it was barely reported on, and when images of matches involving 'them' and not 'us' were limited to newsreels which seemed to cut to reaction shots every other frame.

In Patrick Barclay's words, "There are two sorts of football writers: those who've been influenced by Brian Glanville, and those who should have been." Hyperbole? No. In the course of a prodigious career which has entered its seventh decade — a 19-year-old Glanville, fresh from Charterhouse, ghosted Cliff Bastin's autobiography in 1950 — he has covered every major tournament in which England could

have played from the 1962 World Cup onwards, attended thousands of games (which he still does, be it at the Den or the Emirates), written film scripts (including that masterpiece, *Goal!*, the official film of 1966 World Cup), a play, collections of short stories, 19 novels which ought to be far better-known (of which the most recent, *Dictators*, may be the finest), disproving his own assertion that "had I not been born, it wouldn't have made the slightest difference." Such is Brian's outlook on life and football. He once told me, "the best advice I ever got on football writing was to keep repeating to myself, 'it doesn't matter… it doesn't matter,'"; except that it does, a great deal, to anyone who's read his *Football Memories* or for whom the final whistle hadn't been blown on English pitches until you knew what Glanville made of it all on a Sunday morning.

There'd be no *Blizzard* if there'd been no Glanville, such is the debt all football writers owe him, whether they know him or not. Long before it was a hip (and conventional) thing to up sticks and taste a year or two of life in Barcelona or Berlin, the son of a Jewish Dublin dentist, then a very young man, moved to Florence and started writing in his fluent, highly idiosyncratic Italian for the *Corriere dello Sport*, *La Stampa* and others, sharpening his understanding of British football — and what was wrong with it — on the whetstone of *calcio*. He was later to be found in New York, where he counted Lenny Bruce as a friend, and where Henry Kissinger provided him with a gem or two for his inexhaustible fount of anecdotes. Ha, the stories! Brian, whose memory is frighteningly accurate, has more than most, including hundreds of unprintable Jewish ones, and tells them with the gusto of a born raconteur. As a result, conversations can be a bit one-sided; not that the listener will mind. This is one of them.

● *Could you assign a date of birth to football writing as we know it?*

The 1890s. The real father, grandfather and progenitor of English football writing was JA Catton, who went by the byline of Tityrus, the shepherd in Virgil's *Bucolics*. They all used to do that sort of thing then. His career, largely on the old Manchester *Athletic News*[1] which used to come out twice a week, and was the bible for a very long time, right into the 1920s, spanned the last decade of the 19th century and went right the way through... I think the very early 1930s. He was a tiny little man in a bowler hat; perhaps a little bit rigid and reactionary towards players' rights, etc, etc, but he was a very, very good journalist who got everything right. He saw, very, very early, the significance of the rise of

foreign football. He said England would be overtaken, because others would use more modern methods. I quoted him verbatim in my *Soccer Nemesis*... "Write me off as senile and silly," he said, "but the truth will prevail, and this is the truth." This was probably in 1920 or so. Catton stood alone. He was absolutely right about that, you know. I'm not aware that he travelled abroad. Nobody travelled abroad for football games anyway. He had a great deal of integrity. He didn't write 'stories'. It wasn't expected of him. He'd describe games and express opinions, which were very sensible opinions. He was tremendously respected in the game as well. The point is worth emphasising: if you wrote for a 'quality paper' then, you weren't read in the football world at large.

● *So the best football writing was found in the popular press?*

Once in a while, you'd find something wonderful in the *Times*, like their report on the 1934 Battle of Highbury [England's hard-fought and controversial 3-2 win over the world champions Italy]. Speaking of the Italians, it read, "players who'd previously run wild began to run into position." Oh — that reminds me of what Geoffrey Simpson, the *Daily Mail* columnist, wrote about that game. "Stanley Matthews — nineteen then — displayed the same force of slowness and hesitation that he did in the recent inter-league match. Perhaps he doesn't have the big match temperament."

[1] *The* Athletic News *merged with the* Sporting Chronicle *in 1931, but its* Football Annual, *which had first been published in 1887, survived into the 1940s.*

Matthews... Yes, the finest writers were to be found in the popular press. That's why I wrote *Looking for an Idiom*, as an idiom that would transcend social classes had been found by American — and French — writers, but not here. Catton was followed as editor of the *Athletic News Football Annual* by Ivan Sharpe... heard of him?

⊕ *No.*

He was a fascinating character. He'd been an excellent footballer himself[2] and wrote a superb book, which I recommend, called *Forty Years in Football*. Not a literary masterpiece — but fascinating. He was a wonderful player; he was a left-winger and played in the same Derby attack as Steve Bloomer — probably the most prolific goalscorer there's ever been in English football. And he was the outside left in the Great Britain team that won the Olympic tournament in Stockholm in 1912. There's a marvellous story... I think he was at Watford at the time... he wrote to Jimmy Catton, asking him, "Could you give me a job?" Years and years later, he went to see him and got the job: his letter, unopened, was still on the desk. Sharpe had a wonderful feeling for the romance and the characters of football. Herbert Chapman, a great friend of his, came to him and said, "How do you go to Arsenal? Can you get me to Arsenal?" It's a fascinating book. Do read it if you can get a copy. Sharpe was not a great writer, no, but a superb journalist, a genuine journalist, not one of these freaks that we have now, who have all their rubbish ghosted for them.

There was a great deal of charm in football writing at that time, the 1930s. Some time in the 1950s, when I was researching *Soccer Nemesis*, I went into the British Library to get permission to go to Colindale — the newspaper library. There was a dear old boy behind the desk. "I tell you what's interesting," he said, "*The Football Chat*!" And I found that wonderful weekly, really charming stuff. "The French didn't play football, they frivolled." Roland Allen was terribly good too.

⊕ *Allen...?*

He wrote for the *Evening Standard*, and very well, about things like the Austrian Wunderteam, more or less saying that when they could turn their extraordinary technical talent into something concrete, then they'd be really something. He came up with some nice lines. When the Barcelona then Real Madrid keeper Ricardo Zamora came over and had a shocking game with Spain against England in December 1931, letting in seven goals at Highbury, he wrote, "if Zamora earns £50 a week" — which was a fortune at the time — "Hibbs, the England keeper, deserves a benefit once a fortnight." Allen also briefly wrote a weekly match report in the *Sunday Times* in the 1950s. And there was LV Manning. Ever heard of him?

⊕ *I'm afraid not.*

He was the father of the sports columnist Jim Manning. LV Manning was not quite a god-like figure, but

---

[2] *Sharpe, a genuine amateur, won the Football League Second Division title in 1911-12 with Derby County.*

certainly a... Jove-like figure. When I was at Newlands prep school, he was the great seer of football, an arbiter of the game, a tremendously authoritative figure. I remember, once, when there'd been this so-called "fog farce", when Arsenal played Dynamo Moscow at White Hart Lane in 1945, the butler of our school, Harry Haines — we called him the butler because he and his wife ran the kitchen, saying things like this when he served us fish: "this one wasn't caught; it gave itself up" — told us, "Well, we'll have to see what LVM says about this." He had tremendous prestige, even if, as Cliff Bastin once told me, he was much too hard on players making their debut for England. An example — I was a tremendous fan of Bernard Joy, a great big blond schoolmaster, the amateur centre-half who took over from Herbie Roberts for Arsenal, one of the last amateurs to get a full England cap, in 1936, when they lost 3-2 to Belgium. I was wondering when he'd get another opportunity to play for England. Then he got a war-time game against Scotland. "Joy deserves this belated honour," says LVM in the *Daily Sketch*. But Joy had a very difficult first half against the Scottish forwards. England recovered and scored six. And LV Manning, two days later, wrote, "Joy has had his match." I thought that was a bit much. This said, LVM was awfully good about Dynamo Moscow during their 1945 tour. In the fog, "a thousand men lighted a thousand cigarettes and it looked like a thousand bonfires" — a bit contrived, but that was really rather good. Then, despite a headline reading "Time saves Dynamo from a knock-out" when they drew 2-2 with Rangers, he said that this was another step down in

the decline of Scottish football, which had become very direct and physically challenging, and he could write — this is where Scottish football is going to go, betraying its roots, you know? He died crossing the road on a Saturday morning, in the late 1940s, and JL Manning — his son — succeeded him, not a bad bloke, but very self-important. I don't put that one in my pantheon. A very prominent journalist, but a rather conceited sort of man. His father was far more influential, even if he contradicted himself, within days at times.

🌍 *What did Manning's readers expect from him or from other prominent football writers at the time?*

It was fairly limited. There were no interviews. Bugger all. No press conferences. You never had quotes, you never had to get them, which was great. A blessing. People wrote straight reports, none of that zeroing in on a tiny facet of the game that the manager might have said something about. It was exceedingly rare to have a manager write columns as Chapman did for the *Daily Express*: journalists had the field for themselves. You didn't have to dig up stuff. But we now come to a man worth writing about, Henry Rose, the man who wore a black homburg, a Cardiff Jew, immaculately dressed, perfect moustache, splendid overcoats and suits, who was a complete stuntsman. He was supposed to go to London and work for the *Express*, and he failed there. So they sent him up to Manchester, where he really broke through, because everything he did was a stunt. Which one is he going to pull next? Which is why he had such an immense following. He had practically every station-master and ticket-collector in the area paid. "Station-master for Wilmslow here, Mr Rose! George Radnor of Manchester United has just passed through the turnstile — I think he's on the way to Bury!" When he turned up for a match, he'd go to the hotel and slip a few quid to the porter or the concierge. Then you'd hear, "Telephone call for Mr Rose! Call for Mr Henry Rose of the *Daily Express*!" He'd then glide across the foyer to take the call — which he'd paid them to do. Amazingly self-important man, but fascinating. Whenever he went to Liverpool and turned up in the press-box, the whole of the Kop booed and jeered him. But when he died — in the Munich air crash — had they been allowed to, the Kop would've given him a gangster's funeral. There's nobody like that today. He had a kind of inspired, defiant infantilism about him. Much better than the other *Express* football writer, Desmond Hackett, who wrote unadulterated shit.

Another very fine journalist who died in Munich, one of the best, was HD Davies, who wrote as 'An Old International'[3] for the *Manchester Guardian*. He was funny; there was a strong Mancunian aspect to his writing. "So-and-so tried to dribble. Why didn't he learn? He's got nothing else to do!" He was a very popular broadcaster as well, on *Sports Report*. Every Sunday morning, he'd repair to his study, shut the door, God help anybody who would interrupt him, and he would spend three *hours* on his football

report, which seems monumentally disproportionate to me.

● *What was expected of a football journalist then, between the 1930s and late 1950s? What people would call 'fine' writing?*

No. Take people like Frank Butler, a very successful writer through the war and beyond, who had the most appalling effect on my style. "Ian MacPherson, call him Mac the magnificent!" or "so often surrounded by red Charlton shirts that it looked as if he was addressing a communist meeting"...These are the terrible habits that I had to grow out of. Football writing declined a great deal in the 1950s and 1960s. It's much better now. But now and then, Butler, a very powerful figure in those days, would come up with something really good. He once wrote a piece about the "pimply young men who prepared for the war" seeing their sporting heroes jumping out of planes, landing onto beaches, and then suddenly, to their surprise, it was these pimply young men who were leaping onto beaches while their heroes were still at home, playing football, as the policy was, as you know, to keep them there. A lot of the writing in the popular press was terrible, the most appalling jargony stuff. Catton and LV Manning were exceptions. What was mostly expected was pontificating, or cheap and cheerful, racy and entertaining stuff. Or provocative stunting. On the other hand, a footballer could do what he liked off the pitch, and it wouldn't come out. There wasn't

---

[3] *Davies, once of Port Vale, was capped three times for the England amateur national football team in 1914.*

really any good investigative journalism. As late as 1974, when Keith Botsford and myself investigated the Solti case[4], I wanted everybody [in the English press] to join in.

I said, 'We've done all this, if you come to us, we'll give you everything we've got. We're not trying to make a monopoly for us.'

'No no no, you've done it all, there's nothing we can add.' That shows you. Things have changed since then.

⏺ *Could football journalism be thought of as a true vocation then?*

People drifted into it; as someone like Geoffrey Green of the *Times* did. I'll say this about him: he had this tremendous prestige that he never used. He never led the way morally. He could have been a beacon for the sport but didn't do it. He liked to be liked. Green, an excellent amateur player as well, was very much looked up to by my generation and I'd say that, at his best, he was the best. A great anti-semite, by the way. He was tremendously admired. Geoffrey, who used to ad lib most of his reports, came up with one of the best phrases ever produced by a football journalist, after the 6-3 defeat of England by Hungary in November 1953. "Right where Puskas pulled the ball back with the sole of his foot, Wright passed him by like a fire engine going to the wrong fire." But in his dotage, he started mixing his metaphors in a rather extraordinary way. "They danced like dervishes who've reached harbour." is an example. "There's no will-o-the-wisp, so to speak, to take the game by the scruff of the neck" is another. "The ball's been brought into their court by the stormy petrel." Strange character. There, have a biscuit. Ⓑ

---

[4] *To quote a piece Glanville himself wrote for the Indian magazine* Sportstar *in 2012, "Juventus, through the suspicious Hungarian expatriate and fixer, Dezso Solti, had tried in vain to bribe the honest Portuguese referee, Francisco Marques Lobo, to manipulate the return leg of the European Cup semi-final, when Juventus visited Derby County. We revealed a shameful cover-up by Uefa who, after a fiasco of an inquiry in Zurich, not only exonerated Juve, but thanked them for their cooperation."*

Ireland's Pioneers

This year marks the centenary of Ireland's first victory over England

By David Owen

Saturday, 15 February 1913. Windsor Park, Belfast. The 57th minute. The Ireland debutant Billy Gillespie, already with one goal to his name, sprays a pass to Frank Thompson, his blue-shirted teammate, wide on the left, and heads for the danger zone. Thompson, an FA Cup winner with Bradford City less than two years earlier, draws Bob Crompton, the vastly experienced England back, and centres between the goal area and the penalty line. (Penalty spots didn't come in until 1920.) There follows a "short, sharp struggle between a host of men". This ends when Gillespie hits a firm, low shot into the net through several pairs of legs with goalkeeper Reginald 'Tim' Williamson unsighted.

Thus was scored, 100 years ago, the goal which was at that point the most significant in the history of Irish association football. The *Athletic News and Cyclists' Journal* went as far as to label it "the goal of the century for Ireland". It brought Ireland their first victory over England. At the 32nd attempt. After a sequence that had started with a 13-0 drubbing in Belfast in 1882.

What first drew me to this momentous day in Irish sporting history was actually the team's exploit the following year. In 1914, Gillespie, Thompson and co. managed to build on the promise of

that gutsy initial 2-1 win over England to capture outright the Home International Championship, contested annually in those days by teams representing the four constituent countries of the British Isles, for the very first time. When I first noticed this years ago, poring over *Rothmans*, it made me wonder what had happened to that ground-breaking group of players. I imagined — overly influenced perhaps by a viewing of *Observe the Sons of Ulster Marching Towards the Somme*, Frank McGuinness's haunting World War I play — that the team might have been ripped apart in the hell-holes of Flanders. I was also curious about the side's make-up. Were they mainly Protestant boys from industrial Belfast? Or a more diverse cross-section of the island's 32 counties?

On the first count, I am glad to report that it was the march of time, rather than the slaughterhouse of trench warfare that dulled the team's edge. As far as I have been able to ascertain, not a single one of the 16 men who turned out for Ireland in their championship season lost his life on the killing fields of the war to end all wars. One of them, the forward Johnny Houston, joined the Royal Irish Rifles and was awarded the Military Medal for gallantry. But he managed to appear for Linfield in the replayed Irish Cup final of 1915-16 and by 1919 he was turning out for Partick Thistle. Another,

Bradford City's Harry Hampton, worked for the Labour Corps in Yorkshire. The simple fact is that by 1919, when normal footballing competition began to resume in England, around half of Ireland's champions were over 30. It took 42 years for another Irish team, by then Northern Ireland, to secure as much as a share of a further home international title — and that was a four-way tie.

The men of 1913-14 were also a reasonably diverse bunch, featuring several Dubliners and individuals from Counties Wexford and Laois. In Louis Bookman (*né* Buckhalter), a winger who was yet another of Ireland's Bradford City contingent, the team also included a Lithuanian-born Jew. Though appearing in only one match in the championship-winning season, Bookman — who was a useful cricketer and is featured in Anthony Clavane's recent book, *Does Your Rabbi Know You're Here?*[1] — returned to the Irish side at 30 in 1921, winning a further three caps.

But I'm getting ahead of myself. England enjoyed 70% of possession and won at least 20 corners in that mould-breaking encounter in 1913. However, Ireland showed evidence of qualities that would underpin their triumph the following year. One of these was resilience. England dominated the early stages. This would once have signalled a one-sided game, since as the *Athletic News*'s reporter Tityrus [the pen-name of the doyen of football journalists, James Catton, whom Brain Glanville discusses in his interview with Philippe Auclair elsewhere in this issue] observed,

"Usually the Irishmen have not been checkmated at the beginning, but they have soon exhausted themselves to run down like an old clock." Nonetheless, on this occasion, the match was still goalless after half an hour, with the home side just starting to get into their stride. This was when Huddersfield's Jim McAuley, paired with his former Cliftonville teammate Thompson on the left side of the Irish attack in a partnership of which much was expected, kicked the ground, wrenched his ankle and was carried off. He didn't return. No substitutions were permitted in 1913 and five minutes later Sunderland's Charlie Buchan headed England into the lead. That the 10 men were able to turn the situation around in the 55 minutes remaining and hang on showed evidence of the team spirit and organisation that they would draw on again 12 months later.

This Irish side were good on the ball. The Bohemians player Denis 'Dinny' Hannon, from Athlone in the geographic centre of Ireland, was one of those who caught Catton's eye. "He appealed to me as a frail boy with a big brain and a cunning foot," he wrote, commenting further on his conspicuous "dribbling in midfield to open the game". The red-headed Hannon would not feature in the undefeated campaign the following year. But his international career had an unlikely swansong when, aged 36, he represented the Irish Free State at the 1924 Olympic Games in Paris. The Irish nearly made a name for themselves too, losing in extra time to a 104th-minute goal by Holland in the quarter-finals of what, with 22 countries, was to be the

[1] *The story of one of the key figures in the book, Leslie Goldberg, was told in* The Blizzard *Issue Seven.*

biggest international football tournament for nearly 60 years. Hannon and his teammates had beaten Bulgaria 1-0 in their opening match.

The 1913 side also had tremendous physical presence, notably through a half-back trio who, after a quiet start, played their inexperienced English counterparts off the park. Everton's Val Harris, captaining the team in his 17th international, led the way, tenacious in defence and "a schemer in initiation". Tellingly, two of the English half-backs, both making their debuts in Belfast, never played for their country again. The third, Francis Cuggy, soon to win the league title with Sunderland, only played for England once more — in the following year's Ireland fixture.

The Irish forwards, moreover, were pacy and direct, compensating for their numerical disadvantage with fast, accurate passing. Houston, at outside-right, strayed offside too much in the first 45 minutes but did better in the second half. Gillespie, destined to become a Sheffield United legend, was a revelation. Tityrus's description of his first international goal, which brought Ireland back into the match on the stroke of half-time, illustrates his versatility and predatory instincts. A Thompson corner fell among a cluster of players at "the nearer post. [England's] Utley headed straight up in the air and before it descended Williamson found himself surrounded by three Irishmen and somebody trod on his ankle. When the ball came down, Gillespie headed it obliquely into the opposite corner from where Williamson was standing and

after it had crossed the line, [England's] Benson helped it further into the net."

In the wake of Gillespie's second goal, Ireland had a scare when the 6ft-plus Buchan sent another header thudding against the bar. But they held out without further serious alarm. "The thrustfulness and speed of the Irish forwards," Tityrus went on, "the meddlesomeness of the half-backs and the dourness and sureness of the backs turned the scale in favour of the Green Isle." A Mr RP Gregson, perhaps the only man then alive to have seen all 32 England versus Ireland matches, was said to have pronounced that the winners had never had as powerful a team. As for England, six of the eleven were dropped and never recalled. The FA, meanwhile, were perhaps left to rue their generosity in allowing the fixture to be staged in Ireland for a second consecutive year. This was to help replenish the finances of the Irish governing body, the IFA, left denuded as a result of a dispute with leading clubs the previous season.

In spite of this historic victory, hopes were not especially high the following year as Ireland prepared to meet Wales on January 19 (a Monday) in the opening fixture of the 1914 Home International Championship. For one thing, defeats by Wales and Scotland meant that they had still finished last in the 1913 competition — and this even though they had played all three matches at home. For another, the 1914 Welsh team oozed class in the forwards, their quintet including Bolton's Ted Vizard, in his prime, on the left wing, and the Manchester United stalwart Billy Meredith, then approaching his 40th birthday, on the right. "Ireland have a strong defence and a capable attack," advised the *Athletic News*. "But the Welsh forwards are incomparably the best section in either eleven and they should be capable of elevating the red dragon of Wales."

This was not, though, how events in Wrexham panned out. Vizard's trickery did win a penalty that was converted but the irrepressible Gillespie notched another brace, earning Ireland a 2-1 victory. In a further echo of their triumph over England, the Irishmen were left once again to play much of the match with 10 men, following an injury to their key half-back Val Harris. Among those who played with particular distinction was Fred McKee, an eccentric, often brilliant amateur-goalkeeper-cum-tea-merchant, who sometimes sported a distinctive red, white and blue hooped jersey and deployed an ivory cigarette-holder on at least one occasion during a club match. McKee was a near contemporary of Billy Scott, the great Elisha's elder brother, which explains why he mustered only five full Irish caps, but he started all three home internationals in that landmark 1914 campaign.

The game against England, nearly four weeks later, was the second full international match played at Ayresome Park, Middlesbrough. In terms of shock value it cannot quite compare with the exploits of Pak Do Ik and his North Korean teammates when they saw off Italy in a World Cup clash at the ground 52 years later, but it produced the second most arresting scoreline on the short list of international football fixtures staged on Teesside: England 0 Ireland 3.

The *Times* gave far more prominence to England's 17-12 rugby victory over

Ireland at Twickenham the same day, in "the presence of the King, his Prime Minister and the Chief Liberal Whip". Yet in the 62 words (plus line-ups) it devoted to the upset, even the voice of the British establishment made plain that the visitors had "outplayed their opponents at all points", their "pace, dash and skill" affording a "most pleasing contrast to the dull, spasmodic efforts" of England.

The sports-focused *Athletic News* headlined its lengthier but, for the hosts, equally damning account, "The Debacle at Ayresome Park". It wrote, "Last season, the representatives of Ireland created a sensation by defeating England for the first time in the history of international Association football, on Saturday they caused a thunderbolt to burst by their audacity in actually trouncing the English eleven by three clear goals."

England's hugely experienced rearguard — the back three of goalkeeper Sam Hardy, Crompton and "peerless" Jesse Pennington had a combined tally of 74 caps — did at least apply the offside trap with some success. In those days, the front man of the side in possession needed to have three rather than two opponents between him and the goal-line to be onside and the Linfield duo of Sam Young and David Rollo, the latter pressed into service as a makeshift right-winger, were caught out repeatedly. But with the visitors astutely keeping the ball low to negate the effects of a blustery wind, Thompson and Gillespie once again combined to good effect. This time they were joined by the inside-left Billy Lacey, who scored two goals, the first as early as the fifth minute, and was adjudged the man of the match.

Just as at Windsor Park, the dominance of the Irish half-backs provided a sturdy platform for their success, with Hampton deputising ably for Harris, who was still unfit. Manchester United's Mickey Hamill marked his man out of the match. The centre-half Patrick O'Connell of Hull City was "steady as a rock", "always had a grip on the game" and "pushed the ball forward splendidly". This was the same Patrick O'Connell who, 21 years later, achieved the stupendous feat of guiding the Seville club Betis to the Spanish championship. He went on to manage Barcelona in a period overshadowed by the Spanish civil war. A year after putting England to the sword so comprehensively, and with English league football about to wind up for the duration of the Great War, O'Connell also captained Manchester United in the notorious Good Friday match against Liverpool that was subsequently found to have been fixed. Seven players from the two clubs, though not O'Connell, were eventually banned.

With Scotland and Wales finishing goalless in the interim, Ireland knew well ahead of their final championship match on March 14 that a draw would secure them their first outright title. As it turned out, there was little football played at Windsor Park that day, but the clash with a robust Scottish team wanted nothing for drama. For the *Irish News*, indeed, it was "probably the most remarkable match ever played under Association rules in Ireland."

Belfast is a fine city in many ways, but there are few places that do wet weekends more remorselessly than the Ulster capital. The Scotland match fell on just such a weekend. It was raining on Friday morning when the Scots arrived. It rained all night. And when the players awoke on match-day morning it was to what one correspondent described as a "merciless, storm-tossed downpour". With the deluge continuing as the potentially historic match unfolded, the manner of play was dictated entirely by the state of the pitch.

As detailed by the *Athletic News*'s "Harrisus", this "contained a number of miniature lakes... Until the movements of the players churned the water into mud, their feet splashed the water about by every footprint, the ball spun round in the small pools, and when the mud stage had been reached, the ball had to be really driven along." One, presumably Scottish, contributor to the *Irish Weekly Record*, "John O' Groat", maintained that "No ordinary club game would ever have been started under such conditions, but as we had arranged to catch a train for Larne at 6.30, and could not stop over the weekend, the battle had to proceed." For "Marathon" of the same newspaper, the playing surface resembled "a Kerry moving bog".

Many had particular reason to bemoan the weather. Management from the Linfield club found ways to expand capacity to accommodate the expected bumper crowd. The *Irish News* reported on the day of the match that the ground would hold 50,000 people. Fans expecting to use "the unreserved side" were advised to have the right money ready "as it will be impossible to give change". In the event, with nearby roofs and telegraph poles pressed into service by the determined and impecunious, the attendance was closer to 28,000. Even so, receipts, at over £1,800, were said to be £400 more than "any previous figures for Ireland". The entire Irish set-up must, moreover, have feared that the conditions would play into Scotland's hands by making their habitual swashbuckling tactics impossible to execute. Finally, spectators in uncovered sections now faced an endurance test rather than an enjoyable afternoon's sport, albeit at an event that might still culminate with a real 'I was there' moment. Descriptions of the crowd spoke of a "forest of gleaming umbrellas".

Some very modern-sounding issues reared their heads at various points before and during the match — for example, club versus country. In 1914, country tended to come a pretty poor second and Ireland faced going into this game of games without the talismanic Gillespie because Sheffield United needed him for a Cup match that had gone to a second replay. His replacement, Robert Nixon, was finally chosen at a special selection meeting on the morning of the game. In marked contrast, a cup-tie in Scotland involving goalkeeper Jamie Brownlie's side Third Lanark had been postponed, enabling him to travel to Belfast.

Ireland had opted to spend the night before the match away from Belfast at a hotel in the small coastal resort of Newcastle, County Down. On the way there on Friday morning, the train carrying the team stopped briefly at Frank Thompson's home town of Ballynahinch, whereupon the Irish left-winger jumped aboard. It turned out he had been up since 4am tramping the countryside with his gun. He had

bagged a teal, as the *Irish Weekly Record* revealed, alluding drily to his "novel method of training for an International".

Two bands — the Edenderry Brass Band and the Castleton Pipers Band, in Highland costume — had been hired for the occasion. Attention was also drawn ahead of kick-off by a man carrying a ribboned black cat, "apparently a mascot". When Hamill, the Irish captain, led his men out into the gale, they were greeted by a thunderous roar. Alec McNair, the Scottish skipper, won the toss and asked the hosts to play into the wind. At last, the match kicked off before "a battery of cameras and cinema machines".

Ahead of the game, one focus of attention was the Scotland forward Andrew Wilson and the threat he posed to Ireland with his robust style of play. One article carrying Hamill's byline observed that the Sheffield Wednesday stalwart "carries 13 solid stone... I saw him this season charge Hodge, our full-back, and poor Hodge was tossed at least four yards in the air and fell unconscious." Not that he had been guilty of foul play: it was rather, Hamill said, "a perfectly fair shoulder charge which caught Hodge standing on one leg." A separate piece cautioned that McKee, the Irish goalkeeper, "must watch both his avoirdupois and his shots".

And indeed it was Wilson who emerged as the key figure of a goalless first half. "First of all Wilson fouled O'Connell and then accidentally, while the latter was on the ground, trod on the arm of the home centre half-back,'" said the *Athletic News*. "He had to be led off and for some considerable time he chafed inside the pavilion, but he turned out again after the interval. McConnell was also carried off and Lacey had to go full-back, but before that McKee was also in the wars. Donaldson had put in a very fine centre and Wilson went on to meet it. McKee came dashing out and kicked the ball away just as Wilson was about to kick the ball into the net. The pair also bumped into each other and the man who runs into Andrew Wilson must accept the consequences. McKee was evidently in a bad way, but he pluckily kept his position."

Yet again, then, Ireland found themselves labouring under a numerical disadvantage. Their prospects deteriorated further shortly after the interval when McKee, nursing a fractured collar-bone, gave up the battle, leaving McConnell, the injured defender, to take over in goal, having first struggled to "get into a jersey two sizes too small". To make matters even worse, Harris, usually a key figure, still appeared to be affected by the after-effects of his injury at Wrexham.

Though the Scots were subsequently exonerated from suggestions they had overstepped the mark (football was a man's game, in every sense, in 1914), the crowd were getting restless, with cries of "Play the game, Scotland" reported. This was potentially a matter of some concern. Belfast football crowds had a rough reputation. The presence of firearms was not unknown. Following the most serious disturbance, in September 1912, as Neal Garnham relates in his book *Association Football and Society in Pre-partition Ireland*, among the 50 or so casualties who were later admitted to hospital "more than one was suffering from gunshot wounds". That was at a club game between rivals closely associated with the city's

incompatible nationalist and unionist traditions. But the international team's maiden victory over England was also said to have been accompanied by pistol shots. Moreover, Garnham states that "the practice of firing warning shots and *feux de joie* at matches was apparently becoming so common that...the football correspondent of one Belfast newspaper [claimed] to be able to identify the type of weapon used by its report."

This was not the ideal time then for a goal-line controversy but that is exactly what happened. Thompson, seemingly invigorated by his duck-shooting expedition, had been playing superbly despite being left isolated on the left flank by Lacey's withdrawal to Ireland's back-line. The Clyde man shot hard at Brownlie's goal. Though the goalkeeper parried it, the ball slipped from his grasp, igniting a "wild" — but vain — claim for an Irish goal. Writing a week later, John O' Groat claims to have spoken to Brownlie who "judged the ball's position from the post and it was no goal". The keeper also expressed bafflement at "how the crowd could tell it was through when the line was obliterated."

A few minutes later and the Irish goose looked well and truly cooked. McConnell, the makeshift goalkeeper, dashed off his line but played the ball within range of Joe Donnachie, the Scotland forward. The Oldham player, who had been training at Windsor Park that week, "cutely" returned it into an empty goal to give Scotland the lead. This left the battered hosts with 22 minutes to retrieve the situation.

Some 14 of these had elapsed when O'Connell — playing so well despite his injured arm that the *Weekly Record* assessed his value, "on Saturday's display", at a princely £1,200 "perhaps more" — propelled the ball into the path of Young bursting through a hesitant Scottish rearguard. On his home ground, the 31-year-old Linfield forward thumped in an unstoppable shot to provide the crowning moment of his career and spark pandemonium among the sodden masses. There was a suspicion of offside, but the goal stood. The man with the black cat began to dance. John O'Groat reported the cracking of revolvers behind the Scotland goal.

The remaining minutes were played out with the jubilant and boisterous crowd clustered tight around the touchlines. Houston nearly won the match and the triple crown for Ireland before the final whistle blew and the glutinous pitch was engulfed with humanity. The bedraggled Scots were no doubt glad to escape to Larne.

The *Athletic News* hailed a "new era" and predicted that Ireland's success should prove a "powerful stimulant to the cultivation" of football on an island where, let us not forget, the Gaelic Athletic Association provided an alluring and popular alternative to games imported from the colonial power. The newspaper recalled that football was described as "the noxious Scotch weed" in 1878 when Queen's Park and the Glasgow Caledonians played a first exhibition match on the ground of the Ulster Cricket Club. "When we remember that the senior clubs of Ireland number 10 and that the majority of her best players migrate to England, it is small

wonder that they have not advanced more quickly."

Would this generation of Irish players have enjoyed further success had domestic politics and the disastrous machinations of the great European powers not intervened? It's impossible to be sure but the likes of Hamill, Lacey and Gillespie were in their prime and the great goalkeeper Elisha Scott was soon to establish himself in the Liverpool first team. It could be argued indeed that the Irish team that drew with England in October 1919 after conceding a first-minute goal, in their first clash since the Great War, was more talented than the 1914 vintage, with the likes of Patsy 'Mighty Atom' Gallagher and Billy McCandless in its ranks.

One other name on that 1919 team-sheet illustrates that the pre-First World War championship team could have been even stronger. In 1914, William McCracken, born in Belfast and first capped by Ireland three weeks after his 19th birthday in 1902, was at the height of his powers. A profile, penned by Catton and published in February of that year, asserts that "the honour of being the best right-back in the world unquestionably rests between Crompton and McCracken." The Irishman, Catton wrote, "is probably the most discussed man in football owing to his tactics of throwing forwards offside by constantly advancing behind the outside winger and towards the man who has possession of the ball." And yet, McCracken did not once feature in that 1914 Ireland team, having been ostracised six years earlier in a dispute over match payments. Ah, football and money; the eternal conundrum. **B**

THE FOOTBALL RAMBLE

Football's most entertaining
show—since 2007

Available every week on iTunes and
thefootballramble.com

@footballramble

109

Africa

"The tent packed up and everyone
looked miserable and deflated."

Eat Them Like Bread

Nigeria ended their 19-year wait for a third Cup of Nations but a familiar sense of chaos remains

By Jonathan Wilson

When the news of Stephen Keshi's resignation broke, I was — for reasons far less interesting than you may imagine — standing in the car park of a Johannesburg warehouse that stocked poles for erotic dancing. The story was shocking yet somehow predictable: shocking because a day earlier Keshi had become the first Nigerian coach ever to win the Cup of Nations and only the second man ever, after the Egyptian Mahmoud El Gohary, to win the competition as both player and manager; predictable because he is strong-willed, nobody's fool and had clearly been frustrated with a lot of the nonsense that goes with being Nigeria coach.

Having filed three pieces that morning hailing Keshi's importance, I confess I panicked. By the time I'd negotiated a severe rainstorm to get to the airport, though, it had become apparent that the resignation wasn't quite as definitive as had first appeared and that my vague hints that his position was insecure were enough to render rewriting unnecessary. Keshi had been frustrated by a failure to pay his salary and by the fact that the car he had been promised had never materialised, and also by the constant rumours that he was about to be replaced. Even in the press conference after Nigeria's victory in the final, there were reports that Hervé Renard, the Zambia coach, had been approached.

"Nigerians don't want me to stay," Keshi said. "They don't value what they have. When there's an African coach nobody wants to give you time, they want you to have the job today, build a wonderful team tomorrow and next year win the World Cup. If only we could work out how these things work we could have more success. But most coaches aren't given freedom to work so they are held back."

But Keshi is smart. Behind the ready chuckle and the studiedly relaxed manner there is cold calculation. He knew he would never be stronger than in the moments immediately after victory in Soccer City and so it was then that he faxed his resignation to the Nigerian Football Federation. It denied ever having received it, but it's a body so chaotic and with such a distant relationship with the truth that its statement is all but worthless. The politicians stepped in and, within 24 hours of his resignation, Keshi had unresigned. "While I have had cause," he said, "to express my displeasure over some issues that happened in the course of our participation in the 2013 Cup of Nations, which my team won by the grace of God, especially concerning my relationship with the Nigerian Football Federation, I have since had opportunity to discuss the various issues with all concerned. I am therefore pleased to say that I have reconsidered my position and have decided to continue with my job."

Nigeria can be very grateful, for Keshi's achievement in South Africa were remarkable and, although he insisted he had no unfinished business, it felt appropriate it was in Soccer City that the Super Eagles finally won their third Cup of Nations. It had, after all, been at the last Cup of Nations in South Africa that it all began to go wrong. Nigeria had won the Cup of Nations in Tunisia in 1994 with a side that featured the likes of Sunday Oliseh, Jay-Jay Okocha, Daniel Amokachi and, as captain, Keshi. Two years later, though, they were denied the chance to defend their crown in South Africa when their president Sani Abacha withdrew the side after Nelson Mandela had criticised the military regime for executing the dissident novelist Ken Saro-Wiwa. As punishment, Nigeria were banned from competing two years later and so one of Africa's greatest sides missed two tournaments they might have won.

They lost on penalties in the final against Cameroon on home soil in 2000, when Victor Ikpeba's kick famously struck the bar, crossed the line and wasn't given as a goal but since then the story has been one of perpetual disappointment. When the squads were announced for this tournament, and Keshi named 17 players who'd never played at a Cup of Nations before, including six from the domestic league, few would have expected that to change. Yet their very humbleness would prove their greatest strength.

The rain lashed down. I blundered off the bus, saw a white tent and headed towards it, hoping it was media working area. It wasn't. I found a steward and asked where the media entrance was: no idea. I did a full circuit of the ground and nobody knew. I did a wider circuit and still nobody knew. Eventually I left the stadium compound and, halfway through my third lap found the entrance, by which time I was drenched, my shirt soaked through my jacket and clinging to my skin. It was the start of a dismal opening day.

Having found the media entrance, I followed the small photocopied signs to the media tribune. When I emerged into the stand, though, I assumed there was a mistake. I went back down and asked around. The answer kept coming back: that's it; up the stairs. It was laughably tiny, so small that there were only about 30 desks, all taken up by television and radio commentators. Written media were told to take their laptops and work off their knees in a section of the stand. Occasionally, in smaller stadiums, you accept that, but even at the Cup of Nations it hasn't happened since Egypt in 2006 (with the exception of the chaotic 2010 semi-final in Benguela when Duncan White of the *Sunday Telegraph* and I were caught up in a brawl between Algerian and Egyptian journalists that had to be broken up by riot police). The idea that it should happen at a venue that had hosted the World Cup final two-and-a-half years earlier is laughable. The usual excuse in Cups of Nations is a lack of infrastructure; here it was clearly down to personnel and CAF's habitual ineptitude.

To make it worse, the wind blew the rain into the press seating. I lasted about a quarter of an hour before retreating to a bar inside the stand, by which time the enter key on my laptop had stopped working and I was having to copy and paste. The game did little to lift the spirits. South Africa, seemingly petrified by nerves, were hopeless and Cape Verde never shifted from their defensive game-plan. Morocco's game against Angola, the second part of the double-header, featured a little more in terms of purposive play, but also finished 0-0. The tournament could hardly have got off to a worse start.

So much, I thought sniffily, for the World Cup legacy. It was an issue that dominated the opening days of the tournament — and Luke Alfred offers a South African view on page 123 — and, frankly, the more I looked into it the more confused I became. As in Poland last year, what the tournament had done was to provide impetus for investment that probably would have happened anyway. The highway from Johannesburg to Pretoria, for instance, has been widened from two lanes to four, something very necessary given the increasing car ownership among the expanding black middle-class, while the Gautrain, although it was completed too late for the World Cup, offers a magnificently swift, clean and efficient service. It has not, of course, eliminated poverty — how could it have? — but it may not even have alleviated it beyond the temporary jobs created in construction.

George Tsoari, a youth football coach I met in Soweto, suggested that hosting the World Cup had opened people's eyes to South Africa, had made them realise it was a place it was possible to do business and there may be some truth to that, although his notion that "people thought there were lions in the streets" seems a misconception of a misconception.

Strangely, it was a phrase Neil Tovey, who had captained South Africa to victory in the Cup of Nations in 1996, also used so perhaps the World Cup has reassured South Africans about how others view them, has helped them feel respected, just as Lech Wałęsa said the Euros had raised Poland's self-esteem.

South Africa's 1996 side has come to feel a little like England's World Cup winners, past glory becoming a stick with which to beat the comparative failure of the present team. It was a victory that had great symbolic value — perhaps more so even than the more famous rugby World Cup winners of a year earlier. Mark Williams, who came off the bench to score two goals in the final is even referred to as "Nation Builder". "In terms of what we achieved, that moment was important in the history of the country," said Tovey. "It was two years after we became a multi-racial country and we knew we had a role to play in uniting the country, that sporting achievement could do that. As a young democratic country [the football team] was far more representative [than the rugby team]. That is what proves that it is the national sport. You can add up all the numbers of participants and fans of the other sports put together and they still wouldn't match football."

With those players and greater resources than almost any other nation on the continent, it was assumed South Africa would go on to be one of the dominant forces in African football. They reached the final in 1998, losing to Egypt, and the decline thereafter was steady: semi-final in 2000, quarter-final in 2002, third in the group in 2004, bottom of the group in 2006 and 2008 before failing to qualify in 2010 and 2012. "I think people thought after '96 it would just be a conveyor belt, that they didn't have to do much about it, but now they realise," said Tovey.

Back in 1996, South Africa stepped in to host the tournament after Kenya had been deemed unready, although the suspicion has always been that CAF wanted to use the event as a prelude to a possible bid to host the World Cup, showing off South Africa's infrastructure. This time, South Africa, having hosted the World Cup, had all the stadiums ready to take over when the conflict in Libya meant it was impossible to stage the event there as planned. In a sense, memories of the 1996 triumph are just as much a legacy of the World Cup as having the capacity to replace Libya and host the 2013 tournament was.

The stadiums themselves remain hugely controversial, with the accusation that they are white elephants never far away. Mark Gleeson, the doyen of African football journalism, argues, though, that while the situation is far from ideal, the stadiums as a whole provide a facility that strengthens the South African Premier League, improving South African football, generating jobs and mass entertainment and offering a route out of poverty for those with talent. I heard a radio journalist ask how expenditure on stadiums could be justified when there were people living in shanty towns a mile or two down the road. At first it seems an unconscionable juxtaposition — and in the abstract, of course, it is —but on the other hand, what's the alternative? Stop football until poverty is eliminated? Perhaps the number of stadiums and the size of some of them was ill-conceived — but then arenas are the great public

buildings of the age, a source of civic pride and a means of drawing visitors.

All I knew for sure as I sat soaking on the bus away from Soccer City was that the World Cup had not improved South Africa's national team.

The opening game in Group D, between Côte d'Ivoire and Togo, featured a clash of two of the more baffling managerial appointments: Sabri Lamouchi and Didier Six. Togo, perhaps, were attracted by the glamour of a player from the great France side of the early eighties, unconcerned that his only managerial experience was a few months at Strasbourg in 1986. The Ivorians' decision to appoint Lamouchi, though, a man with no prior managerial experience, made no sense at all. This, after all, is a team blighted by its own underachievement. What was needed, surely, was somebody with experience to soothe nerves — or, in fact, simply to stick with François Zahoui, who came so close to winning last year.

Since they lost on penalties in the final to the hosts Egypt in 2006, Côte d'Ivoire have gone into each tournament as favourites. Each time they have failed. In 2008, they had been the most impressive team in the early part of the tournament, beating Nigeria in the group stage and hammering Guinea 5-0 in the quarter-final. But in the semi-final in Kumasi they ran into Egypt; Kolo Touré returned too quickly from a groin injury and was destroyed by Amr Zaki — and arguably hasn't been the same player since — and Egypt won 4-1. In 2010, they came through the group in Cabinda that had been reduced to three teams when Togo withdrew after the terror attack, and then took a 2-1 lead with a minute to go of their quarter-final against Algeria. But Majid Bougherra headed in a free-kick in injury-time and, stunned, Côte d'Ivoire lost 3-2.

Each defeat and disappointment has added a new layer of trauma and insecurity, made it harder at each passing tournament. Last year, Zahoui stripped their game back to basics, instilling an approach of severe risk aversion. It worked, in so much as Côte d'Ivoire didn't concede a goal in six games; more importantly, though, Didier Drogba missed a penalty with 20 minutes of the final remaining and, as the tension overwhelmed Kolo Touré and Gervinho, they lost another penalty shoot-out. At every tournament, we've asked, "is this finally the time?" and at least since Angola in 2010 we've wondered whether this could be their final opportunity: they've had a lock-in in last-chance saloon.

This time, they began sluggishly, seeming to switch off after Yaya Touré's opener, allowing Jonathan Ayité to level from a poorly defended corner. Gervinho sealed a scarcely deserved victory, crashing in Touré's free-kick with the outside of the right foot. The celebrations seemed almost patronising in their intensity, as though his Ivorian teammates know Gervinho's confidence needs bolstering at every opportunity. Up to a point it worked: he was superb in the 3-0 win over Tunisia in the second game before fading.

Six was apoplectic afterwards, lasting 22 seconds in the press-conference before storming out in protest at a refereeing decision that replays later showed had been entirely correct. Perhaps that

could have been justified as some sort of sub-Fergie mind game, pressuring future officials, had he not abandoned an embarrassed Ayité to face the media alone.

Keshi didn't name names but when he spoke of the ongoing preference for even mediocre or unproven European coaches over locals, it didn't take much of a leap to see he wasn't just talking about Nigeria. "The white guys are coming to Africa just for the money," he said. "They are not doing anything that we cannot do. I am not racist but that's just the way it is. I am never against a white coach in Africa, because I've always worked with white coaches. If you want to bring in a classic, an experienced coach from Europe, I am ready to learn from that coach, because he's better than me, he has more knowledge than me. Meanwhile, we have quality African players, or ex-African players, who can do the same thing, but they're not given the opportunity because they're just black dudes. I don't like it."

Mike Collett of Reuters and I had made good progress on the road from Rustenburg to Nelspruit so we stopped for a coffee. Thank goodness we did. About 10 minutes after setting off again, we joined a line of perhaps two dozen cars travelling at little more than a crawl. There were police everywhere, directing cars into a single lane. The road turned gritty with broken glass. To the left lay the shell of a car, a blanket draped ominously over it. A few yards on to the right was a burnt out engine block and a few yards after that a minivan, its front smashed, straddled the central reservation. Quite how the crash had happened I still can't quite comprehend but its severity was shocking. Given the debris and the number of people hanging around, it seemed the accident had happened recently, about as long ago as it takes to drink a coffee.

Some roadworks also delayed us so we ended up watching South Africa's game against Angola in a petrol station, perched on stools at a coffee bar with two locals who seemed to have come specifically to watch the match. After an anxious opening, South Africa won comfortably enough thanks to goals from Siyabonga Sangweni and Lehlohonolo Majoro. Towards the end, the manager — who was white — came out of his office. "I thought games were 90 minutes long," he said. "Why does it say 93?" As one of the locals explained the concept of injury time to him, I glanced behind me and saw about a dozen staff — all black — peering through the window at the television, hands cupped against the glare.

Ultimately, tournaments are judged more on their drama than on the quality of play. The complaint in the first week of the competition was that it was flat, that there was little to excite the neutral. There was some truth to that but it's a trope of most modern tournaments, the price that must be paid for expansion.

That is not to say that the decision to increase the number of participants from 12 to 16 teams for the 1996 tournament was a bad thing, far from it. Regular competition has clearly raised the level of what might be considered the second-rank of African teams, just as

the likes of Venezuela and Ecuador have improved significantly since South American World Cup qualifying began to be organised on a league basis for the 1998 tournament; regular competitive games against better teams of higher quality (so long as the gulf in quality is not too big) sharpens sides, teaches them how to organise themselves, gives them gamecraft. "You can no longer differentiate so much between which teams are better," Keshi said. "In the old days you could predict how many goals one team was going to score against the other but now you don't know what is going to happen. You might think one side will win but you don't know. I think this is wonderful for African football. The competition is so tight: you look at the likes of Ethiopia and Cape Verde and some of the other countries. I am very impressed with their performances and the standard they are reaching."

The problem is that the early days of a tournament, before the giants, the sides who are perceived as potential champions, start playing each other, can often feel like an extension of the qualifying process. Unless there is a remarkable underdog tale — such as Equatorial Guinea's progress last year — only with the final round of group games, when the objectives are clearly defined, when it becomes go through or go out, does a tournament really get going. This tournament essentially began eight days after the opening game, as South Africa faced Morocco and Cape Verde met Angola in the final games in Group A.

Morocco had been their usual flaky selves, packed with potential yet somehow never quite playing to their ability. After two draws they needed a win to progress, while a draw left them needing the other game to finish in a lower-scoring draw. At half-time, Morocco led through Issam El Adoua's header, while a Nando own goal had given Angola the lead in Port Elizabeth, scorelines that if turned into results would have taken Morocco and South Africa through. Morocco had played well in the first half, dominating a timid South Africa. But then, with 19 minutes remaining, May Mahlangu curled a sumptuous shot into the top corner to pull South Africa level. Suddenly it was the hosts and Angola going through. Fernando Varela bundled in a header for Cape Verde; only disciplinary points separated them and Morocco at that stage. But then Morocco scored again to take the initiative.

Sangweni, after his superb finish in the second game, came up with another, the centre-back emerging inexplicably in the inside-left channel with four minutes to go to arc in a low finish. That meant it was South Africa to top the group (a relief, frankly, having already booked flights to Durban in the expectation of seeing them in the last eight) with Morocco in second — so long as there wasn't a deciding goal in Port Elizabeth. There was. Two minutes into injury time, the Angola goalkeeper Lama fumbled an apparently simple cross and Héldon Ramos slammed the loose ball in. The smallest nation ever to qualify for the Cup of Nations was through to the quarter-finals, while Morocco became just the second team since the tournament switched to its present format 17 years ago to go out having been undefeated in the group stage. Within three days they'd have been joined by two more: the

defending champions Zambia, whose rapid counter-attacking game foundered on the sand of the Mbombela, and DR Congo, who came from 2-0 down to draw with Ghana in their first game but then lacked the guile to break down Niger and went out with a tepid draw against Mali.

Tales of taxi drivers are a lazy journalist's staple, but two I met seemed particularly relevant. The first, who picked me up at the airport in Johannesburg remains the only South African I've spoken to who actually went to a game at the World Cup (journalists excepted). He'd saved up to buy a ticket for the opening game and had then been given a ticket for Holland against Denmark by some Dutch fans he'd driven around, a touching story that suggested that Fifa's corporate ideal of a great family of footballing nations isn't quite such saccharine nonsense as it often appears.

The other took me to Nelspruit airport. He was called Peter, will turn 60 in June, and had once played in defence for a local side called Roger's Black Stars. "Roger owned the farm," he said, "so that's why we were called Roger. We were all black and so that was why we were called black. Stars... well, we had to dream." He was wearing a new Zambia shirt, a present to him from Renard after he'd given him a lift. Somebody in the Zambia set-up also gave him a ticket for the opening doubler-header. He'd enjoyed it, he said, but he wouldn't pay to go back, not when you could watch the matches on television for nothing. This partly explains one of the features of Cups of Nations: low crowds. In the first week of each tournament, I always feel an irritation I confess is unjustified as Twitter and comments sections fill up with questions about half-empty stadiums: I want to grab each poster, whether earnest or snide, shake them and scream, "Have you never watched the thing before?" For the fact is that apart for games involving the host nation and the final, stadiums at Cups of Nations are never full.

In part the issue is economic, less to do with ticket prices than simply the difficulty of travelling across Africa. At last summer's European Championship, for instance, the majority of fans weren't from Poland or Ukraine, but from elsewhere in Europe. For, say, an Ivorian to travel to Rustenburg to watch a game against Togo, though, is much more difficult, both in terms of expense and logistics (even given the vagaries of the Polish rail network), than for, say, a Croatian to travel to Gdansk. Add in the comparative lack of disposable income in Africa, and the low crowd figures are readily comprehensible.

The situation is exacerbated by the lack of a culture of going to games, something Gleeson highlights. The popularity of the Champions League and European domestic leagues means a lot of fans in South Africa (and by extension elsewhere on the continent), have got into the habit of watching matches in bars, or with a few mates over a crate of beers at home, and the fact Didier Drogba happens to be playing 10 miles down the road doesn't change that.

In fact this tournament was comparatively well-attended, thanks in part to large numbers of travelling Algerian fans and in part to the significant

Nigerian and Ethiopian populations in South Africa. The green-and-white clad Nigerians are a feature of Cups of Nations but the Ethiopians, many of them brandishing pictures of Haile Selassie, came as a revelation at their first finals since 1982. The fans were raucously noisy and, while they let themselves down by showering the pitch with vuvuzelas after their goalkeeper Jemal Tessaw had been sent off for a dreadful foul in their game against Zambia, they at least had the grace then to hold up a banner apologising. As a team, Ethiopia looked good in patches and forced a memorable draw with 10 men against Zambia, but an injury to Adane Girma early in their second game, against Burkina Faso, robbed them of their most creative player and a certain defensive rawness eventually found them out.

Only for the final did Nigerian fans really have the confidence to express themselves. Coffins, supposedly carrying the corpse of Burkinabé football were paraded around the aisles (a little gracelessly, given the relative status of the sides — the demise of Nigerian underachievement might have been a more appropriate thing to celebrate). At least two fans brought chickens painted in national colours while another wore a loaf on his head and carried the message, "Eat them like bread."

After Zambia had been awarded a contentious late penalty against Nigeria by the Egyptian referee Gehad Grisha, the goalkeeper Vincent Enyeama dismissed the decision as "one of the worst in football history". It would soon have some competition.

People who regularly watch the South African referee Daniel Bennett say he's usually pretty good, but his performance in the final group game between Togo and Tunisia was awful. Togo needed only a draw to go through and looked likely to get it as Emmanuel Adebayor, breaking a rickety Tunisian offside trap for the umpteenth time, laid in Serge Gakpo to open the scoring. Replays later showed Gakpo was a foot or so offside. So there was an element of evening the score when Daré Nibombé was harshly penalised for a push on Walid Hichri; Khaled Mouelhi rolled in the penalty.

In the second half, Bennett's decisions became increasingly bizarre. He denied Tunisia a clear penalty when Vincent Bossou clattered through the back of Oussmana Darragi. He ignored two decent Togolese shouts for penalties and then waved play on when the goalkeeper Moez Ben Cherifia blatantly tripped Adebayor as the Tottenham forward wandered round him. When the 5'10" Serge Akakpo chopped down Yousef Msakhni, he booked the 6'5" Nibombé, who'd been about 10 yards from the incident. And then, with 13 minutes remaining, he awarded a penalty to Tunisia as Saber Khalifa tumbled in the vicinity of Nibombé. The two Togolese journalists sitting next to me, having passed through anxiety to anger to resignation, giggled at the sheer preposterousness of it. Mouelhi's penalty seemed almost embarrassed, his dink coming back off the post.

So Togo held on to reach the last eight for the first time, an achievement Adebayor, who had a fine tournament, immediately dedicated to the memory of the three men who were killed in the gun attack on the team bus last time Togo had reached the finals, three years ago. Adebayor, terrified for his own life, had cradled his good friend, the press officer Stan Oclo'o, as he died and only came to South Africa after being convinced security would be more stringent than in Angola. "I'm very proud of my country, of what we have been through," said Adebayor. "I think you guys know better than I do that two months ago when we qualified against Gabon we went through a lot of difficult moments, of me coming to the Africa Cup of Nations or not coming. Today I'm here and I'm very happy — I'm part of the history. It's a good thing for the country and a good thing for me."

Tunisia's exit meant that, for the first time since 1992, there was no north African presence in the quarter-finals. The trend is concerning but there were mitigating factors. Tunisia were poor and Morocco were as self-destructive as ever, but Algeria were unlucky, outplaying Tunisia and Togo before losing to both. Football in Egypt, the most successful team in Cup of Nations history, meanwhile, has fallen victim to the political upheaval. With the next two tournaments to be held in Morocco and Libya a swift upturn is likely.

As though inspired by the drama of their final group stage game, South Africa came alive for their quarter-final against Mali. The Moses Mabhida in Durban, by some way the most aesthetically pleasing of the World Cup stadiums, was awash with yellow, while the rendition of the South African anthem sent shivers down the spine (and raised the question, yet again, of why so many countries insist on having a diva on a microphone drowning out everyone else when there is something so moving about thousands of voices raised together in song). South Africa themselves seemed inspired and deserved their 1-0 half-time lead. They conceded a soft goal on the break to Seydou Keita after 55 minutes, though, and wilted, perhaps exhausted by the intensity of their pressing.

As they had at the same stage a year ago in Gabon, Mali, having come from behind against the hosts, went through after a penalty shoot-out. And as he had a year ago, Keita spoke movingly about the ongoing conflict in Mali after the team gave up a percentage of their bonuses to help the war effort. "Giving hope to the country has been priceless," he said. "There is a crisis in Mali and I did my best to give hope to those who are suffering. We have made an effort to help, but money doesn't matter. You can't imagine what it means to play for Mali at this time. I told my government they could reduce our bonuses. My priority is to play for my country."

It was the quarter-final in Rustenburg the following day, though, Côte d'Ivoire against Nigeria, an unfulfilled power against one that had lost its way, that really sent a jolt through the tournament. Everything about it had an epic feel. The day had begun sunny but by an hour before kick off the wind had got up and heavy clouds had rolled over. Curtains of rain draped the hills that surround the east and south sides of the Royal Bafokeng Stadium, while eddies of dust scudded across the veld to the north and

lightning flickered above the platinum mines. The stage was set for the last stand of the Elephants.

That Boubacar Barry has been the first-choice Côte d'Ivoire goalkeeper for six years remains baffling; how can a nation that has produced talented footballers in such numbers have failed to have generated anybody better? He probably has improved over the years and he is certainly capable of spectacular saves but the propensity for skittishness has never left him. The warning was there after 10 minutes as he thumped a Victor Moses shot back into the centre of the penalty area and the mistake arrived three minutes before half-time as he reacted pathetically late to a vicious Emmanuel Emenike free-kick. Mido, harshly but not entirely inaccurately, promptly tweeted that Barry had already won three Cups of Nations for Egypt.

Côte d'Ivoire have had a habit of collapsing under pressure, but this time they fought back. Three minutes into the second half, Didier Drogba was tripped just outside the box, about five yards from the goalline. He took the free-kick himself, dinking it to the back post where Cheick Tioté headed in. The stadium braced itself for a charge but with Efe Ambrose quashing Gervinho and Mikel having the better of his battle with Yaya Touré, it never quite materialised and, with 12 minutes remaining, came vindication for Keshi. Sunday Mba collected the ball just outside the centre-circle, accelerated through two diffident challenges and struck a shot from the edge of the box that glanced off Sol Bamba's backside and looped past Barry. For the Ivorians, it was a setback too far: energy and belief melted away, just as it had in Cabinda three years earlier, and Nigeria were through.

In the post-match press-conference, Mark Gleeson, at 6'8" an unmissable figure, took the mic. "Where have you been?" bellowed Keshi. "I haven't seen you for years."

"I've been covering the big boys," Gleeson replied.

Keshi laughed — as he does a lot — but the point was a valid one. This was probably Nigeria's best result since they beat Spain 3-2 at the 1998 World Cup and, although they'd reached the semi-finals in five of the six tournaments before failing to qualify for last year's competition, it was the first time they'd really looked like potential champions since reaching the final on home soil in 2000.

Before this tournament, Burkina Faso had seemed a classic argument against the expansion of the finals to 16 teams. In 26 previous matches at the finals, they had won only two games, drawing six and losing 18. Away from home soil, they'd gathered four points from a possible 60. The previous year, in Equatorial Guinea, having been extremely fortunate to have been allowed to compete after fielding an ineligible player in a qualifier against Namibia, they were a shambles and lost all three matches.

Burkina Faso's coach Paul Put, who was once banned for match-fixing in Belgium, admitted that when he left Ouagadougou, he'd have been happy just to win a game. But this side proved rather better than that: it was solid

at the back — aided, perhaps, by the awful pitch at the Mbombela where they played their first five games —and had, in Jonathan Pitroipa, an intelligent winger, and, in Charles Kaboré, a languid midfield passer. For 125 minutes, it also had the most devastating forward in the competition: Alain Traoré. He came off the bench to equalise in the opener against Nigeria and then scored with two thunderous strikes in the 4-0 victory over Ethiopia but suffered a thigh injury early in the final group game, the goalless draw against Zambia that took the Stallions through. They still had enough to overcome Togo in extra time in the quarter-final but few thought they had much of a chance against Ghana in the semi-final.

Yet Ghana, essentially, were a team of reputations. Without Dédé Ayew, omitted for failing to show up on time to have a hamstring strain assessed (he didn't miss a minute for Marseille between the restart of the French season and the end of the tournament) and with Anthony Annan carrying a knee injury, they lacked drive. Emmanuel Agyemang-Badu battled manfully in midfield, Christian Atsu sparkled intermittently and Kwadwoh Asmaoah always projected danger, but he never had a settled position, being shifted from left-back to play off a striker and back again. The biggest disappointment, though, was Asamoah Gyan. There were glimmers of his talent in the 3-0 win over a poor Tunisia but for most of the tournament he looked exactly what he is, a good player gone soft by playing at too low a level.

It took a couple of odd refereeing decisions to get Ghana through a quarter-final against Cape Verde; their coach, Lucio Antunes, an air-traffic controller in Praia, had sung in delight after their progression from the group, but after his side's 2-0 defeat he wondered openly whether referees had been instructed to help the big sides go through. His words took on yet greater significance after the semi-final.

Slim Jedidi, the Tunisian referee, was even worse than Daniel Bennett had been in the game between Togo and Tunisia. Bennett had at least been awful both ways, although Togo probably just got the worst of it; Jedidi, with the exception of booking Keba Paul Koulibaly for kicking out at Gyan when he should have sent him off, seemed to give everything Ghana's way. Burkina Faso were denied two penalties, had an extremely dubious penalty awarded against them, had a goal disallowed after some anodyne tussling between Préjuce Nakoulma and Asamoah and then, worst of all, when that second penalty was denied them, four minutes from the end of extra time Pitroipa was booked for diving. It was his second yellow of the game, so off he went, which meant he would be suspended for the final if Burkina Faso got through the penalty shoot-out.

They did, and they deserved to. There had been an assumption that Ghana would get going when they really needed to but they never did. Their coach, James Kwesi Appiah, tightened up the defensive laxity that had been apparent in the 2-2 draw with DR Congo, but they never attacked with any verve or fluency. They were fortunate to go ahead against Burkina Faso and, although Gyan did hit the post in the second half, extremely

fortunate not to lose the game. Aristide Bancé, leading the line in the absence of Traoré, was a revelation, his weirdly perpetual fury for once focused. He is not the world's most natural finisher, but he scored one, drew one fine save from Fatawu Dauda and had a header cleared off the line by Harrison Afful. In the shoot-out, it was he who had the nerve to panenka his kick.

When Badu's effort was then saved by Daouda Diakité, confirming Burkina Faso's victory, Bancé made straight for Put. There is a wonderful photograph of the two, one peroxide blonde, the other with his sandy hair bleached by the sun, both with mouths wide in triumph, arms outstretched like long-lost lovers, about to embrace as dozens of moths flit around them, illuminated in the floodlights like a flurry of snow. Whatever his sins in Europe, Put has done a remarkable job in Burkina Faso.

But that was as far as the Burkinabé fairy tale went. Nigeria had cruised by Mali in the semi-final, Victor Moses, Emmanuel Emenike and Elderson Echiejile all superb in a 4-1 win. One of the criticisms of African football for years has been the lack of creative wide play but Nigeria won with two wingers and an attacking full-back in superb form. The only concerns were injuries to Moses and Emenike: Moses recovered and played in the final; Emenike did not.

It hardly mattered. Nigeria were comfortably the better side and took the lead five minutes before half-time as Mba flicked up the dropping ball after Moses's shot had been blocked, hurtled into the box and volleyed it into the corner. His goal in the quarter-final had made him the first player from the Nigerian league to score at a Cup of Nations since Emmanuel Okocha in 1990; his winner in the final, and the superlative form of Godfrey Oboabona at centre-back, fully vindicated Keshi's much-criticised decision to select home-based players.

Only anxiety on the break in the final minutes denied them further goals and Keshi felt secure enough in the lead to give his squad captain Joseph Yobo, a veteran of six Cups of Nations, a cameo. "The difference with this squad is that there's a lot of unity and a lot of potential at the same time," Yobo said. "Other squads I've been with, the unity has not being that strong — we've always had problems because we have different cultures and we're from different places. What brought us closer is that nobody thought we had a chance from the start. We were hurt and that gave us confidence and the unity was very strong."

Within the team, maybe, but, as Keshi's subsequent actions showed, not within the federation. His genius was to make Nigeria prepare like underdogs; he made them champions by persuading them they were not champions, by throwing out the egos and insisting on a work ethic and tactical discipline. In 2006, in Cairo, on one of the rare occasions when the relaxed façade slipped, he announced, "Some day I will be coach of Nigeria and then they will know what a coach is." The players do, the fans do, perhaps even the usual hypercritical journalists do. The federation and the politicians still seem in some doubt.

After the Circus

What was the legacy of the World Cup for South Africa?

By Luke Alfred

We have three relics of the 2010 World Cup in the Alfred home. Our youngest son, Thomas, has his Zakumi duvet. He also still has his increasingly weather-beaten Panini sticker album. Finally we have a framed artwork of the family's ticket stubs: yellow for the family as fans, blue for me as a journalist. There are 14 in all, arranged in chronological order. We are proud of them in the way that families are proud of what they have witnessed and what they have experienced collectively. Of our World Cup relics, this is the one which visitors comment on most often.

Such are the relics, what of the memories? Mine gather around the high emotion of Siphiwe Tshabalala's opener against Mexico, the months of exquisite expectation leading to the competition itself, my fingers freezing to my keyboard one cold weekday night at Ellis Park when North Korea made life awkward by patrolling a thick defensive wall against Brazil with — dare I say it? — old-fashioned Communist rigour. I remember an appalling match report after the Australia versus Ghana game in Rustenburg, the amusing but slightly farcical ebb and flow of a Diego Maradona press conference, something potentially wild and bizarre always lurking off stage. I remember the late nights and the travel, the shitty meals, the endless queues, arriving early at the Germany versus Ghana game and looking out of the bus window thinking that there is nothing quite as beautifully empty as one of those bleached Highveld afternoons in winter.

Such is the shape of memory that there are millions of others besides, a quiet river of anecdote and individual and shared feeling. Two and a half years on, my abiding impression of the World Cup, though, is of an alien visitation, something strange and surreal. I am amazed at how little changed, at how little disruption there was, how, like an old-fashioned circus, the big top rolled into town, the elephants and the acrobats performed, the clowns juggled. Suddenly, after all the fun, it was over. The tent packed up and everyone looked miserable and deflated. The only evidence there was of anything exciting having happened was a patch of discoloured, flattened veld as the circus and its entourage disappeared over the horizon in the direction of Brazil.

Yet this isn't quite right, is it? We have a legacy of fine stadiums, with their best practice insistence on chic changing-rooms, good referees' and officials' facilities and billiard table pitches. We have the World Cup Trust fund (Fifa's contribution to South Africa from World

Cup ticket sales) and the roll-out of approximately 50 artificial turf pitches across the country; we have a number of improved airports, part of the Gautrain link and some better roads, off-ramps and junctions than we once had.

We made friends and a few enemies but the World Cup wasn't the unmitigated disaster that some of the world's media were predicting. It was largely crime- and disaster-free, largely happy and peaceful. Why, with all these tangible improvements, all this concrete and steel, do things seem so unchanged? Why does it feel that the rewards are so intangible and difficult to quantify? Why the sense of slipperiness about legacy?

Some of the gloss has undoubtedly been taken off the event by the local newspapers' exposure of a massive match-fixing scandal involving the local football association (Safa) and a group of conmen led by the Singaporean Wilson Raj Perumal in the months immediately before the tournament. Just over a year ago my newspaper, the *Sunday Times* in Johannesburg, led a massive investigation into the scandal, the infiltration by Perumal's organisation, Football4U, of Safa, and the complete dereliction of duty and general tardiness he encountered. Four pre-World Cup friendlies were apparently fixed as Perumal's associates chose, paid and instructed the referees. A fifth match might have also been fixed, but minutes before Bafana's last World Cup friendly, against Denmark, the referee was changed in the tunnel. Steve Goddard, a slightly long-winded but essentially decent and honest Yorkshireman, was the Safa official who had his doubts from the very beginning about the fixtures.

He made them known to his superiors and eventually to Chris Eaton, once Fifa's head of security. At time of writing — and despite the publication of a 500-page Fifa report into the fixed matches — Goddard is the only man to have lost his job at Safa. Those fingered by local media reports and the Fifa investigation have recently been re-instated, an act which does little to convince an already cynical public that the association is graft-free and as selfless as it likes to portray itself.

More germane, perhaps, has been the fact that although standards are inching upwards, there's no great improvement in local football, a dizzy fare high on tempo but usually low on possession and sophistication. The fans who came to the World Cup matches haven't come to local football and any sense that the excitement and dynamism of the World Cup would be transferred to the domestic game has long been lost. The stadiums are making a go of it, hosting everything from rugby matches to Christian extravaganzas. Still, Port Elizabeth has no Premier Soccer League (PSL) franchise and Cape Town's several PSL sides have turned their back on Cape Town Stadium for financial reasons. There is only just enough sport to keep some of the World Cup stadiums in the smaller centres like Bloemfontein, Port Elizabeth, Polokwane and Nelspruit going. It's not easy to predict a problem-free future for any of them, despite the fact that the latter three have played a role in the 2013 Africa Cup of Nations, Port Elizabeth doing so because the city council directed funds usually earmarked for essential services towards the stadium and the tournament.

Much of the slightly depressed post-World Cup feeling must also be down to the ossified structure of South African football. The organising committee for the 2010 tournament was a temporary body, with the situation before and after reverting back to the traditionally hostile one between the PSL, who are in charge of professional football in South Africa, and Safa, who control national teams and grassroots development. The two figures central in each camp — Irvin Khoza, chairman of the league, and Danny Jordaan, who still plays an influential behind-the-scenes role at Safa — are the local game's two most influential power brokers. The two have historically been real and imagined antagonists, Khoza pulling himself out of the mire of poverty in Alexandra, a township east of Johannesburg, by deeds good and nefarious. By contrast, Jordaan has taken a more respectable political road to the top via his home town, Port Elizabeth, and his involvement with the ANC. Khoza remains the most powerful man in South African football, while Jordaan's star has fallen dramatically since the World Cup. His proxies, such as the Safa president, Kirsten Nematandani, and the CEO, Dennis Mumble, are arguably as influential nowadays as he was in and before 2010, despite the fact that they have an internal investigation about the match-fixing scandal hanging over their heads.

The influence and reach of the two camps (and the fact that most in local football either line up in one camp or another, whether by conviction or association) has resulted in a kind of stalemate, a situation similar to the Cold War. Advances in the sport are not discussed on their merits, therefore, but on how they will impact upon and benefit the camp proposing the advances. The PSL is effectively a gentleman's club, with the club owners' making up the board of governors; Khoza is both owner of Orlando Pirates and league chairman, and as such he is precluded from making impartial decisions on what is best for the league. It's a corporate governance mire.

Safa's executive are forever attempting to storm the higher moral ground, reminding the public and the football community at large that they're elected officials with the game's best interests at heart. But the reinstatement of some of the banned officials before Safa's internal investigation into the pre-World Cup match-fixing scandal, leads one to wonder about their motivation and honesty.

Such negativity has undoubtedly been bad for football (it led to an acrimonious stand-off between the PSL and Safa about players' availability for the African qualifiers for the 2012 Olympics) and will continue to inform much of what passes for governance. The World Cup — and the 2013 Africa Cup of Nations — has also brought home just how scarred the current generation of footballers are by the legacy of apartheid and its attendant tragedies. Our national teams play without reservoirs of confidence and, by and large, play a callow, fragile game. Bafana's current inability to score a goal is bordering on the pathological. Muti men and witchdoctors have been consulted but you rather feel it will need more than chicken bones and donkey blood to find a world-class striker. The World Cup should have led to greater self-respect and belief from our players. It seems to have done the opposite: a demonstration that South Africa has a frighteningly long way to go if she is ever going to find herself regularly in the world's top twenty.

Interestingly, part of the magic key all South African football fans are looking for must involve the tens of thousands of expatriate Africans domiciled legally and illegally in the country. The Cup of Nations showed that there are healthy reserves of football-loving Africans sprinkled all over South Africa. Invariably they come from places with rich football traditions and, even if they don't play, they follow. A PSL side of decent expatriate Africans would do much for standards — and standards of interest — in the local game and prove, as Jordaan so often said before 2010, that South Africa's World Cup was dedicated to the continent itself.

The Great Administrator

How Ydnekatchew Tessema led the fight to have African football taken seriously

By Tom Dunmore

"I'm issuing a call to our general assembly that it affirm that Africa is one and indivisible: that we work towards the unity of Africa together... that we condemn superstition, tribalism, all forms of discrimination within our football and in all domains of life." Ydnekatchew Tessema, speaking as the President of the Confederation of African Football (CAF) at its 1974 Congress in Cairo, Egypt.

In the summer of 1936, the Ethiopian emperor Haile Selassie made a dramatic speech to the League of Nations' general assembly in Geneva, Switzerland. He warned that his country had been subjected to a relentless and brutal occupation by Italy since its 1935 invasion, who were now "proceeding to the systematic extermination of a nation by barbarous means", sending aircraft to spray "a fine, death-dealing rain" over vast areas of countryside.

The speech created headlines worldwide as Selassie called for the principle of collective security — which the League precariously existed to protect — to be defended. He would be named Man of the Year by *Time* magazine in January 1937.

Selassie's speeches had little immediate practical effect, as the League of Nations failed to act against Italy in any substantive manner. In Addis Ababa, the capital of Ethiopia, Selassie loyalists launched a failed attempt to assassinate Viceroy Graziani on 19 February 1937; in the aftermath, Italian brutality was taken to new extremes as perhaps 30,000 Ethiopians were slaughtered by knife, gunfire, petrol bombing and worse in a two-day pillage by the occupying forces.

In the St George area of Addis Ababa, under siege from the Italians, Ydnekatchew Tessema and his family found safety in the home of a Greek immigrant family near St George cathedral. They were spared from the massacre outside because Italian troops would not enter the homes of foreigners.

Two men had thrown the bombs at Graziani that sparked the retaliation. One of them, Abrha Deboch, was known to Tessema as a prominent fellow player among the pioneer footballers of Addis Ababa. Football had been an immediate casualty of the Italian occupation. The first notable Ethiopian game of football had occurred just before the invasion. In 1935, a visiting French naval team played against a select team of the best players in Addis Ababa. Tessema — who had taken up the sport with enthusiasm himself — was one of those selected for a squad that played in numerous practice games as preparation, employing as referee a man Tessema later described as "a huge and fat Negro American who found it difficult to conduct on foot and therefore had to be on horse-back for the purpose."

That select team was formed from all of Addis Ababa's communities, indigenous and immigrant, but an all-Ethiopian team — the St George Team — was created in December 1935, playing against Greek and Armenian teams in the city. Football seemed set to grow in Ethiopia after a decade of gestation. But within six months, the Italian invasion had succeeded and Ethiopia was merged with Italian Somaliland and Italian Eritrea to form Italian East Africa. Ethiopian football, along with the rest of its culture and society, was subjected to a massive assault.

The Italian occupiers played football, but initially only among themselves: all the existing Ethiopian teams were disbanded. As Tessema later put it in a book celebrating the history of football in Ethiopia, "eager Ethiopian fans had to satisfy their desires and love for the game by watching the Italians play from hideouts around fields."

The Italian occupation was based on racial segregation in cultural realms such as football. In 1937, in the aftermath of the assassination attempt on Graziani, a separate "Sports Office for the Indigenous" was set up by the Italian Directorate for Political Affairs. The political nature of it soon became obvious, Tessema recalled, even as Ethiopians were at least allowed to play

football again: "So it was made that we conduct our games in our place, everything separate, separate fields for football, separate spectators, even separate seats for bicyclists."

Tessema's St George team was Italianised and renamed Littorio Wube Sefer. Tessema, 16 at the time, was assigned to work in the Directorate's Sports Office, translating football rules and regulations. Despite his age, Tessema remembered that "I did not find it difficult to understand that the Italian policy was morally bankrupt." The Office's aim was clearly not to further sporting ethics, but to separate and divide communities.

On the football pitch, this meant that when two junior Ethiopian teams met for the first time on a previously "whites-only" field, the Italian officials and spectators goaded the players into fighting each other. "Encouraged by a wild mob, we became gladiators in a Roman arena and I tell you it turned out to be one spectacular fight," Tessema recalled. "So we had a mighty battle in the field, the Italians had a roaring time and we went home without having played the game, licking our wounds."

In his teenage years as a sport administrator and footballer playing under Italian rule, Tessema developed a commitment to equality on and off the pitch, a belief in fairness and a steadfast determination to face down the sort of devastating manipulation of the game he loved that he experienced until the Italian occupation ended in 1941.

Following the end of the occupation, Tessema rapidly became an extraordinarily prominent figure as a player, coach, referee and administrator in Ethiopian sports, especially football. He had a gift for organisation, an ability to manoeuvre politically, and no little talent in playing and managing that earned him the respect and admiration of his peers, even at a young age.

Tessema played a critical role in helping to found Ethiopia's first national sports office in 1943, leading to the formation of what became the Ethiopian Football Federation that year. Tessema was its first Secretary General, translating its statutes into the Amharic language himself. His team, St George, was one of four teams to compete for the first Ethiopian Football Championship, held in 1943 with ex-pat Greek, Italian and British teams. On 5 December 1947, Tessema captained the first Ethiopian team to play an international (the 1935 game against the French naval mission notwithstanding), as neighbouring Dijbouti were dispatched 5-0 in the presence of the Ethiopian emperor.

Tessema played in a total of 15 games for his country between 1948 and 1954, but his more significant impact would come as a coach and as an administrator. The year before Tessema retired as a player, Ethiopia officially joined the international stage, as its Federation joined Fifa, the fourth African nation to do so (after Egypt, Sudan and South Africa).

In 1957, the Confederation of African Football (CAF) was formed to represent Africa as a continental block within Fifa, with Tessema representing Ethiopia at the founding meeting. Egypt, the richest federation, led the way, with CAF's headquarters in Cairo and the Egyptian General Abdelaziz Salem chosen as its

first president. Along with Egypt and Ethiopia, South Africa and Sudan joined the fledgling organisation. Tessema was a significant figure behind the scenes: he helped draft CAF's statutes and was elected to its executive committee.

The same year, the Africa Cup of Nations was inaugurated. Ethiopia was one of three nations to take part, losing in the final to Egypt. Five years later, Tessema coached Ethiopia himself and took them one step further, winning the competition on home soil — still the country's only major title. By then, Tessema was well-known for his opposition to the apartheid policies of South Africa. Without Tessema's insistence, all four founding nations may have been at the inaugural Africa Cup of Nations in 1957: the Ethiopian had successfully pushed for South Africa's exclusion as its federation, the Football Association of South Africa (FASA) insisted on sending either an all-white or an all-black team to the competition — but under no circumstances, a mixed team. In 1958, CAF expelled South Africa. It was Tessema, his fellow CAF delegate Abdel Halim Mohammed commented, whose "firm stand" ensured CAF was the first international organisation to isolate South Africa for its apartheid politics in sports.

CAF, led by Tessema, demanded that Fifa similarly recognise that the participation in international competition of a federation governing a racially segregated sport in its own borders was not only morally wrong, but against Fifa's own statutes. CAF demanded South Africa be suspended from the world's governing body until it integrated its national team. Fifa did so in 1961, but under the new leadership of Sir Stanley Rous — elected as Fifa president the same year — South Africa's suspension was lifted in 1963 after a visit to the country by Rous, against the fierce opposition of CAF and Tessema.

Rous was reported by the *Johannesburg Star* as saying that "All we are interested in is to see the controlling body of soccer in this country furthering the cause of football to the best of its ability." Fifa saw the issue of South Africa's racist politics, including the impact it had on sport, as none of its business. Its federation, according to Rous, was only following orders. Indeed, Rous asserted that taking action against the racial segregation of football in South Africa was itself bringing politics into sport. "Beneath a veneer of apolitical universalism," David Goldblatt wrote in *The Ball is Round*, "lurked an unreflective racism so deep that collaboration with apartheid was deemed a firmer moral and practice basis for the development of football than resistance to it."

Rous, though, could not control a Fifa Congress that was now increasingly populated by newly independent African and Asian nations. The Congress operated on a one member, one vote policy and by 1965, CAF had 26 members, up from four five years earlier. Led by Tessema, they were determined their voice should be heard. African nations, according to John Sugden and Alan Tomlinson in *FIFA and the Contest for World Football*, viewed the platform of world football as a key way to establish international recognition of their independence: "In the absence of economic and military might, newly independent African nations discovered in football a medium through which to register their presence in the international arena both on and off the playing field."

The African demand to be heard was impossible for Fifa to avoid in the run-up to the 1966 World Cup, to be hosted by Rous's homeland, England. The 1964 Fifa Congress was held in Tokyo in conjunction with the Olympic Games, making it far easier for delegates from poor African sporting bodies to attend. With broad support from Africa, Asia, South America and the Soviet bloc, and led by Tessema — now a Vice-President of CAF — the Fifa Congress voted to suspend South Africa once again, to Rous's considerable chagrin. CAF threatened to walk out of the next Congress if Rous attempted to lift the suspension once more.

Sporting injustice was also on the agenda in Tokyo. As the 1966 World Cup approached, CAF now had nearly 30 member nations — but only half a spot at the World Cup to chase, shared with all of Asia, the winner of each region's continental competition competing for the lone qualifying berth. Rous and Fifa were not disposed to shift the distribution of qualification spots, fearing greater participation from Africa would weaken the standard of the competition. Brian Glanville summed up the view of the European establishment, commenting that, "It is quite true that football in countries such as the USA and Ethiopia would be encouraged by World Cup participation, but only at the expense of cheapening the World Cup, a pretty heavy price to pay when this tournament is, or should be, the very zenith of the international game."

As well as participation in the World Cup, Rous was blunt about his belief developing nations did not deserve an equal standing in the Fifa Congress:

"Many people are convinced that it is unrealistic, for example, that a country like England, where the game started and was first organised, or that experienced countries like Italy and France, who have been pillars of Fifa and influential in its problems and in world football affairs for so many years, should have no more than equal voting rights with any of the newly created countries of Africa and Asia."

Tessema was curt in his response to this patronising attitude. "Although we acknowledge the role played by certain continents in the creation of Fifa, its development and their moral, material and financial contributions, we estimate that democratic rule dictates that all rights and duties that form an international organisation should be the same for all. This is why in the framework of legitimacy, and by following a process consistent with the interests of world football and its unity, a progressive equilibrium of the representation in the heart of Fifa and its competition is required."

As well as successfully defending the one nation, one vote policy at the Congress, Tessema led the charge to expand the World Cup beyond the Eurocentric horizons of Rous, engaging in lengthy correspondence with him to push Africa's case for a direct qualification spot to encourage the development of the game.

With Fifa intransigent, Africa boycotted the 1966 World Cup. Fifa reacted by fining the threadbare African associations thousands of francs each, but by the 1966 Fifa Congress, CAF had clearly won the war and was awarded a full place at the 1970 World Cup. Even that concession only came after CAF

had threatened to withdraw from the Congress, when a leaked memo showed Rous was supporting a proposed breakaway from CAF by a southern African federation including South Africa and Rhodesia.

Tessema's role in propelling African football's interests on the world stage soon saw him take on further responsibility, joining Fifa's Executive Committee in 1966, elected as secretary general of the Ethiopian Olympic Committee in 1967 and as president of CAF in 1972. As well as speaking Amharic, Tessema was fluent in English, French and Italian, a huge advantage in the hallways of international sports administration, navigating the complicated politics of Africa's Anglophone and Francophone blocks with consummate skill.

In the 1970s, Tessema was at the peak of his power. The struggles of the 1960s over apartheid in South Africa and African representation at the World Cup had shown the drain of fighting what CAF officials saw as a reactionary, Eurocentric Fifa leadership on issue after issue. What was needed, Tessema knew, was a shift in the axis of power inside the Fifa Executive. Rous was continuing to enrage CAF with his ongoing support for South Africa and Rhodesia in the late 1960s — CAF had expelled the latter in 1965 for its politics of racial discrimination in sport, but it wasn't until 1970 that Rhodesia was suspended from Fifa.

It was clear to Tessema that for CAF to continue to further its aims — increasing its number of places at the World Cup, growing its share of Fifa's revenue in development funding and opposing racial discrimination in sport — Rous would need to be replaced as president of Fifa.

As the 1974 Fifa Congress approached, Rous was challenged by João Havelange, the president of the Brazilian federation, who aimed to ride on the wave of discontent directed at the Englishman and promised to realign world football to the southern hemisphere: he visited 86 countries in his campaign, concentrating on African and Asian votes with promises to exclude apartheid South Africa from Fifa forever and to increase the number of World Cup places, allowing more berths for every confederation. Rous's campaign was distinctly — perhaps even proudly — amateur by contrast. He offered nothing new of benefit to CAF members.

Havelange was, therefore, the obvious choice for Tessema to throw his influence behind. Tessema used this leverage to force Havelange to withdraw Brazil from a 1973 sports festival in South Africa aimed at giving the apartheid regime international credibility. As Rous himself wrote, "The Brazilians withdrew, I am told on good authority, because Tessema, the president of the African confederation, threatened that Mr Havelange would lose the support of the African associations in his fight against me for the presidency of Fifa."

In his book *Africa, Football and Fifa*, Paul Darby argues that by supporting Havelange, Tessema and CAF seized an opportunity to reshape the poles of power in world football: "The fact that Tessema was in a position to threaten the withdrawal of African support for Havelange's presidential challenge illustrates that CAF was not only gaining

confidence to assert itself within world football politics but was also beginning to recognise the potential that its voting powers offered the African continent. Indeed, it is clear from African accounts of the 1974 Fifa Congress … that the African nations did not see themselves merely as pawns in a power struggle for the control of Fifa. Instead, they saw Havelange as the means through which to achieve a realignment of the distribution of power and privilege within world football which would more adequately reflect their growing stature."

With Havelange in office, having defeated Rous in the 1974 Fifa presidential election by 68 votes to 52, Africa did reap obvious benefits and many of the goals of the 1960s were reached in the late 1970s without the need for the boycotts and fierce infighting within the halls of Fifa that had defined CAF's relationship with the governing body previously. Symbolically, the shift was seen with Havelange's inaugural Fifa executive committee meeting held in Africa for the first time, in Dakar, Senegal.

The two big issues of the 1960s were soon resolved positively from CAF's perspective. At the 1974 Fifa Congress in Frankfurt, Tessema put forward a motion that was passed requiring the automatic expulsion from Fifa of any country that practiced "ethnic, racial and/or religious discrimination in its territory," thus ending — to the chagrin of Rous — the ambiguity that surrounded South Africa's suspended membership. Ahead of the Congress in Montreal that year, Tessema wrote that he hoped the Fifa delegates would "have the courage to uphold the Fifa regulations which were not aimed at either white or black people in South Africa, but only against racial discrimination." South Africa were expelled from Fifa by a vote of 78 for to nine against.

Progress was also made in terms of CAF's goals on the field. In 1978, without the need for a vicious fight or a boycott, Africa's World Cup berths were doubled to two as the World Cup expanded to 24 nations for the 1982 competition in Spain. By the 1980s, the flipside of Havelange's regime had also begun to become apparent: Fifa's embrace of commercialism had begun to shift its priorities towards maximizing income at the expense of sporting integrity, while a belly-full of corruption bubbled barely below the surface. What Tessema, who by all accounts was himself unimpeachable, made of this is unclear. Did he ever regret his support for Havelange, despite the progress his regime had brought in fighting apartheid and increasing Africa's number of World Cup berths? Or for the successor he supported at CAF, Issa Hayatou, still in charge of the confederation today?

Tessema certainly had serious concerns about the direction of African football. He had long been sceptical about what professionalism might mean for the integrity of sporting competition; as a supporter of amateur football in the Olympics (he was made a member of the International Olympic Committee in 1971), he held closer beliefs in this area to the traditionalist Sir Stanley Rous than to the rapacious commercialism that was coming to define Havelange's Fifa.

Not long before his death from cancer at the age of 65 in 1987, Tessema issued a warning as he saw the flood of young African players leaving the continent for Europe, many in futile quests to make their fortune, and the impact that had on the development of the sport in Africa itself. "African football must make a choice!" he said. "Either we keep our players in Africa with the will power of reaching one day the top of the international competitions and restore to African people a dignity that they long for; or we let our best elements leave their countries, thus remaining the eternal suppliers of raw material to the premium countries, and renounce, in this way, to any ambition. When the rich countries take away from us, also by naturalisation, our best elements, we should not expect any chivalrous behaviour on their part to help African football."

Tessema, a man whose career had been defined by his fight for fairness on and off the field, was all too aware that his approach was the exception and not the rule in world football. **Ⓑ**

Bamako Twilight

Away from the war, football goes on in the Malian capital

By Stuart Roy Clarke

Late last year, as the conflict in Mali worsened, the photographer Stuart Roy Clarke travelled to the capital, Bamako. There he found a football culture undiminished by the slide towards civil war.

Badala is on the bend of the river in Bamako. The usual scene: people washing their clothes, washing themselves, collecting water to irrigate their crops. Along this riverbank are beauty and scruffiness, the natural and the artificial, the water-carried and the human-discarded. There, here, where I am fortunate, there are two goals, with crossbars, bound together by twine.

At 5pm every night — with no abandonment or postponement conceivable as the weather is always much the same: hot or hotter or really hot or hot with thunderclaps as God says, "That's quite enough heat," — the young men of the area filter out from alleys and workplaces on mopeds, scooters, bikes and on foot to greet each other and then argue the team selection and the toss. A man, an elder nowadays, in a turquoise cape, wags his finger and utters lavish much-loved nonsense, mostly to the smaller boys who actually try to listen to him. Another man, with a club foot, who casts himself out of team selection,

bangs the ground with a spare goalpost. Through the haze lies the other bank of the River Niger (the third longest in Africa), a tallish building (the tallest in West Africa) and the first of several bridges that seems always laden. Iman Mohammed, my hotel's faithful gardener, will miss the game. Because of the conflict, he is having to work overtime as a security guard. He is unhappy at this, only, for he never misses a match.

The stage is set. The daily washing removed. The pitch is 50m of bumps, big humps, hollows and pools of River Niger overspill flanked on the near side by prickly bushes and a few spectators. No dogs. One team are made to go bare-chested and one player still has his vest wrapped over his head when another nutmegs him. The game is underway and it's a passing game... with some dribbling, then an uncalled for bicycle-kick, then a clutch of players jumping for... a shoe — the ball is elsewhere.

The powerful Skins team are 2-0 up in barely a blink of an eye. Arguments-cum-discussions abound. The smallest boy — as usual — is sent to retrieve the ball from a pond. He is lectured about keeping his head up. And to get on with it, by a ring of Skins eager to get a third goal. A family arrives and Papa, on learning that the team his end are 2-0 down, urges his wife and toddlers "to go look at the river." He rolls up his sleeves and starts reorganising his team.

The second smallest boy, perhaps fearing that go-get-the-ball-out-of-the-water service will soon be upon him, commits a series of fantastically badly-timed tackles sending the stars and giants of the game crashing, looking up at him. Even his own captain. Had there been a referee, he would have walked.

Another incident — a high-speed slip on donkey dung sends the player with the fanciest footwork into a murky pool. His luminous vest is not so eye-catching now. The fightback, however, is on. The scores are level. Another small boy, in goal, saves a thunderous shot in his midriff and with tears in his eyes completes a second reflex save. But not a third. Odd T-shirts abound and when the crumpled boy eventually stands up his reveals the slogan, "Tell Santa not to speak to my teacher."

A player called 'One Love' sets off on a dazzling run, sidestepping and skipping over all challenges, donkey dung, pieces of hose, plastic bottles, fishing nets and lost shoes to pass twice and score: 3-3. High fives. The toothless witchdoctor in the turquoise cape is beside himself, storming onto the pitch finger-pointing. There is so much laughter all around about everything, he won't be heard.

Now the ball is in the bushes and five players, ignoring the scratches appeared on their legs, hack it out mercilessly. One turns, arguing for a throw-in. It's taken quickly, leaving behind the four fighting the bush. It becomes an exquisite move — the throw to a foot, a chip, a passing header and a cannonball of a volley with complete follow-through.

The light is fading, mouths and eyes are smiling and, somewhere, mothers are silently willing their boys home not too far past the curfew.

144

"When art is commercialised, its creative content becomes driven by monetary success, stifling innovation and instigating cyclical ideas that stunt the development of culture, producing docile consumers of repetitive art. Sport can never be reduced to this state."

In Praise of Football

For all the commercialisation and scandal, football remains the purest and most demotic of cultural modes

By Alex Keble

Football has received significant bruising over the past twelve months: racial abuse cases, the re-emergence of match-fixing scandals in Italy, Turkey and elsewhere and increased concern over foul play, underhand tactics and abusive competitors have given outsiders an ugly impression of the sport. This image was only exacerbated by London 2012, as the state of modern football was held up against the 'Olympic spirit', highlighting, for some, that football is the vulgar relative of the idyllic summer games. But if we look beneath the problems, we can posit that football is not the barbarous culture of animosity it is sometimes made out to be.

At first glance, increasing corporate ownership and monetary obsession and the decreasing moral values of the sport look like legitimate reasons for abandoning the Premier League. I do not agree. Watching live football is, I believe, fundamentally a unifying experience with infinite scope for social change and artistic beauty. Being given the opportunity to witness this first hand is a privilege that should not be taken lightly.

The moral core of the sport is not in decline, despite increased media focus on prejudice; football is arguably still the most egalitarian of sports and one that continues to set a positive example for the rest of the world.

Prejudice saturates — dominates — every sector of human society; those critical of football's regressive attitudes reflect a perverse misunderstanding of the sport's representation of social reality. There is no evidence to suggest that the percentage of football fans that perpetuate racism is any higher than the percentage that perpetuate it in the general population. The reason figures appear higher than other major sports is that no other sport is as classless, universal and representative of society as a whole. Tennis, for example, does not need to confront racist chanting; the nature of the sport means its prejudices are played out more subtly than in crude chants. Football does not have a racism problem, society does; the problems within the sport are a reflection of deeper societal issues.

Football is not prejudiced. A minority of its supporters are, a minority of people are. The persistent condemnation of their actions by the educated governors of the sport is likely to reform perverted world-views and align supporters with the egalitarian principles that the sport is built on. It should be celebrated that acts of prejudice are called out so fiercely by competitors, officials and fans within the game. Football is not declining morally — it is growing. It is still the sport we look to to instigate social change and unite communities.

The post-structuralist Terry Eagleton once remarked that football is "several light years ahead" of socialism, providing an "experience of solidarity[...] to the point of collective delirium". Football offers the tantalising possibility that it could have been you that made the grade. And it could have. In a world in which the disparity between rich and poor is increasing, football remains the biggest industry in which the truly impoverished individual is given the platform to display imagination and artistry, with the chance of being rewarded with a wealth and status ordinarily reserved for the bourgeoisie (to use 'bourgeois' in its strictest Marxist sense).

With the measly possessions of a Coke can and two jumpers, a group of individuals is instantly transformed into a united cooperative, capable of remarkable displays of selfless teamwork and individual skill. Children from poor backgrounds demonstrate a level of intelligence and technical precision they will rarely be given the opportunity to show outside the football pitch; an opportunity to validate their self-worth. A street child begging in an African village can, through an ingenious weaving of condoms into a bouncing sphere – a creation built by street children across East Africa, find a sense of purpose in one of the few art forms available to them to express their creativity, passion and human will.

The sport is becoming increasingly corporate; ruled by sickening quantities of money, football increasingly

resembles the ultimate capitalist venture. Clubs become businesses; fans become customers; athletes become commodities. Elite sporting occasions are glossed with phoney narratives by corporate TV executives. Moments of stunning athleticism are repackaged as Hollywoodesque plastic perfection and used to sell newspapers.

The key difference between football and other art forms is that it can never be fully commercialised. The Marxist academic Theodor Adorno described the modern culture industry, in particular Hollywood and pop music, as "a machine rotating on the spot". When art is commercialised, its creative content becomes driven by monetary success, stifling innovation and instigating cyclical ideas that stunt the development of culture, producing docile consumers of repetitive art. Sport can never be reduced to this state. Just as the child escapes daily concerns on a football pitch, so too do the athlete, and the spectator, escape the corporate net; the white lines of a football pitch symbolise the absolute severance of monetary obsession and artistic endeavour. Granted, players may play for win bonuses, for better contracts, for offers from richer clubs — but the art form itself, the creativity on display, the performance that we come to watch, is not *defined* by these factors. Money may drive individual player interest but it does not direct the discipline itself, as, for example, the pop music industry drives the style of music created. Money can dominate the politics of the sport, but once on the field, the game is indistinguishable, in principle, from children playing on the street. Corporate dominance is not a valid reason to stop watching such talented athletes.

In our postmodern world, supposedly devoid of objective meaning, sport offers something concrete amid the chaos of daily life. Western industrialised society has come to represent a bitter environment of individual greed, the ultimate climate of wealth disparity, a place of alienation — in short, the antithesis of a 'big society'. Georg Simmel's belief that the metropolis generates indifference, apathy and an alienating monetary obsession, that "one never feels as lonely and as deserted as in the metropolitan crush of persons", rings as true today (for some of us) as it did in the early 1900s[1]. But for 90 minutes people from contradictory backgrounds become a collective force sharing in the universal language of football. 22 people kicking a ball on a patch of grass becomes the primary focus and concern of thousands of people united in a shared moment of solidarity. It is a brief glimpse of utopia.

And what spectacle is it that defies the regular organisation of society? It is a performance by 22 immaculate athletes. If corporate ownership is ruining competition, at least the increased monetary concern has dramatically advanced investment in technical ability. Within seemingly narrow parameters, individual athletes display remarkable moments of innovation and technical assurance. The scope for creativity — utilising a ball with a 22cm diameter on a pitch roughly 110m long and 70m across with 21 other autonomous players providing countless other variables — could be seen as equivalent to the scope for an artist painting on a canvas.

This theory has been proposed by the writer David Foster Wallace, whose theories on tennis are equally valid to football: "match play is not a fractal matter of reducing chaos to pattern, but of expansion[...] each well-shot ball admitting of n possible responses, $2n$ possible responses to those responses, and on into a Cantorian continuum of infinities of possible moves." The number of variables, folding on top of one another, makes each moment in sport uniquely creative. Athletes are artists, blending a unique mix of human intelligence, integrity, skill, courage, unity and creativity. It is a spectacle that celebrates an extraordinary species capable, somehow, of a subtle blend of ferocity and beauty. In the words of Foster Wallace, "Beauty is not the goal of competitive sports but high-level sports are a prime venue for the expression of human beauty. The relation is roughly that of courage to war."

The highest adulation is given to those world-class athletes who combine the sublime with the tactical; a complex combination of highly refined technical artistry and semi-illogical moments of creativity. This is the beauty that Foster Wallace speaks of. There is logic behind the collective satisfaction in a well-timed pass or ingenious finish; they require a high geometric intelligence and instinctive vision comparable to that of the painter or the poet.

There are few moments in life that compare, emotionally and spiritually, to the feeling of witnessing a goal. When else have you jumped up and down

---

[1] *For further reading, see Georg Simmel,* The Metropolis and Mental Life, *1903*

in life, through nothing else but pure pleasure? The purity of the emotional impulse of a goal is beyond the descriptive capabilities of language. It is abstract and irrational and it is because of this, not in spite of this, that the feeling of ecstatic joy, euphoric completeness, is rarely replicated in any element of human life. It is a momentary glimpse of salvation, a fleeting emotion of euphoria that brushes with a feeling of oneness. In this way, more than any other, can football be considered a religious experience. Crucially, this experience is not the worshipping of a super-human deity, but the celebration of our own species' creative potential.

Corporations may be masochistically driving the sport towards obliteration but, for now, they cannot touch the complex and enigmatic art displayed on one small patch of grass. It is an art form, an experience, that is rarely replicated in any other aspect of. The image created in the media, particularly in light of the Olympic Games and the positivity that surrounded it, is not necessarily a fair reflection of our game. Ⓑ

Financial Fair Play?

How Champions League revenues can devastate competition in Europe's smaller leagues

By Steve Menary

On 3 July 2012, less than two months after Chelsea dramatically clinched the Champions League title in Munich, Europe's richest club competition was underway again. Spain had won Euro 2012 only two days earlier but there are no players from the European Championship at the Stade Jos Nosbaum in southern Luxembourg or involved in either of the two other ties played on the same day, in Belfast and Malta.

The first qualifying round is a world away from the glitz and glory of Munich. A crowd of just over 1000 sit in the Luxembourg sun to watch a one-sided thrashing. F91 Dudelange's opponents Tre Penne of San Marino look what they are: amateurs. No club in Luxembourg has a squad of entirely professional players, but F91 — the number relates to the year of the club's formation from a merger of three old Dudelange outfits — have more full-timers than most. In the two decades since Dudelange were created, the club has dominated the game in the Grand Duchy and won the double again last season.

Investment from the club's owner, the financier Flavio Becca, is one reason for this dominance. The other is Uefa prize money. Dudelange have won the Nationaldivisioun title in 10 of the last 13 seasons and are regular European competitors. In 2005-06, the club became the first Luxembourg side to win a European Cup tie in 42 years by beating NK Zrinjski of Bosnia & Herzegovina 4-1 on aggregate. In 2012-13, Dudelange went even further.

After hammering Tre Penne 11-0 on aggregate, Dudelange faced a Red Bull Salzburg side then linked with a move for the German legend Michael Ballack. Awash with money, Austria's most dominant side completely misjudged F91. The tie finished 4-4 with Dudelange going through on away goals. Dudelange lost 5-1 against Slovenia's Maribor in the third round but still banked €620,000 from Uefa; their usual turnover is around €1.2 million a year.

Two decades ago, when Europe's governing body began to transform the European Cup into the Champions League, clubs like Dudelange were not on the agenda. The G14 group of major clubs were pressuring Uefa for a greater share of the income and cared little or nothing for small-fry like Dudelange. The G14's constant threat to Uefa was a breakaway pan-European league. That pressure has certainly worked but it has had unforeseen consequences.

In the 2011-12 season, Uefa paid out €754.1 million to participating clubs. Chelsea's Munich victory earned

Abramovich's play-thing €59.9m from Uefa to add to £54.4m from the Premier League in broadcasting payments for 2011-12. This helped produce a record annual turnover of £255.7m. So winning the Champions League was worth 19% of Chelsea's annual revenue. That ratio will be more like half at Flavio Becca's bauble in the 2012-13 season. "Uefa prize money can go a long way here," agrees Paul Philipp, head of the Fédération Luxembourgeoise de Football (FLF), choosing his words carefully, wary of openly criticising his country's dominant side.

In Luxembourg and many other places further down European football's food chain, scraps from the Champions League banquet can have a huge effect: the further away from the real prize, the more disproportionate the impact.

Last season Apoel qualified for the Champions League for the second time in three seasons. After reaching the group stages in 2009-10, Apoel received €10 million from Uefa giving the club a playing budget of €9 million in 2011-12. This helped Apoel to become the first Cypriot club to reach the quarter-final, which generated Uefa prize money of €18.1 million.

Money obviously does not guarantee success in west London, Luxembourg or Nicosia and Apoel surrendered their title to AEL Limassol and were consigned to this season's Europa League. But with €18.1 million banked, the club has substantial foundations to fund further success in the future.

Reaching the group stage is just as rare for Hungarian clubs with only two sides having done so. When Ferencváros qualified in 1995-96, the rewards on offer were vastly different to those earned 14 years later by Debrecen. In 2001, the Hungarian businessman Gábor Szima secured majority control of Debrecen. Four years later his club won their first Hungarian title and, in 2009-10, joined Apoel in the group stages. Debrecen departed pointless but with €9 million from Uefa.

That is a substantial sum in Hungary's fragile sporting economy. According to a survey conducted by the journalist Mihály Muszbek, in 2011 Debrecen had an income of 975 million forints (€3.4 million). To put the value of that Uefa money into perspective, a new TV broadcasting agreement is expected to give each club in Hungary's OTP Bank Liga around €620,000 a year.

Club owners can spend this windfall on whatever they like. Debrecen have taken six out of the last eight Champions League places available to Hungary but Szima, who owns hotels and a brand of mineral water and regularly plays five-a-side, saw a wider picture. The Uefa money built an academy — but if owners want to pocket the money or to use it ensure no other domestic club can compete in terms of wages that is up to them.

What the owners of the Israeli champions Hapoel Ironi Kiryat Shmona spend their 2012-13 windfall on will be telling. Kiryat Shmona's budget is around 25 million shekels (€4.9 million), reputedly the highest ever for an Israeli club. After overcoming MŠK Žilina of Slovakia in the first round, Kiryat Shmona cruised past the Azeri champions Neftçi PFK 6-2 then lost in the play-off round against BATE Borisov, who have taken every Belarusian slot in the Champions League since 2007-08.

Kiryat Shmona will get €2.1 million and a place in the Europa League. That is less lucrative than the Champions League but the rewards are still substantial for a poor club from near the Lebanese border whose ticket prices are in the region of €3.

When Michel Platini was elected as president of Uefa in 2007, he was backed by many smaller associations, whom he helped by tinkering with the qualification rules to make it easier for them to get into the group stages. In 2008-09 Anorthosis became the first Cypriot side to reach the last 32. The same season BATE became the first Belarusian side to do so, but plenty of Uefa's 53 members are – despite Platini's tweaking – yet to produce a side capable of doing the same. For many national associations, the prospect of a team reaching the group stage is far from enticing.

Clubs from Montenegro only entered the Champions League in 2007-08. Last season, FK Budućnost of Podgorica became the fifth Montenegrin champion in a row to fail to qualify for the group stages. Budućnost have a budget of €1.5 million and a full-time squad; according to their general secretary, Nikola Prentić, the €340,000 'compensation' from Uefa for losing after one round is not huge. But if a Montenegrin club ever reached the group stages, the impact would be immense. "It would be a football revolution in Montenegro," said Prentić.

In small, mainly part-time leagues any trailblazers reaching the group stages

leave a trail of domestic wreckage. "Should a team from Iceland qualify, we would without a shred of doubt see total monopolisation of the domestic league by that team," said Ómar Smárason of the Icelandic federation (KSI).

The Icelandic champions KR got a bye to the second round this season. The only return on the pitch was Emil Atlason's 74th minute strike at home to Finnish champions HJK Helsinki, who won 9-1 on aggregate. Off the pitch, the return was better. KR also pocketed €340,000 for playing a single tie.

Icelandic sides have played in Europe for decades. Uefa money is vital in a country in which turnover at top-flight clubs ranges between €1.25 million and €2.5 million a year. "Qualifying for Europe makes a huge impact," Smárason said. "A club playing in Europe year after year, even just in the qualifying rounds like most of our clubs do, they are in a very strong position."

In the Faroe Islands, annual revenue at clubs in the Effodeildin is about €270,000. A big side turns over around €540,000. This season, B36 from Tórshavn played the Northern Irish side Linfield in the first round. No one found the net in either leg; Linfield won on penalties and B36 left with €340,000.

"There is very little money from gates or sponsors. There is some from private sponsors but Uefa money is major for them," said Brian Kerr, the Irishman who managed the Faroes national team from 2009 to 2011. Kerr also highlights another vital role that Uefa club competitions play, one that the KSI confirms holds true in Iceland. The Faroe Islands Football

Association runs an Under-21 team but can only afford to play competitive matches. With clubs and agents unwilling to fly to Tórshavn, European games offer a chance to get promising players seen, such as Jóan Símun Edmundsson, who joined Newcastle in 2010 from the Toftir side B68.

At the very tip of this inverted pyramid are clubs in San Marino and Andorra, who like the Montenegrins, were allowed a first sniff of the Champions League honey pot in 2007-08. Two years later a restructuring introduced an extra qualifying round. This gave the likes of Linfield a chance to win not just the odd game but a tie. The extra qualifying round means that clubs winning a first-round tie receive another €140,000 for progressing. After beating B36, Linfield went down 3-0 to Limassol. Having failed to score in four Champions League ties, Linfield earned €480,000, a significant sum in Northern Irish football.

In 2010, the Maltese champions Birkirkara travelled to Andorra to play Santa Coloma in the first round but the pitch was unplayable. Birkirkara were awarded a 3-0 walkover and subsequently won 7-3 on aggregate. Santa Coloma were fined €10,000 and banned from Europe for two years but still had their prize money — for playing one game.

This season, Tre Penne of San Marino fielded a side including a number of forty-somethings against Dudelange. After a 7-0 humbling in the first leg, Tre Penne lost 4-0 in San Marino but earned €340,000 for doing little more in sporting terms than turning up. According to Uefa's own research, the average club revenue in San Marino is €86,000 per

year. So for a Sammarinese club, just qualifying for the Champions League can quadruple their annual revenue.

What Uefa is doing says something about the European body's priorities. Clubs that can prove to Uefa and the Club Financial Control Body that their income and expenses are below €5 million in the two years before qualification are 'potentially' exempt from the break-even clause in the Financial Fair Play (FFP) regime. That could remove a whole swathe of clubs from across Europe.

"The break-even rule objectives are particularly addressed at the impact of individual clubs' behaviour on club football as a whole and to rebalance the spending and investing of larger clubs, which has been defined in the 2012 regulations as €5m," Uefa explains. "In practice a club with total relevant expenses of less than €5m a year is unlikely to have much of an influence on the sustainability of club football as a whole."

With FFP, Uefa is trying to combat big-spending patrons and make the game more sustainable; an admirable notion and one that surely still applies in places like Luxembourg.

Interestingly, when the FLF proposed a rule ensuring clubs in Luxembourg have a minimum number of players with football licences issued in the Grand Duchy, Dudelange protested. Becca's side insisted the rule was discrimination against foreign players, the best of whom were cementing Dudelange's domination. The FLF went ahead anyway and a level of local opprobrium remains focused on Dudelange, a club with little tradition but lots of money.

Dudelange and any other side qualifying for the Champions League still need a Uefa licence and are monitored in a number of areas. If any trigger an alert — if, for instance, the ratio of wages to revenue passes 70%, then more information is requested from the club, who are trusted to provide a honest answer. Whether clubs like Chelsea and Manchester City comply with FFP or not will be examined by hordes of international media and fans. Who will be verifying Dudelange's answers, or those from Tre Penne?

Crucially, to secure a licence, clubs must demonstrate "relevant income and relevant expenses". For regular European participants such as Dudelange that is not a problem: Uefa prize money from the Champions League or the smaller monies derived from the Europa League qualify as relevant income.

Those clubs wanting to keep up a domestic challenge are left scrabbling to compete against a new local hegemony funded to a significant extent by Uefa's own generosity and then left unregulated.

What happens if these dominant clubs in smaller countries then fall off the Uefa gravy train? If clubs fail at a domestic level because this money has been spirited away or mismanaged? If they no longer fall under Uefa scrutiny, are they simply forgotten? How does that meet the objective of sustainable club football that the Uefa president Michel Platini is using as a platform for his long-expected bid for the Fifa presidency? What is sustainable about creating a two-stream Europe with financially bloated smaller clubs simply allowed to pass quietly under the most significant part of the FFP radar?

We're celebrating our 2nd birthday!

Issue One
June 2011

Issue Two
September 2011

Issue Three
December 2011

Issue Four
March 2012

Issue Five
June 2012

Issue Six
September 2012

Issue Seven
December 2012

Issue Eight
March 2013

First and Second Year Collections are available at
www.theblizzard.co.uk

156

Fiction

"From my hands and knees I could see them lining up like a firing squad. 'Why d'you want Hastie's to lose?' I gasped. 'Why are you doing all this?'"

The Limping God, part 3

His football career ended by injury, John Brodie's life is going nowhere until he is sucked into the world of crime

By David Ashton

The story so far. I, John Brodie, washed-out, weak-ankled, boozed-up, ex-Junior Footballer had been hired as guardian angel to a young talent, Billy Gourlay. This enigmatic boy was the great hope of Hastie's Works team in next Saturday's final. He was seen by me wrapped in the warm embrace of a bookie's wife in a blue Triumph Herald. Mamie Dunlop, the wife, had been beaten up by her husband Donny and this presented as an accident. Billy was scared out of his wits. I had been put on the case by an Irish gambler Frank Carlin who had just as quickly taken me off again. Mamie had recovered, was apparently seeking vengeance and had pointed me towards a premises owned by a friend of Donny's where all proof of his nefarious deeds were concealed in a certain filing cabinet. I was after Donny — he had insulted the memory of my dead father. I wanted to take him down.

The security to White's Garage had proved surprisingly feeble, the hasp of a rusty padlock springing easily and the old blunt chisel I had brought prising open the lock with such ease that I almost fell into the damned place.

The door jammed back shut to give some semblance of normality to any passing outside eye, I fumbled for the light switch and activated a single bare bulb high above. Luckily the windows were blacked out so nothing would give me away. So why was my heart pounding?

The afternoon conversation I had with Bob Adamson, once a centre-back in the same school team now a sergeant in the force for law and order, did not lessen the anxiety level.

Donny Dunlop had connections, said Bob. Hoodlums. Hard men. The polis knew he was into crime, robbery and violent assault for starters but proving it was another matter. He pursed his lips and shook his head — if I was thinking of poking into Donny's affairs, I'd better buy a Sherman tank. Or a suit of armour.

Here I was with neither. As I moved forwards I noticed that the Triumph Herald was still waiting for a panel beater — the neatness of the radiator dent now explained by Mamie as a cover up for a different kind of beating. In the world of working men someone who hit a woman was the lowest scum — old fashioned maybe but that was the deal. Of course Mamie could be lying and possibly Donny's eyes had filled with tears when he heard of my father's demise but for some reason I believed her at least on that one. The raw anger had not faded — the pain was deep — and for once it wasn't directed totally at myself.

Another small door led into a back room as I pushed it open and the light above spilled in enough to reveal an array of filing cabinets like standing like tombstones. As I hesitated a voice sounded from behind me.

"Take your pick, eh?' said Donny Dunlop.

The thought that I should have known better echoed in my mind as I turned to see the poison dwarf himself plus three goons. They must have concealed themselves in one of the other alcoves and now appeared in all their glory.

I still held the blunt chisel but prospects of transmutation into Excalibur disappeared when one of the goons lashed out with a long stick and jolted it from my hand. My knuckles crunched in the blow and as I lurched over with the pain, Donny grinned like a rat.

"Not so clever now, John — eh?" Then he waved a lordly hand at the three squat-faced bruisers to command, "All yours boys, any way ye like."

I avoided the first kick with a nimble sway of the hips but forgot to allow for the second punch, which took me deep in the guts and doubled me over to get a knee in the face that I part blocked but it still sent me sprawling onto my back. The men pinioned my hands and feet and Donny approached fitting on a neat pair of kid gloves.

"Led by your dick, my friend," he said.

"At least I have one to point the way."

For a moment Donny's eyes narrowed, then he grinned again.

"By the time we're done," he announced pleasantly enough, "you will not see the match tomorrow, no more smart comments, balls kicked to buggery and if you're lucky end up on a fish lorry for Stranraer. They can leave you in the sewer pipes."

He looked down. "Now which was the bad foot? Left I think." Donny sighted carefully. "By the way Mamie did tell one thing true. Your father belonged in the cludgie. I would have dumped on him and then pulled the plug."

Having got that off his chest he crunched down on the weak ankle with all his weight, grinding the high sharp heel of his boot into the fragile bone. The pain was excruciating and I let out a scream then somehow managed to wrench myself free to end up crouching like a dog against the metal cabinets. But there was no way out.

"There's nothing in them anyway," Donny laughed. "Just Geordie White's tax receipts."

From my hands and knees I could see them lining up like a firing squad. "Why d'you want Hastie's to lose?" I gasped. "Why are you doing all this?"

"None of your fuckin' business," came the response, then Donny worked his mouth till he got enough saliva to spit over me. "Now the fun begins," said he. "Now the fun really begins."

I scrabbled at my inside pocket and pulled out a small metal object, put it to my lips and blew. Donny initially flinched at the shrill blast then he and the goons chortled happily.

"What will that accomplish, John? Ye looking for a fucking sheepdog?" Donny asked.

"It's a referee's whistle," I gasped, agony shooting through me from the splintered bone. "I borrowed it. Usually signifies — start of hostilities."

A boot crashed open the outside door and three huge bodies stumbled inside like so many bad-tempered bears. Neilly Forsythe with his two brothers Shug and Jaffa. Neil was the brain of the family, the other two were bricklayers with hands the size of hods and granite knuckles. It may have been the spam fritter diet the family enjoyed but they made the goons look like pipe cleaners.

"Mamie was inviting," I said, a cold sweat pouring down my face. "But I was taught, in respect of the fair sex, always to take precautions. In case I got into trouble. So I brought some friends."

To tell truth, it wasn't much of a fight. They were minced. The Forsyth brothers almost absent-mindedly battered the goons like a fish supper. I managed to lever myself up in time to see Jaffa hit one so hard he lifted the man clean off the floor to the detriment of his jaw.

As the thugs huddled together in a broken heap, a white-faced Donny ran for the door and disappeared as if the hounds of hell were on his trail. We could have chased, hauled him back, lit matches under his immaculate fingernails, ripped the badge off his blazer and tortured the truth out of him, but why lower yourself to the level of the beast? See what tomorrow will bring.

I nodded solemn thanks to the other two giants, ignored the rabble on the floor and addressed myself to Neil.

"You better get to bed," I commanded. "You have a cup final on your plate. Hastie's need you at the back — you have a winger to kick in the air."

"Whit was it all about anyhows?" he asked.

Keep it simple. "He insulted my dad," I replied.

"That's no' decent,' said Neil. "If you canny keep decent — whit the hell's the prospect in life?"

Broomhill Park. Swirling wind, stinging rain. The lower pitch had a high fence to keep the ball on the park and an improvised stand had been set on the higher. A big crowd and Hastie's were getting pulverised by the enemy.

All parties on the scene, present. Donny with a new squad of goons on the opposite side of the pitch with Mamie huddling into him as if he were man of the moment. No sign of Geordie White, after what happened in his garage he would be keeping his head down. Frank Carlin further along on my side, camel-haired coat glistening with water, his hat drooping forlornly over the plump face as he watched Lithgows' nuggety little team run rings round their shipwrecked opponents.

Hastie played in Glasgow Rangers blue, the others in an orange that glowed in the sleety downpour like a twelfth of July parade — no religious divide then but so far the game resembled a massacre of the innocents.

Well into the second half and by some miracle, Hastie's were only two goals to the bad. Also down to 10 men as the centre-back had ricked a calf-muscle in a desperate lunge and Big Neilly had been drafted into that position. In fact it suited him fine, less ground to cover and he was playing a blinder, but the rest were chasing shadows. As the puddles formed on the pitch, they slid and skidded like seals at the circus.

Billy Gourlay was the worst player on the park — a phantom in midfield — avoiding the ball as if it had the pox. The Hastie's supporters screamed abuse at him, the side, the referee, the weather, the skittering seagulls that landed insolently onto the pitch, especially at the Lithgow's end which was untouched since they'd kicked off for the second half — but it made no difference. Their team was defeated, a look of shame on every man's face as he realised that they were beat. Slathered in mud, still chasing but beat. Humiliated. I know that feeling. To the bones.

Donny's teeth gleamed triumphantly across and I longed to be on that pitch running down the wing but what a bad joke. I had to take the bus to get here and my ankle was still in agony from last night's pounding. A heavy hand landed on my shoulder, followed by one on the other side. It was Jaffa and Shug their big faces solemn with gloom.

"This is fuckin' terrible," they announced in unison and then Jaffa continued solo. "Can ye no' do something John? Neil says you're dead clever. Like your dad. Neil says."

My attention switched away from the game and I had a sudden memory of a family Hogmanay when the neighbours came round and after my mother had jigged into *Frankie and Johnnie* and I followed with *Sixteen Tons*, the sentiments of which my father totally approved, he then launched into *The March of the Cameron Men*, a lugubrious ballad of highland warriors following a totally lost cause. He was tone deaf, no sense of rhythm but he sang it to the end. Every verse an affront to the ear. But he sang it to the end. No mercy.

A shout brought me back to see the ball, leaden with mud, hurtling in my direction as the Lithgow's defence disdainfully repelled one of Hastie's sporadic attacks. I instinctively stuck out a foot — the wrong one as it happened — to trap the ball and suffer agony at one and the same time. I bent over painfully to pick it up and when I straightened I was looking into Billy's eyes.

"Gie's the ball," he said.

"No," I replied. "You don't deserve it."

The silence that followed was probably seconds but seemed an eternity. I gathered up what pitiful strength I had available and leant in, wiping the dirty ball down the front of his strip — it was clean because he'd done bugger all and the mark was left all the way down his front.

There were a few shouts but the majority of the crowd had fallen quiet as if they realised something was happening.

Billy held my stare but only just. I made my play.

I don't exactly know what happened that night Billy but you've been running ever since and maybe you even think you're a wee bit in love. A bad combination. You betray yourself, you'll never forget it. You betray the game, that's even worse. She doesn't care for you Billy — you're just a performing monkey. She'll go which way the wind blows.

In the silence a shrill laugh sounded; Billy turned and I looked past to see Mamie slide her arms round Donny's neck and stick what seemed a considerable tongue down his throat. His quiff quivered and his face registered sublime satisfaction.

Billy grabbed the ball, threw to a teammate who promptly lost it and the game lurched into the morass once more. Lithgow's hit the bar and Big Neilly booted it desperately out into unknown territory. Billy had somehow appeared in the centre-forward slot, the rightful occupant hirpling on the wing. Gourlay took the ball down and in the one motion swung a lazy foot like a golfer chipping a ball greenwards. It sailed in a graceful arc and looped over the goalie like a falling star into the top right-hand corner. Goal! The orange hordes uttered a strange mangled sound of incomprehension and the Hastie's lads howled approval.

Ten minutes to go, two-one and it should really be six-one but God is good even if your father's a communist — Lithgow's had another shot that the Hastie's goalie somehow clawed away and our right-back in a moment of delusion actually passed the ball. It reached Billy who hitched one shoulder, then went the other way and for some reason half the Lithgow's defence went with the shoulder.

He bore down on goal tracked by the centre- and right-backs but managed to poke the ball between them and wriggle after it. The goalie came rushing out and there was a sickening thud as they collided but the ball went on its merry way over the virgin goal area of Lithgows and then it slunk almost apologetically over the line.

Two goals — all in the mix but the cheers were muted. Billy was stock still on the ground with a crowd of players and the ref, Sammy Workman peering down. Sammy was one of the best in the division, handsome as an Italian film star, always dressed in black, hair neatly parted and a first aid expert. He announced the boy was winded — give him a breather. Sure enough Billy slowly got his feet amid relieved Hastie's cheers and walked back for the kick-off with a big smear of red running down from a gashed cheekbone.

"He's been blooded," said Shug wisely. "They dae it wi' foxes."

Then it was a few minutes to go and we were in trouble because if it went to extra-time, Hastie's were buggered. The team were out on their feet, a man down and the fag smokers especially, which meant most, were coughing up nicotine remnants whereas Lithgow's had hardly broken sweat.

Billy wriggled to the by-line and was thumped unceremoniously over the line with the ball. As he prepared to take the corner, I turned and called to Neilly who normally had a nosebleed if he crossed the half-way line unless it was to take a penalty.

"Forsythe!" I shouted in a voice that for a moment was uncannily like my father's.

"Ye've biled yer can long enough, get up there and make a name for yourself!"

Neil's face turned purple and he began lumbering like a mudslide from his own penalty area until he reached the dizzy heights of the halfway line, then he ploughed on like a behemoth with the crowd beginning to chant his name.

Sammy Workman turned round, grinned and then blew the whistle to signal Billy. Neilly actually began to growl like a bear — a fearsome noise and sight as he charged into the penalty area. Billy sighted like a surveyor and swung that deadly right foot. Over came the heavy missile. Neil hadn't the puff to jump. He just stood there, the ball banged him on the head and flew into the net the opposite way to where he was facing.

Bedlam. Final whistle. Pitch invasion. No one tried to hoist Neil up, even in their delirium. I looked over. Donny was gone. Down to the side, Frank similarly vanished — hell mend them, neither was a football man. Shug and Jaffa lifted me onto their shoulders and Neilly waved like a berserk. I didn't deserve to be up there but was not about to argue with two happy bricklayers.

Way off to the side, Billy was standing alone. Our eyes met, he spat some blood out that had seeped into his mouth, and nodded. I nodded back. Talent. The boy had talent. Game over.

A lot can happen in a week.

Donny Dunlop went bust. A pile of money had been bet on Hastie's to win,

one large wager in particular, and he had been so confident that the odds offered were more than generous. Not only that but it turned out that he had broken the sacred rule of bookmaking. Never gamble on cuddies or cards. Fancied himself as a poker shark and was in big to some heavy Glasgow casinos — they had come to collect and Donny was absented in the twinkling of an eye. My own bet for a destination was the Sewer Pipes of Stranraer. A song I'm sure I heard once in a folk club.

As fate would have it, all his house and fiscal possessions were in Mamie's name for tax reasons and so she was sitting pretty. I would like to have seen the moment when the goonless, helpless, bankrupted Donny pleaded with her to sell it all up to settle the debt and she pointed silently at her still faintly discoloured eyes.

As for me, I was just getting off Jimmy Lapsley's borrowed scooter on the Lyle Hill having waited in the dark till Mamie emerged from the awfy nice house in Ardgowan Street, got into the renovated Triumph Herald and sped off to the upper reaches.

She stopped at a secluded part of the park where the trees leafy dripping branches hid many a tryst and a shadowy figure appeared to slide in beside her.

I waited while the owls hooted and the drenching rain soaked me through, and then walked softly to the car to rap upon the window.

"Can I see your licence, if you don't mind?" I announced in my best policeman tones. The window slowly wound down and I shone my pocket torch in to reveal the startled faces of Mamie Dunlop and Frank Carlin.

A smudge of lipstick at the side of his mouth but no doubt it would rub off. All things do in time.

I was now sitting in the back of the Herald, sucking happily on a spangle while in the manner of Marlowe I laid out the disreputable deeds committed by the two sick faces I could see in the windscreen mirror. This is how I read the cards.

Frankie and Mamie were lovers. In it up to their necks. A devious plan was hatched.

Frank laid a heavy bet with Donny Dunlop on Hastie's winning the cup; of course not in his own name, through trusted friends let's say. Eagerly accepted because Hastie's had no chance. But our Irish friend played a flanker — he wangled Billy Gourlay into the factory office because he knew that with the boy's talent anything was possible. So far so good.

Mamie decided to keep the boy sweet by the generous offer of her charms but perhaps grew more fond of that body swerve of Billy's than Frank had warranted.

Donny noticed that Hastie's were sailing through the preliminary rounds, saw Billy in action on the pitch and also noted that his wife had a glow on her face that had little to do with Max Factor. He had her tailed and caught up with them not far from this very spot perhaps, took them back to White's Garage, smacked Mamie around and put the fear of god into Billy

by threatening to chib her face to mince if the boy didn't do what he was told. So far so good.

But Mamie was a resourceful girl. When she saw Billy talk to me during the match and him turn round, she screeched with laughter, did the anaconda on Donny, figuring it might tip the scales but even then she'd swing both ways. If her husband won, she'd be stuck with the horrible little creep but there'd be other times, other plans. If Frank won, she'd be in the position she now commanded.

That is — in clover. Along with Mr Carlin who was gambolling in the same papilionaceous pasturage.

And as for me? Frank hired me as insurance to keep an eye on Billy and I proved to be both a spanner in the works and a useful contrivance. When I was getting too close for comfort Mamie was happy to contrive with Donny to set me up and take me out of commission.

Because whoever was going to lose, it was never going to be Mrs Dunlop. The only thing out of her control was when Donny caught her out and beat her up. But she knew his tongue was still hanging out for her — it didn't take long to make the midget dance once more.

When I finished there was silence. Mamie's face was like the Sphinx but Frank swallowed hard. "How did you figure it all out?" he asked.

"It was the only story that made any sense," I answered. "After I visited Mamie in hospital she rang you. One was to let you know what had happened and she could still pull it off, the other was to get me off the case. You both used the same phrase, 'accidents will happen'; it got me thinking."

"You were a menace, John," said Mamie quietly.

I looked at Frank who had a strange shifty expression on his face.

"Please don't tell me you're going to leave the happy home to set up with the blonde bombshell, here?" I muttered. "Please don't."

He wouldn't meet my eye in the mirror and glanced away.

"She'll spit you out like a lemon pip, Frank."

His head did not turn. I shook mine and gazed into Mamie's hazel eyes. "What is it you really want?" I asked quietly.

Mamie gave that serious consideration. "I like horses," she said finally. "Ponies. Show jumping. I could breed them."

"Frank can clean out the stables," I answered. A bubble of laughter had been percolating for some time and I suddenly let it out in a loud guffaw.

"What a palaver, eh?" I announced and leant forward to hook Frank's wallet from the inside pocket, extract two fivers and flip it back to him. "My resignation fee."

"But I took you off the case," he protested.

"Yes. But I didn't agree at the time. Now, I do."

Mamie shrugged. They were in the clear, nothing could be proved. Other than the mishap when she was found with Billy, she had run the game from start to finish. The girl had brains and no scruples; perhaps a soft spot for the cuddies but other than that, she was lethal.

I opened the car door and prepared to depart the scene — they both turned round to look at me and I felt a weird surge of compassion. Frank looked lost at sea and Mamie as if she'd won everything and nothing at the same time. Now they were stuck with each other.

"I was very fond of your mother," Frank said, with a Catholic desperation.

"Light a candle for her Frank," I replied. "And make your confession to Father Scanlon, he's a betting man. I'm sure he'll understand."

And then I left. I could have berated them over the myriad lies told, the fact that I nearly got my head kicked in and my ankle was shooting shafts of pain on an hourly basis but in a strange way, I was grateful for the corruption. It got me out of bed.

As I hauled myself up the stairs towards the attic room, Jimmy Lapsley's smile kept coming in to my mind. I had returned the scooter to him at the Willow Bar and told him to put my name down as his partner for the next domino tournament. He almost bought me a drink but then thought better and slid me a shandy instead. But he couldn't keep a daft grin off his face.

It doesn't take much to make folk happy; it's just maintaining the damn thing that is a problem. It takes stamina. Like a run from midfield — no guarantee the ball will come your way, it all depends on luck.

As I reached the landing, listing slightly to compensate for the dud ligaments, there was a note pinned to the door. Perhaps the offer of another case? No. Even better. The fair hand of Rosalind Connor, her spiky handwriting like a left jab.

I come off the night shift at 10 tomorrow morning. You better be fit for purpose.

A lightning calculation. Wind the alarm clock. Up at seven, general tidy-up, hide the Russian books, don the one white shirt missed so far by the moths, out for bacon and eggs courtesy of Frank's fivers, soft rolls from Auld's the Bakers, start the fry-up at precisely 9.45, the girl would be looking after ill people all night in the hospital and ravenous as hell. Scour out the pot, best quality leaf-tea — play it cool. Let sophistication be my byword.

I could feel a foolish smirk creeping over my phizog and tried to rectify matters. I had just survived beatings, triumphed over violent adversity, won a football match, solved a case — I would play it cool.

A picture of my parents walking in the hills came into my head, my father with that familiar half-smile on his face swiping at the daisies with an old piece of stick and my mother with a daft pink beret, always askew, and a checked two-piece suit that was loud enough to scare a flock of crows.

I felt some kind of moisture in my eye but Greenock is full of moisture.

Deep breath. Key in the lock. Rosalind's note in the top pocket. In I go. Close the door behind.

And that was me — gone.

THE END.

166

Greatest Game

"The only thing that unites us is
[to]" defend the colours of Boca."

Boca Juniors 2 Real Madrid 1

Toyota Intercontinental Cup final, National Stadium, Tokyo, 28 November 2000

By Rupert Fryer

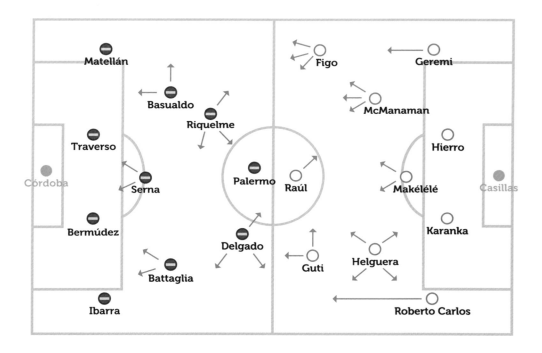

"If we have to travel from A to B, most of us take the six-lane highway and get there as quickly as possible. Riquelme would choose the winding mountain road, the scenic route which takes him six hours instead of two." — Jorge Valdano

On 28 November 2000, Juan Román Riquelme invited the world to join him in Japan on what was perhaps his greatest trip of all. However, it would

be the man who you'd find speeding down that six-lane highway whose goals would ultimately crown Boca Juniors world champions. The greatest night in the club's history would be the tale of Argentinian football's odd couple and one which would remind us all that football takes all sorts.

Real Madrid arrived in Asia on the cusp of a revolution. Luís Figo had joined the club from Barcelona for the biggest fee in the game's history. Two years previously, the team with which Alfredo Di Stéfano defined the European Cup, had their hands back on those big ears, defeating Juventus to end a 30-year wait. *Los Blancos* followed up that victory by seeing off Héctor Cúper's Valencia at the Stade de France to claim a second European title in three years. It would be Boca Juniors, however, who were the ones on the edge of the greatest decade in their history: their penalty shootout victory over Palmeiras in June 2000 would be the first of four Copa Libertadores to arrive in *La Boca* in the 2000s and this victory over Real Madrid the first of two world titles.

Club world championships, we're told, are little more than an inconvenience[1] for Champions League winners (at least, that's what the Anglophone press would have us believe); a trip to the Far East that serves only to disrupt the season. That certainly wasn't the case for Florentino Pérez and his ambitions of world domination. Steve McManaman recalls the president's reaction to their defeat in his book, *El Macca*: "Pérez thundered, 'How are we ever going to conquer the Asian market with performances like that?'"

The Galácticos era would ensure those ambitions were eventually realised, though the *Zidanes y Pavones* approach would produce little in terms of

silverware. Boca's expansion into the world market would instead owe a debt to on-field achievements, though their golden era would arrive via a not dissimilar *modus operandi* under new president, Mauricio Macri. He, too, intended to hoover up the best talent available, but in contrast to Pérez, Macri was playing the long game. "We made a 180-degree turn," admitted Macri in *Boquita*, Martín Caparros's story of the club.

Boca were in extreme financial difficulties in 1995 when Macri was elected president and his first act was to implement a complete overhaul of the club, radically transforming the business model — or perhaps more accurately, finally introducing one, as *IESE Insight Review* noted: "Efforts were made to optimise the resources coming from members and season ticketholders via telephone service centres, a decentralised ticket sales system and, for companies, a special section with corporate box seating at the stadium. A professional management system akin to that of a private company was instituted, while the club, in accordance with Argentinian law, remained a non-profit organisation."

On the field, Boca would rely on their academy, promising teenagers they managed to pinch from around the country[2] and the most talented players

[1] Something with which Carlos Bianchi vehemently disagrees: "I don't [believe that]," he said in 2004. "What's true is that the European sides try to talk down the competition whenever they lose. I saw the 1996 final in Rome between Juventus and River Plate and after the Italians had won, the players celebrated wildly and the result made front-page headlines."

[2] Juan Román Riquelme was one of 15 youth players purchased at a total cost of around US$3 million; they were later sold for around 10 times that much.

from other top clubs in Argentina that carried resale potential.[3] In 12 years under Macri, Boca would earn close to €100 million through player sales — the majority of whom headed for Europe. Like Pérez, the Intercontinental Cup held importance for Macri's plans for global expansion, but while his financial achievements would help him to be named mayor of the City of Buenos Aires in 2007, it was the 16 trophies[4] that defined the Macri era — nine of which would arrive under the man who proved to be his greatest signing of all, Carlos Bianchi[5].

A prolific striker in both Argentina and France, the Larry David doppelganger moved from Vélez Sarsfield — via a short and unsuccessful stint with Roma — having led the Liniers outfit to three league championships and the club's only Copa Libertadores and Intercontinental Cup titles. *Los Bianchi Boys*, as his Boca team are now known, came and went according to Macri's blueprint[6], but the titles kept arriving. Bianchi says the Intercontinental Cups

a chance to "prove that you and your team are capable of reaching the next level. Facing the European champions with their star-studded internationals and often-limitless financial clout is extremely motivating for us South Americans." This defeat of Real Madrid would signal the start of a dynasty.

"Much of the pre-match talk had surrounded the world's most expensive player, Figo, who was making his first appearance on a global stage," said the report in *World Soccer* magazine. "But Real's £37.5m Portuguese star was eclipsed by two Boca players in particular — Palermo and Riquelme."

Martín Palermo is Riquelme's antithesis. There are statues of both at La Bombonera, but that's where the similarities end. The latter was blessed with an immense talent and is defined by his unquenchable thirst for the aesthetic. Sensitive, demanding, quixotic, cerebral, delicate and enigmatic, Román is an artist masquerading[7] as a footballer. The

---

[3] *Martin Palermo, Hugo Ibarra and Walter Samuel are just a few of those acquired from elsewhere in Argentina and exported for profit.*

[4] *An unprecedented period of success their fierce rivals River Plate refer to as "proof" that Boca "have only existed since 1998."*

[5] *Who, curiously, grew up a fan of River Plate.*

[6] *31 different players contested Boca's three two-legged Copa Libertadores finals between 2000 and 2003*

[7] *That football itself (by which I mean what actually occurs on the field of play) isn't considered a mode of cultural expression akin to literature, sculpture and painting, is something that continues to baffle me; with millions around the world taking to the pitch every day, there appear few more fitting scenes in which we can attempt to further our understanding of the human condition.*

former is all heart. A warrior. *El Titán*, they called him. He's visceral and emotive. Palermo cared only that the ball found the back of the net; how it ended up there was an irrelevance. In his study into Argentinian masculinities, the anthropologist Eduardo Archetti ponders the "the contradictory character of Argentinian football... [where] male individual virtues are transformed into contrasting styles and moral attitudes." Never were they more contrasting than between Boca's two most famous sons.

"The only thing that unites us is [to] defend the colours of Boca," admitted Palermo in 2010, and their very public falling-out undeniably contributed to the three barren years for *Los Xeneizes* prior to Julio César Falcioni's arrival as coach in 2011. Each with their own clique of dedicated disciples, they split the dressing-room in half during that period[8]. It's difficult to pinpoint exactly when the relationship between the two soured, but their philosophical differences are believed to have come to a head during Boca's 2008 Copa Libertadores semi-final exit at the hands of Fluminense. Riquelme was sensational that evening, twice putting Boca ahead. He "painted the pitch with the most beautiful colours football has known," said the report in *Olé*. The same could not be said for Boca's goalkeeper that night, as Pablo Migliore's error gifted Flu an equaliser

from which Boca would not recover. Riquelme was furious and made his feelings known to Migliore at the final whistle. For Palermo, who always placed the collective above all else, it was the final straw.

Both would leave Boca after receiving plaudits from around the world for their respective performances against Real Madrid in Tokyo but it was never in doubt that both would one day return. Riquelme joined Louis van Gaal's Barcelona in 2002 for around €11 million after leading Boca to a repeat of their Libertadores success. He claims he never wanted to leave Boca in the first place but when the offer arrived from Catalonia he was told that if he truly loved the club, he would make the sacrifice. He went but he left Barça a year later[9], having made little to no impact at Camp Nou, to join an emerging Villarreal, where he would enjoy a much more productive spell.

Riquelme's role in hoisting *El Submarino Amarillo* to within a penalty of the 2006 Champions League final can not be overstated. Surrounded by South Americans and forming a formidable partnership with Diego Forlán, he led the club to a third-place finish in the 2004-05 season, notching a career-best 15 goals along the way and earning a nomination for Fifa's World Player of the Year. So integral was his role, there was

---

[8] *Boca went through four coaches and six managerial changes in two years before Falcioni's appointment*

[9] *Legend has it that upon his arrival Van Gaal greeted him with a child's Barcelona shirt for his newborn son, along with the words, "He'll get to wear it more than you wear yours." Boca, Tigre and San Lorenzo all finished level on 39 points.*

something oddly Romántic about the moment when Jens Lehmann dived to his left to stop his weak penalty; of the moment Riquelme stopped dead in his tracks, looking around him as he tried desperately to ascertain what had just happened. "It was one of the saddest memories of my career and one I will always remember," he said. "I thought we were stronger than Arsenal and deserved to play in the final."

He came home a year later, following one of the many clashes with figures of authority that characterised his career, this time with Villarreal's Chilean coach Manuel Pellegrini. There were multiple offers from top European clubs, including genuine interest from Tottenham Hotspur but, for Riquelme, they were never an option. Home was always where his heart was. He publicly thanked Spurs for their interest, but confirmed Boca as his only possible destination. During his initial loan spell back in *La Boca*, Riquelme led the club almost single-handedly to its fourth Copa Libertadores of the decade, finishing second-top scorer with eight goals (including three of Boca's five during the two-legged final against Mano Menezes's Grêmio) before sealing his permanent return by agreeing to the biggest contract in Argentinian football — a deal that stipulated he would play his final season without pay.

"I love Boca," he reminded the fans as the club went into decline after winning the 2008 apertura title[10]. "If I didn't, I wouldn't be working here for free. I'm the only idiot who works for free, so I don't think anyone can come and lecture me about my responsibilities." It wouldn't be the only time he'd play without a wage. Less than a year into a new deal so controversial that then club treasurer — and now club president — Daniel Angelici resigned from his position, Riquelme once again managed to climb above his superiors to the safety of the moral high ground by donating his wages for the season back to the club after injuries significantly restricted his appearances in Falcioni's 2011 apertura-winning side, saying, "I want this money to go to help the kids at Boca or to fix the dressing-rooms."

Palermo returned in 2004 following three-and-a-half mostly miserable years in La Liga, first with Villarreal and then with Real Betis and Alaves. The running joke in Argentina is that God is directing his own movie and has chosen Palermo as the star. It's a concept that fits the remarkable life of an extraordinary man, one who seems to seek out adversity only so it can be heroically overcome. He was hot property following the 2000 Intercontinental final and was sold to Villarreal for €7.5 million soon after. A barren spell for his new club finally ended one November evening against Levante. As his joy and frustrations poured out in front of the away support, the stadium wall gave way. The structure, and a fair few of the Valencian community, rained down upon him, breaking his tibia and fibula.

Palermo also infamously failed with a hat-trick of spot-kicks against Colombia

---

[10] *For the first time in history, a three-way playoff was employed to find an eventual champion after Boca, Tigre and San Lorenzo all finished level on 39 points.*

in a World Cup qualifier in 1999. While most scoff at his failings, the events may actually be held up as testament to the desire of a man so willing to put everything on the line in the quest of his goals. Few would have the courage to step up for the second, while he may well be the only one with enough steel to take the third. Then there's the famous one-legged goal, or 'gol de las muletas' — the goal on crutches. During Boca's 2000 Copa Libertadores quarter-final against River Plate, following six months spent on the sidelines after ripping an anterior cruciate ligament, Palermo (literally) hobbled on for the last 15 minutes and somehow managed to score in what would be the pivotal moment of the Libertadores-winning campaign that booked their clash with Real Madrid.

His most emotional moment of all, however, arrived in 2006. "Following his newborn son's premature death [on the Wednesday], he asked to play the following Sunday," wrote Marcela Mora y Araujo in the Guardian. "People criticised this decision: at a time of mourning, he should have been at home with his family, they said. Boca fans praised him: his loyalty and commitment unswerving." He scored twice that day and left the field in floods of tears; thousands joined him. In Riquelme's absence, Palermo helped Boca to two more continental crowns, scoring in both finals as they claimed 2004 and 2005 editions of South America's secondary club competition, the Copa Sudamericana. The Libertadores, however, would evade him until Román's triumphant return.

By 2010, three years and another league championship after Riquelme came home, the true extent of the breakdown of their relationship was exposed in the most dramatic of settings. "I am not a friend of [Riquelme's], I have no relationship [with him]," Palermo told Argentinian radio just days after becoming Boca's all-time top-goalscorer with two goals in a 4-0 win over Arsenal de Sarandí. It was supposed to be Palermo's moment, the one in which he wrote himself into history, the one that would cement his legacy as one of the all-time greats. The Boca fans had a huge banner on which they had repeatedly updated El Titán's total following every strike that season. It was the moment everyone had been waiting for, perhaps the greatest of his life. But one Riquelme would deny him. Instead, the aftermath of that goal has become the defining image of their turbulent relationship.

Riquelme had drifted unnoticed to the edge of the Arsenal box in time to receive a square ball from Cristian Erbes. He looked up and played a smart one-two with Nicolás Gaitán, before shrugging off his marker to find himself one-on-one with the keeper from 12 yards. Gol de Román, gol de Román, cried TV Publica. Riquelme, though, had other ideas. As always, Palermo was lurking. Riquelme popped the ball off with the outside of his boot, leaving Palermo a tap-in for goal 219. For history. Hoooy, Martín, Martín, Martíííííín. Riquelme peeled away, arms outstretched... in the opposite direction. Palermo set off after him, at first looking slightly bewildered. His stare then morphed into a look of utter contempt as he gave up the chase. Half the Boca side embraced San Martín. The other formed a group hug with El Diez firmly in the middle.

Boca's two greatest sons had torn the team in half. It's said that tensions grew after the game, with Riquelme quipping, "Anyone can score goals like that." From that moment on, La Bombonera was no longer big enough for the both of them. "I won't talk about it," Palermo told *Radio de la Red*. "What happened is out there for all to see." Something had to give. It finally did when Palermo called time on his glittering career in 2011. "Now only the football side of things is discussed and that does us good," admitted Sebastián Battaglia.[11] "Martín's exit defused the previous situation of who was with one and who was with the other."

It's a context that makes that evening at the National Stadium in Tokyo all the more special, for it would be one of those magical nights when the two came together; one could not have achieved what he did without the other. Both teams lined up with what can most accurately be described as variations of a 4-3-3. Carlos Bianchi went with an interpretation of the archetypal Argentinian 4-3-1-2 but with Riquelme drifting from a starting position on the left and Marcelo Delgado supporting Palermo from the right, meaning the shape would morph in and out of a 4-3-2-1. Vicente Del Bosque opted for a lop-sided 4-3-3, with Guti rarely anywhere near the left wing, ostensibly vacating the space for the onrushing Roberto Carlos, who would be Madrid's biggest goal-threat throughout.

Palermo and Riquelme proved the difference but it was Bianchi who provided them with the platform. In terms of talent, Boca couldn't compete and so Bianchi did what he could: he devised a system that improved his side's chances. "It wasn't exactly '*la nuestra*'," the Argentinian football writer historian Ezequiel Fernández Moores said. "It was '*la suya*', [or] 'Carlito's way'... Riquelme and his careful ball possession was *la nuestra*, but Boca's pragmatism was not. [They were] cautious, and when you think that your team is inferior, you just defend and wait for your rival's mistakes." Bianchi's side was broken, conceptually a 7-1-2. The back four was obdurate, its full-backs showing little desire to get forward. The midfield three behind Riquelme were stoppers, intent solely on restricting space for a talented opposition. Boca would work hard and look to counter. Riquelme carried the creative burden and was charged with intermittently providing those around him with much-needed breathers.

There was little respite in the opening stages, however, as the game started at a frantic pace that saw Boca take the lead inside three minutes. Geremi won a throw following a tussle with Riquelme on the halfway line — pretty much all the Cameroonian would win from Boca's *enganche* all evening. He held the ball above his head and looked for an option as the television director turned his attentions to *El Diez*. By the time said director's interest had returned

---

[11] *Despite losing a huge portion of his career because of injury, Sebastián Battaglia holds the accolade of being Boca's most successful player, with seven league titles, four Copas Libertadores, two Intercontinental Cups, a Copa Sudamericana, three Recopas Sudamericanas — as well as being listed as a Copa Argentina 2012 winner, despite not making a single appearance in the competition.*

to the game, Geremi had thrown the ball straight to Colombian destroyer Mauricio Serna. The Madrid full-back didn't react to the transition; Delgado did, instantly running off Fernando Hierro's shoulder and making straight for the space behind. Senna cushioned the dropping ball to the 37-year-old José Basualdo, who spotted Delgado's run and curled a wonderful pass outside of Geremi and into the channel behind. Delgado was away. He headed straight for the byline before looking up to see Palermo darting in between Aitor Karanka and Roberto Carlos, who himself had been caught too high up the pitch. To say Roberto Carlos was twice as quick as Palermo may be doing the Brazilian an injustice; it may be equally unfair to Palermo to suggest his instinct for goal was twice as keen as the Brazilian's was to defend. The goal was — well, it was very Palermo. Delgado delayed and delayed, allowing his labouring strike partner to reach the six yard box before his perfect square gifted *El Titán* a tap-in. *Delgado el centro para Palermo. Gol. Gooooooool.* Breath. *Gooooooool.* Breath. *Gooooooyyyooooool de Boca* cried Telemundo. *Paleeeermo! Boca uno, cero Real Madrid.*

"I don't think we underestimated them," Del Bosque told reporters later that night. "They just started better than us — with devastating consequences." Madrid remained calm, however, and initially appeared to react well to the opening goal. Having identified that Battaglia was more intent on holding his position to the right of Boca's midfield three than attempting to look for the ball further up the field, Roberto Carlos positioned himself between Battaglia and the right-back Hugo Ibarra for the rest of the first half. McManaman drifted over to that side in an attempt to free the Brazilian and, just two minutes after going behind, the two combined to win a throw.

Roberto Carlos lofted the ball to Raúl, but his chest down to Guti was short. Battaglia nipped in to rob him on the edge of the Boca area before nudging the ball forward to Riquelme[12]. By this point, like Delgado just three minutes earlier, Palermo was already off and running, dashing between Hierro and Geremi and straight for the Madrid half. Riquelme's first touch allowed him to turn and open up his body. He took the briefest of glances upfield and effortlessly sprayed his pass all of 60 yards. By the time the ball had dropped, around 25 yards from Iker Casillas and the Real Madrid goal, Geremi had caught up. But Riquelme's pass was as perfect as they come. Leaning as he sliced across the ball, Román achieved sufficient backspin to have the ball grind almost to a halt as it bounced up off the turf. Had it run on another full circumference, Palermo would probably have lost the race with Geremi. Had it required a first touch to be taken, you doubt whether Palermo would have possessed the technique to evade his defender. But so perfect was the ball, Riquelme's first forward pass

---

[12] *David Beckham was once asked about Madrid's approach during his time with the club. His answer was simple: "Give it to Zidane. He's better than the rest of us." That became a trend of Riquelme's career: no matter how close the man in possession or in what position on the field, the rule was simple: if Román was free, his teammates gave him the ball.*

of the night, he didn't have to. Palermo didn't even have to check his stride. As the ball sailed over San Martín's head, you wondered where on earth Casillas was. Why did he never come? At that moment, his decision to stay on his goal line seems poor. Two seconds later, however, as the ball's trajectory was drastically altered by the backspin as it bounced up in front of the Boca forward, it became apparent that Madrid's young keeper, whether by calculation or not, had made the right call. Had he rushed from his goal, that bounce would have left him in no man's land. The ball bounced just once more, travelling no more than four or five yards. Palermo had just one thing on his mind. The only thing that was ever on his mind. He managed to hold off Geremi and struck the ball on the second bounce, sending it across goal and underneath the diving Casillas.

Palermo hit the deck. Arms clumsily stretched out in front of him, he slid across the turf before popping up to peel away along the touchline, glancing back at his colleagues — who were still halfway up the field — with a look of immense joy and shock. The cry of '*gol*' that followed on Telemundo wasn't one for the scrapbook. It was staggered. Broken. The tone akin to that of the teenager who works in every shop that Homer Simpson wanders into. Over on Radio Mitre, Alejandro Fantino was thanking God, over and over again. Five minutes in and Boca were 2-0 up against the mighty Galácticos. Against Figo, Raúl, Hierro and Roberto Carlos. *¡Increíble!* "To be honest, no one prepares for that, it was a surprise, especially against a team like Real Madrid," Palermo admitted immediately

after the game. "I am used to scoring but this was very special, a spectacular start for which nobody could have planned. I will remember this night for the rest of my life."

"We were our own worst enemies," said Del Bosque. "It was very unusual for us to be caught twice like that so early." But caught they were. The commentator still hadn't recovered his breath by the time a frenzied opening almost produced a third goal just 90 seconds later. As Madrid put together their first extended period of passing, Claude Makélélé exchanged passes with McManaman and Karanka before laying the ball off to Hierro, who was intent on spraying one of his trademark long passes. He looked up, elbows sticking out like chicken wings in that renowned stance of his, but decided against it, instead rolling his foot over the ball and pushing it to his left. It was then that he saw his pass.

Vicente Del Bosque's setup asked Roberto Carlos to man the entire left flank, and he spent most of the evening as wide forward. Spotting the Brazilian, Hierro floated a 40-yard pass right onto his colleague's chest. Hugo Ibarra's position was good, he planted his feet and got square on, but, anticipating the Brazilian would chest the ball down in front of him, the Boca defender committed. Roberto Carlos, eyes never once leaving the ball, saw Ibarra stepping towards him and chested the ball up and over the defender's head. It dropped onto his 24" right thigh before settling on the deck. Jorge Bermúdez rushed to close him down, but a drop of a shoulder took him away from the tackle before his right foot smashed a shot against the bar. So hard was it struck, the ball had almost cleared the penalty area by the time it returned to earth.

The warning signs were there for Boca. And if their two goals arrived as something of a shock, Roberto Carlos's certainly did not. And with the way in which the game had begun, neither was it a surprise that Madrid would get back into the contest so soon. Whether instructed by Bianchi or not, Battaglia dropped increasingly deep in an effort to help Ibarra with the flying Brazilian, but their attempts proved futile. This time the move began at left-back, as Roberto Carlos's attempt at a long pass almost took Battaglia off his feet — a blow from which the midfielder hadn't recovered by the time the ball flew past Óscar Córdoba a couple of minutes later. Having taken the wind out of the Boca man's sails, the ball ballooned up into the air before Riquelme calmly cushioned it back to Senna, who played square to Basualdo. As Delgado and Riquelme switched flanks, returning to their starting positions either side of Palermo, Basualdo appeared caught in two minds, and laboriously scuffed his pass between the two of them and straight to Geremi.

Riquelme's unwillingness to track back at first appeared insignificant — indeed, Basualdo's key function on the left of the midfield three was to provide cover for such an eventuality, and the veteran instantly slotted back in front of left-back Aníbal Matellán — but it would lead to an overload on Boca's right which would eventually provide Figo with the time and space to deliver a deep cross that would result in the equaliser. Between them, Basualdo and Matellán could chase and press Geremi and

Figo. A problem arose when Makélélé joined in. With Riquelme wandering aimlessly further up the pitch, Basualdo was eventually drawn infield, leaving Matellán facing two Madrid players. To compensate, Boca's entire back-line essentially shifted across.

Anticipating a deep cross, Raúl allowed Guti to dart into the space at the near post and preoccupy Bermúdez and took up his own position against the shorter Ibarra at the far post. As the ball sailed over Raúl's head, Ibarra should simply have headed the ball out of play for a corner. By that stage he was well aware that Roberto Carlos was playing as a de facto left-winger and that the Brazilian was likely to be lurking. Instead, the Boca right-back aimlessly headed the ball up into the air. Roberto Carlos took the ball down on his chest and hammered a thunderous volley inside Córdoba's near post and into the top corner. The Boca keeper got a hand to the ball and should probably have kept it out. But he didn't. Madrid were back in the game.

The Spaniards continued to pour forward and the opening quarter of an hour nearly produced a fourth goal when Guti was allowed to drift untracked between the lines to pick up a pass from Makélélé and charge at Boca's for once unprotected backline, before laying the ball off to Raúl on the edge of the box. Guti darted to his right for the return, but Raúl instead turned to his left and opened up his body to drive a shot at goal before electing to attempt one of his trademark chips. Córdoba was beaten. But the man who would go on to become Madrid's all-time top goalscorer got too much on it and sent the ball a yard over the bar.

Boca were on the ropes and looking increasingly in danger of being overwhelmed. They needed something. One moment just to reassure themselves that they weren't out of their depth. That they could compete. They looked to their talisman. To their one individual who appeared to be on a level playing field with the millionaires in white. That moment arrived on 20 minutes, after Hierro had beaten Palermo to a lofted ball forward and stabbed it straight into Riquelme's path. *El Diez* turned to play the ball to his right as Geremi approached, but instead executed a Cruyff turn and headed toward the left wing. Geremi poked out a foot, Riquelme rolled his own over the top of the ball and out of the Cameroonian's reach. Figo drifted back, sandwiching Riquelme between the two. Riquelme checked to pass the ball back down the line, then checked again, leaping over another Geremi lunge and heading for the by-line, stroking the ball with the outside of his boot in order to get that all important half a yard in front of his marker that would allow him to get across the defender. He did — and Geremi hauled him to the ground. "Riquelme can change the game," Telemundo reassured its audience.

Riquelme himself took the free-kick, some five yards in from the touchline, and curled a shot for the far top corner. Casillas rose and beat it away. But it was a chance. A chance created from nothing. And in 40 seconds, Riquelme had levelled the playing field somewhat, reminding his side they too could still pose a threat. There were more chances before the break. Palermo was inches away from converting a Delgado cross at the far post. Riquelme tested Casillas

with another set piece. At the other end, Raúl headed a McManaman corner wide from a few yards out after Córdoba was lost underneath the ball's flight. Makélélé made an unusual surge forward to find space inside the box, but wasted his chance. Boca tired as the break approached, but remained steadfast.

The second half almost saw Boca instantly restore their two-goal lead, but Riquelme's wonderfully curled free-kick brought the save of the game out of Casillas. Riquelme took the resulting corner and his wicked inswinger was just inches away from providing Palermo the chance to head into an almost empty net at the far post. It served as another reminder to Madrid that the Argentinians had more to give. The next goal had to go Madrid's way if they were to salvage anything from the game. But Boca were carrying out Bianchi's plan to perfection. "The tournament coincided with the end of our football season. That meant training had to be fairly light and mostly tactical," Bianchi explained. Never was that more evident than 12 minutes into the second half when, for the only time all evening, Boca showed just how well-drilled they were by perfectly executing an offside trap that saw Geremi's headed equaliser ruled out.

Del Bosque had identified that Boca's right side was where most joy would be found and McManaman moved increasingly left to join his great friend Roberto Carlos in an attempt to go two-on-two with Battaglia and Ibarra. And it was from that very situation that Madrid went within inches of an equaliser. McManaman committed Battaglia before his short pass left Roberto Carlos one-on-one with Ibarra. The Boca full-back stood off, reluctant to commit and allow the Brazilian's searing pace to exploit the space behind him. That allowed Figo the time to come across and receive the ball on the edge of the box before spinning Serna and rolling in Raúl, who dispatched the ball past Córdoba and high into the corner of the same net Palermo had twice made bulge. But the flag came to Boca's rescue once again, with replays showing Raúl's leading foot just half a yard beyond Matellán.

McManaman was then withdrawn, replaced by the Brazilian Savio, who took up his position as an orthodox left-winger, offering balance to a shape that became symmetrical, with specific instructions to get at Ibarra whenever possible. Within two minutes, Ibarra was booked for shoving Savio off the field. Figo's ambitious effort from the resulting free-kick almost caught Córdoba out, with the Boca keeper having to scramble across goal to tip the Portuguese's dipping effort over the bar. Madrid continued to probe, but Boca constricted, forming a seven-man blockade in front of their goal.

As Diego Estévez puts it in his book recording over a century of Boca Juniors, *103: Más de un Siglo Azul y Amarillo,* "The rest of the match was played out between the attacks of Real Madrid and the counterattacks of Boca Juniors." Fernando Morientes replaced Makélélé to offer a focal point as Madrid began crossing into the box more frequently. Raúl went close to heading home from a few yards after Savio had beaten Ibarra to cross to the far post; Delgado wasted a golden opportunity to make it three after getting in behind on the right, while Riquelme's corners continued to create chances for Boca.

In between those transitions, however, the importance of Riquelme's performance would be truly realised. There was little dynamism, few slaloming runs and shots at goal or threaded through balls. There was just calm. In the second half, Riquelme was, in some ways, the ultimate team player. While those around him panicked, Román brought serenity. Time and again, his languid, leisurely style encouraged all around him to relax, to pass and move; he reminded them that the game can be simple. The best form of defence is not attack, but — as Barcelona have emphatically proved in recent times — possession. He just refused to lose the ball, an attitude most aptly illustrated two minutes from the end when he picked possession at left-back and skipped way from Guti, then turned Geremi three times on the touchline before being bundled to the ground to win a free-kick. As he crashed to the turf, Riquelme fell on top of the ball, embracing it in his arms, refusing to let go until the Madrid players had retreated and Basualdo arrived to take the free-kick. The ball was his.

His survival instinct had kicked in: Riquelme only exists when his side have the ball. His reaction to being marginalised may be the only visceral emotion this complex and fragile being brings to the game with which he seeks to define himself. And what made his contribution so poignant is that it wasn't purely the fact that he retained possession, but that what made the difference was that which he holds above all else — the aesthetic. Calm, composed and, and with the elegance of Alessandra Ferri, he elevated his side when they needed it most. "Riquelme played the sort of football which we Argentinians like and which really typifies the South American style," said a gushing Diego Maradona[13].

Combined with the resolve of his teammates, his display would be enough. "We played better for the next 85 minutes, but Boca are a good side," said Del Bosque. Battaglia was withdrawn two minutes into stoppage time and replaced by a young Nicolás Burdisso, who slotted into a back five just in time to see Raúl mis-control Geremi's lofted ball into the Boca box. And when Hierro attempted to stop one final counter-attack by hammering the ball back up the field and out for a goal kick, it was all over. Córdoba lofted his goal kick downfield. Casillas attempted to hammer it back and that was that. *'Boca es el campeo del mundo,'* they cried. Again and again.

The bench emptied. The celebrations began — both in Tokyo and back home, where half of Argentina plus one leapt for joy[14]. "Boca said they were the greatest team in Argentina," recalled Fernández Moores. Now they were champions of the world. "That their rival was the legendary Real Madrid made the victory all the more important." It was Bianchi's second world title in six years. "It is hard to compare the two," he told Fifa when asked where this victory stood in relation to Vélez's 1994 defeat of Fabio Capello's Milan. "Both are special for different reasons. But this victory is not only for Boca, but for Argentina. We were able to prove that Argentinian football is the best in the world."

Looking back on the game now, perhaps the most striking image of the night arrives after Palermo hauled himself off the ground following his second. It took what felt like forever for his teammates to arrive. When they finally did, it was Riquelme who was first on the scene, grabbing him by the waist and hoisting him high into the air. Despite all we know and all we've seen since, it's a snapshot many of us would like to hold up as symbolic of their lives together — one representative of their shared achievements, of Boca's odd couple.

Following Palermo's retirement, one reader of *La Nación* likened them to Guns N' Roses (hugely popular in Argentina, where the mullet still rules): "Riquelme is the melody, the artist, like Slash; Palermo is the strength, the voice of the goal, like Axl Rose." Martín Palermo and Juan Román Riquelme are two polar opposites that came together that night to make Boca champions of the world. "They are very different, both on and off the pitch," said Fernández Moores. "Their coexistence shows that football is a collective sport and

---

[13] *The harmony between the two would dissipate as time went on, with Riquelme's international retirement being swiftly followed by an argument that simmers to this day; most recently in the press conference to confirm he wouldn't play for Boca again, when Riquelme said he didn't care what the "muchacho" said — a term perhaps best translated as "that guy".*

[14] La Mitad Más Uno: *the club claim that half of any given group of people in Argentina, plus one, are Boca fans.*

that you need the one who can create and the one that will score."

Palermo sealed the victory; Riquelme made it beautiful. They're illustrative of the game's great binaries; of passion and flair. Individually, they provide two contrasting images of football, art and of the world itself. But they need each other. And we need them both. Because together they encompass everything it takes to win a game of football. And perhaps a whole lot more. Ⓑ

182

Eight Bells

"...first it was time for war, glasses
of juniper juice and a nice long
boozy snooze."

Football on TV

Key moments in the history of televising the game

By Scott Murray

 Football at the Arsenal (1937)

Exactly how much effort the BBC put into television during the medium's infant years is a moot point. Take the opening day of their regular service, on Monday, 2 November 1936. At 3pm, the curtain went up for pompous welcoming speeches by various BBC grandees, blowhards and windbags. After a whopping 25 minutes of programming, the station paused for its first interval. Another 35 minutes and it was time for closedown, followed by large G&Ts all round, then a siesta. Thanks, BBC, you pissed-up shower of indolent toffs!

Media historians today will tell you that the most memorable and spectacular performance put on by the BBC Television Service during the 1930s came on 1 September 1939, when Germany invaded Poland and the entire department swung their boots up onto their desks in choreographed unison, having been presented with the perfect excuse to do bugger all for the next six years. Though in fairness, between 1936 and 1939, at least a little work had been undertaken to advance the cause of live televised sport.

On 14 April 1937, the BBC studios at Alexandra Palace played host to the first television demonstration of snooker, an exhibition of play by Horace Lindrum and Willie Smith. The programme lasted 10 minutes, whereupon it made way for *Daffodils* ("a display of various types of daffodils from the Daffodil Show" — *Radio Times*). Another couple of months down the line, and the BBC were off to Wimbledon for the first time. And then, on Thursday 16 September, it was the turn of football, and the world's first live televised match.

The game had admittedly limited appeal — George Allison's Arsenal were taking on Arsenal reserves at Highbury — but then only a few hundred houses close to Ally Pally in north London could receive BBC pictures anyway. Arsenal were the natural choice for the BBC's experiment anyway: Highbury was the closest ground to Ally Pally and had a bespoke gantry for telly cameras in its fancy new East Stand.

"The players will be introduced by Mr George F Allison, manager of the club," began a breathless preview in the *Manchester Guardian*. "The television demonstrations will show tactics on the field, shooting in goal, dribbling and goalkeeping. Three cameras will be used, one being on the stands to give a comprehensive view of the ground and two others near the goalmouth to give close-ups of the play and players and visual interviews. No film will be used, transmission being by radio direct to Alexandra Palace which can actually be seen from the ground."

Not much action was shown. The BBC were still persisting with their one-hour afternoon schedule, and, with most of it gobbled up by *Fancy That!* starring the camp comic Douglas Byng, the programme only lasted 15 minutes. But the BBC had proven that football could work on the small screen and within the year, an England-Scotland international and an FA Cup final had been shown live. It was certain football would become a fixture in the schedules, although first it was time for war, glasses of juniper juice and a nice long boozy snooze.

 ## International Football (1957)

In late 1946, the folk at BBC Television yawned, scratched their arses, reluctantly put the crossword down and did some telly. Over the next decade, their memorable output would include a few FA Cup finals when they could be bothered, live coverage of a German aristocrat being given a shiny new hat, a potters wheel, a kitten playing with a ball of wool, and, er, that's it! (Note for the purposes of clarity: *Er, That's It!* was not a vehicle for the camp comic Douglas Byng.)

But then ITV came along in late 1955 and shook the whole scene up. Within two months, they'd shown live coverage of floodlit friendlies between Hibernian and Manchester City, and Wolverhampton Wanderers and Dinamo Moscow.

Another couple of months down the line, and live FA Cup ties between Bedford Town and Arsenal, Chelsea and Burnley, and West Ham and Spurs were under their belt. The coverage was live, exclusive and only of the second halves: ITV weren't allowed to show domestic games in their entirety lest attendances be adversely affected.

But they were given free rein to transmit full coverage of ties in the new-fangled European Cup. The 1955 champions Chelsea had cravenly kow-towed to pressure from the xenophobic Football League chairman Alan Hardaker, who infamously didn't want his clubs consorting with "wogs and dagoes", but their successors at Manchester United were having none of Hardaker's sorry shit. United were in the centre of a perfect televisual storm: their manager Matt Busby was effectively in control of a sleepy boardroom and insisted on participation in Europe; his Busby Babes side were fantastic to watch, perfect fodder for casual armchair viewing; the biggest and richest company in the new ITV was Granada, based in Manchester; and the owners of Granada, the Bernstein brothers, were, as the company name suggests, hispanophiles. Oh look, here come Real Madrid!

The second leg of the 1957 semi-final between United and Real at Old Trafford thus became the first match to be transmitted live in its entirety on ITV. Well, almost. Only the second half of *International Football* [sic] was networked nationally; it was just lucky viewers in the north-western Granada region who were offered the full game. And even then it didn't quite work out like that. The first four minutes of the match were lost to an advertising break. Unlike in later years, when the network regularly blocked out important goals through sheer incompetence — the Dan Gosling / Tic Tac affair, for example, or England's one moment of glee at the 2010 World Cup — this wasn't ITV's fault. The referee had simply started the game early, as he couldn't be bothered to hang around in the chilly Manchester air — and who could blame him.

3 The Big Game (1960)

ITV kept pestering the Football League for the right to show First Division action and in 1960 they wrote a large enough cheque — £150,000 — for football's principles to be hoicked out of the window. A compromise was struck. Televised games wouldn't kick off until 6.50 on a Saturday evening and ITV wouldn't join the action until the last few minutes of the first half at 7.30pm, allowing supporters from the afternoon fixtures time to get back to their armchairs. ITV announced that on 10 September, the First Division match between Blackpool and Bolton Wanderers would be the first edition of the centrepiece of the network's new Saturday evening schedule: *The Big Game*. "It's viewing with a KICK!" promised Val Parnell, the guy who lent his name to the contemporary hit *Sunday Night at the London Palladium*, and one of the many magnificently entertaining cigar-toting chancers then running ITV.

Parnell, an impresario schooled in the ways of the theatre, was merely whipping up the public like a good showman

should. But his act consisted solely of a man talking through his hat. Before *The Big Game* even kicked off, it had all, well, kicked off. Turns out the League had snaffled the cash greedily without considering the wishes of the clubs. The very thought! Tottenham Hotspur — the runaway league leaders and sexiest team of the era — were hosting Aston Villa a fortnight after the opening show, and the fixture had been lined up as the third edition of *The Big Game*. But the Football League hadn't banked on Spurs telling them to shove their agreement with ITV up their centre circle.

Arsenal quickly followed suit. They'd been pencilled in for the second edition, as hosts to Newcastle. And the other glamour clubs of the day — Wolverhampton Wanderers, Aston Villa, Birmingham City, West Bromwich Albion, Manchester United, Manchester City, Everton, Sheffield Wednesday and Nottingham Forest — were all also expected to revolt.

With the whole affair threatening to descend into freeform farce, ITV crossed their fingers and hoped that the Blackpool-Bolton curtain-raiser would wow the nation and make a few recalcitrant clubs change their stance. Oh dear. Even that was doomed to failure before the get-go. "A leg injury keeps out Stanley Matthews," reported the *Daily Express*, "the only player capable of putting £150,000 sparkle into a match which lacks crowd-pulling appeal." ITV's production staff placed the main camera behind one of the goals at Broomfield Road, which ensured that, according to an apoplectic *Daily Mirror* review, "the pitch looked 200 yards wide and only 50 yards long!"

That may or may not have been a bad thing, because it would have required psychedelic levels of distortion to maintain the viewer's interest in a drab 1-0 win for Bolton. "There was no point in commentators Peter Lloyd and former England skipper Billy Wright trying to kid us that we were watching a smasher," continued the empurpled man in the *Mirror*. "Mr Lloyd hadn't checked his facts. He referred to the packed crowd — when there were 17,000 in a ground that can hold more than twice that. And his identification of the players was sometimes late and sometimes wrong. It all added up to an unnecessary irritation." To add insult to injury, the Arsenal game which had been lined up for the following week but already blacked out, would subsequently be a five-goal spectacular.

Live football on British television would have to wait another 23 years. The first game, inevitably, would be at Spurs. On ITV. If only Val Parnell had still been around to talk it up.

4 This Is Your Life (1961)

And in a seamless segue, so to someone who made it his life's mission to talk it *down*. Danny Blanchflower packed up playing in 1964 and having devoted his life to the glory, glory game as a player, decided to bring a little of his trademark vitality and honesty to the world of journalism. He was as singular in his new profession as he had been in his old one, telling it as it was, rather than how people might like to hear it. Which may explain why he wasn't exactly a roaring success as a 'color man' for US network CBS, who snapped him up for

the inaugural season of the National Professional Soccer League.

Blanchflower was tasked with the job of selling soccer to a new American audience. Sadly for CBS, the quality of the new league was piss-poor, and their color man was not of a mind to kid the audience that the fare on display was anything other than monochrome. "Blanchflower killed every soccer sportscast for us," moaned CBS producer Bill Bergesch. "He pointed out all the bad things. He was so honest it hurt us. His job was to promote the sport. That's what we were paying him to do."

He was eventually hauled into the offices at CBS after going to town on a goalkeeper from St Louis who had dived over a dribbler from distance. "We think there are two truths, a positive truth and a negative truth," they said to him. "You could have said it was a good shot. We want you to say it was a good play rather than bad."

Blanchflower — who as a journalist would keep a resignation letter in his pocket to produce during arguments over articles which had been toned down by spineless editorial staff — was not going to take that lying down. "I had never met men before who worshiped two truths," he wrote in *Sports Illustrated* a year later, after inevitably getting the boot. "Why had such inventive souls stopped at only two, I wondered? Why not four truths? Or 10? The philosophical winds of it swept through my mind. If they had two truths they must have two gods... But if there was no bad, how could there be good? What would their reactions have been if I had said of the goalkeeper at St Louis: Well, folks ... that sure was good negative play on his part, making it easy for them to score that great goal."

It all makes one wonder whether CBS had done much research into Blanchflower at all. The man, after all, was famous in Britain not just for captaining Spurs to the double, or hilariously berating Alf Ramsey throughout the sixties for his pulseless brand of football, but also for being the first celebrity to turn down an appearance on *This Is Your Life* in 1961. "Basically I did not want to expose myself to the public without the right to say yes or no," he later explained. "You get shanghaied into this situation where you are suddenly exposed to something." He declined a second BBC offer later in the year.

Viewers were not shortchanged, though. Instead of the planned Blanchflower programme, the makers of *This Is Your Life* had a spare in their back pocket, and the nation was treated to the story of Dr Robert Fawcus, a GP from Chard in Somerset, who pootled around the town on his "famous round-tank motor cycle" in order to get to "every emergency, whatever the time or weather". Eamonn Andrews's big red book went on to note that the kindly Dr Fawcus was "smiling and tolerant", which if nothing else goes to show the BBC didn't just lazily fill the Blanchflower-shaped hole like for like.

 Match of the Day (1964)

Having viewed the freewheeling debacle of *The Big Game* with detached amusement, the BBC had steered clear of live football, major international set-pieces and FA Cup finals apart. The

Football League was more trouble than it was worth. However, they didn't shy away from highlights reels, and had shown short clips from Football League matches regularly of a Saturday evening since 1955, in programmes such as *Sports Special* and *Saturday Sport*. By 1962, a couple of regional ITV companies — Anglia and Tyne Tees — had started knocking together highlights programmes of their own. This clearly got the BBC thinking, and when they set up BBC2 in 1964, then quickly realised they had bugger all to put on it, they decided it was time for action.

And so, at 6.30pm on August 22, the opening day of the 1964-65 season, BBC2 transmitted the first edition of *Match of the Day*. The programme did exactly as it says on the film tin, consisting of one match, and one match alone, played earlier that day: reigning champions Liverpool playing host to Arsenal. That *MotD*, as it wasn't yet known, could be out and over the airwaves in less than two hours of the final whistle was down to new-fangled video and editing facilities.

Less impressive was the fact that nobody who went to Anfield that day would have been able to see the programme: BBC2 had been on the air for a mere four months, and could only be received by a select few with expensive new 625-line sets in the London area. Viewers in Liverpool had a choice between *The Travels of Jaimie McPheeters*, a western on BBC1, or another western on ITV, *Sugarfoot*. The Beeb's generously rounded-up viewing figures: 20,000, less than half the match's 47,620 attendance. Like 1937 all over again, then, albeit this time Arsenal got their arses felt in a 3-2 defeat.

Shame, because the programme was a good one. Kenneth Wolstenholme stood pitchside before the game to introduce the very first edition, with "She Loves You" and "Hippy Hippy Shake" hooting over the PA system. "As you can hear, we're in Beatle-ville!" ran the commentator's now-famous introduction. Liverpool flew into a two-goal lead through Roger Hunt and Gordon Wallace, Geoff Strong and Joe Baker levelled with two goals in 45 second-half seconds, and Wallace grabbed his second, Liverpool's third, and the winner with three minutes to go.

"Phew, well I'd call it the match of the century, I don't know about Match of the Day," quipped Wolstenholme after the game, pitchside once more. The colour analyst Walley Barnes — formerly of Arsenal, and more willing than Danny Blanchflower to do television's bidding — stepped awkwardly into shot in Cholmondley-Warneresque fashion and agreed with the presenter that "match of the century is probably very right."

6 Pay-TV (1966)

There are no new ideas. Sky Sports staged the biggest song and dance routine performed outside the MGM studios when they launched Premiership Plus in 2001. It was their first foray into pay-per-view, and as such was sold, to a myopic generation who only avert their gaze from their navels in order to have the occasional quick peek up their own fundaments, as a groundbreaking enterprise.

Which, in fairness, it was for the majority of the country. It was the UK's first nationwide pay-per-view channel; the first game armchair viewers had to stump up ready money for was Chelsea versus Newcastle United. Boudewijn Zenden scored on eight minutes, Clarence Acuña equalised on 77. Can we have our £8 back, please?

However, it wasn't the first PPV football match to be transmitted in the UK. Back in January 1966, 2,000 residents of Westminster and Southwark in London had their television sets fitted with slot boxes which allowed the transmission of non BBC and ITV programming in exchange for coin. Usually the programmes on offer were the sort of horror flicks which were nothing more than borderline bongo, but there were other treats: racing from Kempton, a bout between Muhammad Ali and Henry Cooper, and a show from St Pancras Mortuary for the benefit of medical students at the Royal Free Hospital.

The experiment was then rolled out to Sheffield in October, and within a month the UK's first-ever PPV game was transmitted: a friendly between Chelsea (see, nothing is new) and the newly crowned champions of Europe, Real Madrid. The star of the show was Ferenc Puskás — who the *Guardian* noted was "perpetually 39 to all his questioners these past four years, tubbier now, but with much of his old grace and a deal of his old skill" — but it was Chelsea who prevailed thanks to goals from Tony Hateley and John Hollins. Not bad for 10 shillings.

Pay-TV was forced to close down less than two years later, pay television as a concept having made no serious advances into the national psyche. There had been one other live match, a 3-3 cracker between Burnley and Arsenal in the 1967-68 League Cup quarter finals, but the viewing figures were so low the entire enterprise has been almost completely forgotten today. Shame the same can't be said for those excruciating PremPlus back and forths between Marcus Buckland and a brazenly disinterested George Graham.

The Big Match Live (1983)

Just over 23 years after their first attempt, the ITV network finally got their wish: live league football. It was part of another experimental deal, a two-year agreement with the Football League, in tandem with the BBC, both stations getting five live matches a season. The BBC decided to put theirs out on Friday evenings, but ITV, who opted for Sunday afternoons, went first.

They picked Tottenham Hotspur versus Nottingham Forest at the start of October, moving the game to Sunday 2nd. Unlike the Blackpool-Bolton farce of 1960, the cameras were in the right position and they caught a minor classic, Colin Walsh giving Forest an early lead, Gary Stevens levelling with a bullet header midway through the second half and Steve Archibald grabbing the three points for Spurs with five minutes to go.

But the match — as Tottenham manager Keith Burkenshaw wryly noted, with reference to posters advertising the event with "the game a little item down

the bottom of the bill" — was almost a secondary consideration. Spurs, as the aforementioned posters suggest, had sold the day as a family gala, worried that the TV cameras would seriously affect the attendance. As it was, the draw of 30,596 was the biggest First Division crowd of the weekend. Whether the size of it had anything to do with the pre-match entertainments on offer — skydivers, a stroll out for a man on world-record stilts and music from Chas 'n' Dave — is a point that will forever remain moot.

The best two moments of ITV's transmission were down to their up-and-coming stars *Saint and Greavsie*, who weren't half as bad as you remember them to be. Halfway through the first half, the co-commentator Ian St John announced that "it's better to be here than sitting at home yelling at your TV." Brian Moore, on the main mic, issued him an immediate bollocking: "I'm not sure you should be saying that." Then at the end of the game, the studio pundit Jimmy Greaves told anchorman Jim Rosenthal that he was "going home to watch the *Winds of War*", the Robert Mitchum vehicle on ITV later that evening. "And I already know what bloody happened in that. You never knew what was going to happen out there today."

Soccer AM (1995)

So, football on television has never, ever been perfect. Still, something went wrong somewhere, didn't it?

Contributors

The Blizzard, Issue Eight

Luke Alfred is the author of two cricket books, *Lifting the Covers, the Inside Story of South African Cricket* and *Testing Times, the Men who Made South African Cricket*. He is the sports editor of the *Sunday Times* in Johannesburg.

Craig Anderson is a Scottish football obsessive and a statistics PhD student. He combined these two passions to create the @SPLstats Twitter account where he shares trivia about the Scottish game. Although he is a Kilmarnock fan, he has contributed articles to Motherwell FC's matchday magazine as well as the STVSport website. **Twitter: @craig_killie**

David Ashton is a playwright, TV and film screenwriter; creator of the BBC Radio 4 series, *McLevy*. He has written four novels, the latest being *Nor Will He Sleep*. Also an actor, he played Dr McDuff in *Brass* and the father in *The Last King of Scotland*. His website is **www.david-ashton.co.uk**.

Philippe Auclair is the author of *The Enchanted Kingdom of Tony Blair* (in French) and *Cantona: the Rebel Who Would Be King*, which was named NSC Football Book of the Year. His biography of Thierry Henry has just been published. He writes for *France Football* and *Offside* and provides analysis and commentary for RMC Sport. He also pursues a parallel career in music under the name 'Louis Philippe'. **Twitter: @PhilippeAuclair**

Sheridan Bird writes for *Champions, World Soccer, Creative Review, Sporting iD, FourFourTwo* and the Manchester United and England match programmes. He has written for *Gazzetta dello Sport* online and appeared on Italian state radio RAI 1 during Euro 2012 **Twitter: @SheridanBird**

Mike Calvin is a columnist on the *Independent on Sunday* and host of *Life's a Pitch*, BT's football podcast. He has twice been named Sports Reporter of the Year, and has also won the Sportswriter of the Year award. His last book, *Family: Life Death and Football*, a season spent behind the scenes at Millwall, was shortlisted at the British Sports Book Awards in 2011. **Twitter: @CalvinBook**

Stuart Roy Clarke is a photographer who has prodiced six picture-books under the umbrella title of *The Homes of Football*. His collection was housed at Ambleside but is now the only contemporary collection of photographs held at the National Football Museum, Manchester. **Twitter: @homesoffootball**

Tom Dunmore is an editor of *XI*, a North American soccer quarterly. He lives in Chicago and is currently working on a history of the United States national team. **Twitter: @tomdunmore**

Rupert Fryer is a freelance journalist and co-founder of SouthAmericanFootball. co.uk. He has written on South American football for the likes of *Fox Sports*, the *Guardian*, the *Observer* and *Sport360*. **Twitter: @Rupert_Fryer**

Gary Hartley is a West Yorkshireman exiled in London. He performs poems that read like lists and co-edits *The Alarmist* magazine. He draws much Byronic suffering from following Leeds United, and occasionally rambles on about it for fanzine *The Scratching Shed*. **Twitter: @garyfromleeds**

Roy Henderson is the editor of RedAndWhiteKop.com and contributes to *The Anfield Wrap* from time to time. **Twitter: @royhendo**

Alex Keble is a freelance journalist who has written for FourFourTwo.com and the *Guardian*. **Twitter: @alexkeble**

Iain Macintosh is the author of *Football Fables* and the *Everything You Ever Wanted To Know* series of sports guidebooks and a co-author of *Football Manager Ruined My Life*. He writes for the *New Paper* in Singapore, si.com and anyone else who'll pay him. **Twitter: @iainmacintosh**

Steve Menary is a regular contributor to *World Soccer, When Saturday Comes* and playthegame.org. He is also the author of *Outcasts! The Lands That Fifa Forgot*, which was shortlisted for the NSC Football Book of the Year award. A new edition of *Outcasts!* has just come out on Kindle.

Scott Murray writes for the *Guardian*. He is author of on-this-day football miscellany *Day of the Match*, and the preposterous but amusing Phantom of the Open: Maurice Flitcroft, The World's Worst Golfer.

David Owen spent 20 years with the *Financial Times*, finishing as sports editor. Now freelance, his book, *Foinavon: the Story of the Grand National's Biggest Upset*, is published next month by Bloomsbury, under the Wisden Sports Writing imprint. **Twitter: @dodo938**

Cyrus Philbrick is a writer of journalism, fiction and other forms. He writes about football, science, art, and education. He is open to exotic and harrowing assignments. Website: www.cyrusphilbrick.com **Twitter: @cyphilbrick**

Lars Sivertsen is a Norwegian writer based in London. He is Premier League Correspondent for TV 2 Norway and a regular contributor to *Josimar*. **Twitter: @larssivertsen**

Jacob Steinberg writes for the *Guardian*. **Twitter: @JacobSteinberg**

Jonathan Wilson is the author of *Inverting the Pyramid*, a winner of the National Sporting Club's Football Book of the Year and the Antonio Ghirelli Award, *Behind the Curtain, The Anatomy of England* and *Nobody Ever Says Thank You*. His latest book is *The Outsider: A History of the Goalkeeper*. He writes for the *Guardian, The National, World Soccer, Foxsoccer, ESPN Star* and *Sports Illustrated*. **Twitter: @jonawils**

Blizzard Subscriptions

Subscribe to the print version of The Blizzard, *be the first to receive new issues, get exclusive Blizzard offers and access digital versions of all back-issues FREE*

Subscription Options

Set Price for Four Issues

Get a four-issue subscription to *The Blizzard* — for you or as a gift — for a flat fee including postage and packing (P&P):

UK:	£35
Europe:	£45
Non-Euorpe:	£55

Recurring Pay-What-You-Like

Set up a quarterly recurring payment for each edition of *The Blizzard*. The recommended retail price (RRP) is £12, but pay what you like, subject to a minimum fee of £6 plus P&P

See www.theblizzard.co.uk for more

Digital Subscriptions

If the cost of postage is prohibitive, or you just want an excuse to use your new iPad or Kindle, you can set up a subscription to digital versions of *The Blizzard* for just £3 per issue.

See www.theblizzard.co.uk for more

Information for Existing Subscribers

Free Digital Downloads for *Blizzard* Subscribers

Whether you have taken advantage of our set price or pay-what-you-like offer, for the duration of your subscription to *The Blizzard* you are entitled to download every issue FREE.

See www.theblizzard.co.uk for more

We very much value the commitment of our print subscribers and have a policy to make available new issues, special offers and other limited access events and benefits to print subscribers first.

About *The Blizzard*

Distribution & Back Issues
Contact Information
About Issue Eight

Buy *The Blizzard*

We want as many readers as possible for
The Blizzard. We therefore operate as far
as we are able on a pay-what-you-like
basis for digital and print versions.

Digital Version
(Current & Back Issues)

All issues of *The Blizzard* are available to
download for Kindle, Android, iOS and PC/
Mac at: *www.theblizzard.co.uk.*

- *RRP: £3*
- *Pay-what-you-like minimum: £0.01*

Printed Version
(Current & Back Issues)

Purchase a physical copy of *The Blizzard*
in all its luxurious, tactile, sensual glory
at: *www.theblizzard.co.uk.* If you haven't
felt our rough textured cover-varnish and
smelled the inner genius, you haven't
properly experienced its awesome true
form. Read it, or leave it on your coffee
table to wow visitors.

- *RRP: £12 (+P&P)*
- *Pay-what-you-like min: £6 (+P&P)*

Contact *The Blizzard*

**All advertising, sales, press and business
communication should be addressed to the
Central Publishing Office:**

The Blizzard
Ashmore Villa,
1, Ashmore Terrace,
Stockton Road,
Sunderland,
SR27DE

Email: info@theblizzard.co.uk
Telephone: +44 (0) 191 543 8785
Website: www.theblizzard.co.uk
Facebook: www.facebook.com/blzzrd
Twitter: @blzzrd

About Issue Eight

Editor	Jonathan Wilson
Publisher	The Blizzard Media Ltd
	www.theblizzard.co.uk
Design	Azure
	www.azure-design.com

Copyright

Grass Roots Football

"FOOTBALL IS MADE OF LEATHER, LEATHER COMES FROM COWS, COWS LIKE GRASS."

"IF GOD HAD MEANT FOOTBALL TO BE PLAYED IN THE AIR HE WOULD HAVE PUT GRASS IN THE SKY"

Replica kits - expensive, generic and polyester, little room for creativity and individuality other than a name and number on the back (at more cost!). A Cult Zeros shirt is your creation, your freedom of expression, your style. Any team, any player, any era, we'll do our best to put it on a shirt. We'll even do your team mates in your Sunday League team. And if you are a connoisseur of food, we do do XXXL sizes!

We're on Facebook & Twitter

www.cultzeros.co.uk